Subnational Partnerships for Sustainable Development

NEW HORIZONS IN ENVIRONMENTAL POLITICS

Series Editor: Arthur Mol, *Chair and Professor in Environmental Policy, Director, Wageningen School of Social Sciences, Wageningen University, The Netherlands, Professor in Environmental Policy, Renmin University, Beijing*

The New Horizons in Environmental Politics series provides a platform for in-depth critical assessments of how we understand the many changes in the politics of nature, the environment and natural resources that have occurred over the last 50 years. Books in the series question how the environment is (re)defined, debated and protected; explore differences between countries and regions in environmental politics; analyse how actors do and do not collaborate around environment and natural resource conflicts; describe who wins and who loses and in what ways; and detail how to better study, analyze and theorize such developments and outcomes.

The series is designed to promote innovative cross-disciplinary analysis of the contemporary issues and debates influencing the various dimensions of environmental politics. Covering a diverse range of topics, the series will examine the political, economic and ethical aspects of environmental policy, governance and regulation. It brings together cutting edge research on environmental politics worldwide in order to shed light on, and explain current trends and developments.

With oversight from the Series Editor, Professor Arthur Mol – a noted specialist in the field of environmental politics at Wageningen University, The Netherlands – the New Horizons in Environmental Politics series comprises carefully commissioned projects from experts in the field including both academics and professionals. The audience for the series is global, and books in the series are essential reading for students, academics and professionals – in short, anyone with an interest in understanding the vital issues affecting environmental politics in the 21st Century.

Subnational Partnerships for Sustainable Development

Transatlantic Cooperation between the
United States and Germany

Holley Andrea Ralston

Blue Ridge Community and Technical College, USA

NEW HORIZONS IN ENVIRONMENTAL POLITICS

Edward Elgar
Cheltenham, UK • Northampton, MA, USA

Published by
Edward Elgar Publishing Limited
The Lypiatts
15 Lansdown Road
Cheltenham
Glos GL50 2JA
UK

Edward Elgar Publishing, Inc.
William Pratt House
9 Dewey Court
Northampton
Massachusetts 01060
USA

A catalogue record for this book
is available from the British Library

Library of Congress Control Number: 2013946816

This book is available electronically in the ElgarOnline.com
Social and Political Science Subject Collection, E-ISBN 978 1 78254 914 7

ISBN 978 1 78254 913 0

Typeset by Servis Filmsetting Ltd, Stockport, Cheshire
Printed and bound in Great Britain by T.J. International Ltd, Padstow

Contents

Acknowledgements

This book is the outgrowth of a PhD dissertation project written at the Free University of Berlin, Germany (D 188). I would like to thank Prof. Dr Miranda Schreurs, whose guidance was instrumental for both the project's completion and for its further development and publication. This book has also benefitted from the support of numerous people over the years. I would like to thank PD Dr Lutz Mez, Jim Ralston, Connie Ralston, Tyler Ralston, Jorn Bramann, Renate Hackler, Erich Hackler and Hania Merrill. Finally, and above all, I would like to thank and dedicate this book to Dirk Hackler.

1. Introduction

One of the more exciting developments in international environmental protection has been the proliferation of initiatives at the subnational level. An important but not so well-known component of this is the international partnerships between US and German subnational governments, states and *Länder*, respectively. The primary aims of these partnerships include drawing lessons from as well as transferring innovative policies and technologies. The partnerships relate to global governance for sustainable development. This concept stems from the United Nations Conference on Environment and Development (UNCED) and related approaches and processes, such as the International Organization for Standardization's (ISO) environmental management standards, the climate change regime, and the push for ecological modernization. The partnerships suggest a true multi-level dimension to global governance for sustainable development, as called for at the UNCED, from the international to the subnational, in which ideas and policies move in both a downward and an upward fashion (although not necessarily hierarchically) as well as horizontally.

The 1992 UNCED marked a new era of environmental protection in a globalized world. It was at this summit where the emerging principle of sustainable development became solidified. The focus was development of a long-term strategic approach to environmental protection that includes all relevant sectors and environmental media at all levels of government; in other words it was a multi-actor, multi-level governance approach. This multi-level depth is largely missing in the competing philosophies on options to address global environmental issues (the dimensions generally do not go beyond the national and international levels).

Subnational governmental activities in countries such as the United States and Germany are critical to the achievement of sustainable development goals, as they are primarily responsible for the successful implementation and achievement of environmental policy objectives. They often take the lead and establish more effective actions than are created by their respective federal governments. Additionally, they have some autonomous decision-making capabilities that are relevant to the international sustainable agenda, such as designing and implementing policies to promote renewable energy, land use and infrastructure decisions (choices that affect emissions for decades), and other areas ranging from agriculture to waste management.

In the 1990s, both states and *Länder* took the leadership role in putting forth policy that is relevant to the international agenda of sustainable development and climate change. In many cases they created innovative policies and became frontrunners in certain policy areas, such as in land use, renewable energy initiatives and climate change policies. This is particularly the case regarding US states and climate change. Interestingly, this phenomenon largely went unnoticed until the early 2000s when this gap in awareness was exposed by a slew of reports that came out on the issue, mostly regarding the US states and climate change (CCAP, 2002, 2003; Herbert and Blechschmidt, 2001; Jörgensen, 2002; Pew Center, 2004, 2006; Rabe, 2000, 2002, 2006; WWF, 2003). And even now, such subnational leadership is not widespread public knowledge.

Remarkably, these subnational climate change efforts do not stop at the border. A couple of states have signed partnership agreements with European countries on climate change (California Office of the Governor, 2006; NJDEP, 1998b). Likewise, in 2001, a regional group of states formed an alliance with a group of Canadian provinces to reduce their greenhouse gas emissions (NYSERDA, 2002). Some states attended international conferences and negotiations. States involved in the Clean Energy States Alliance went to the 2004 International Conference for Renewable Energies in Bonn to find transatlantic partners to help in their efforts to create markets for renewable energy technologies (CESA, 2004). Likewise, members of the Regional Greenhouse Gas Initiative (RGGI) – a coalition of Northeast and Mid-Atlantic states that formed a cooperation to design and implement a regional greenhouse gas cap-and-trade program – traveled to Buenos Aires to the Conference of the Parties 10 (COP10).[1] On this basis there was talk of 'linking up with the Europeans in a backdoor trading scheme on emissions' ('Some States', 2004).

These actions are in line with other observations on the increasing role of subnational governments in 'foreign affairs', 'international relations' or 'international arenas' (Aldecoa and Keating, 1999; Fry, 1998; Kaiser, 2002, 2005; Lecours, 2002). Most of these activities have been in the economic arena, although not exclusively so. The evidence can be seen in their representation abroad where they lead trade missions, participate in regional and international organizations, enter into relations with other subnational governments, and sign agreements (Lecours, 2002). The World Bank has summed up the situation as a 'widespread movement towards devolution' (Canaleta et al., 2004, p. 90). As of the turn of the century, 95 percent of democratic countries had elected subnational levels of government (Canaleta et al., 2004; Lecours, 2002; Ohmae, 1993;

Richards, 2004). And as for governments that already have subnational levels, for example federal systems such as the United States and Germany, the movement has been for a stronger subnational role.

There is growing interest in the literature related to the driving factors for subnational activities or arrangements on the environment. Increased state activity and network and regional actions, such as the aforementioned state or province collaboration to address climate change, are important new developments in global environmental governance (Rabe, 2008, 2009; Selin and VanDeveer, 2005). Driving these actions are international scientific and political debates and immediate signs of climate impact. Other motivations include changing incentives for politicians; civil servant, state agency, non-governmental organization (NGO) advocacy coalition influence; and economic development opportunities (including the desire to be first-movers).

Studies indicate how certain subnational environmental activities are fitting into the larger multi-level system or how the decentralization efforts in the federal systems themselves have contributed to shifts in the roles of government (Brown, 1999; Jörgensen, 2002; Kern, 2008; Kraemer, 2007; Kraft and Scheberle, 1998; Rabe, 2000, 2007; Schreurs, 2008; Schreurs et al., 2009; Vogel et al., 2005). It is not just states but also cities that have become active policymakers in many countries, oftentimes before central governments; both NGOs and businesses have established programs to influence the public and policy as well as technological developments to help curb greenhouse gases (Andonova et al., 2009; Schreurs et al., 2009). Subnational activities and new forms of governance are altering decision-making patterns and dynamics within federal and multi-level systems (Betsill and Bulkeley, 2004; Blatter, 2001; Kern, 2008; Kern and Bulkeley, 2009; Kern et al., 2007; Kern and Monstadt, 2008; Rabe, 2007, 2008, 2009; Selin and VanDeveer, 2005; VanDeveer, 2010; Vogel and Swinnen, 2011). The findings show that there are different types of horizontal and vertical interactions and coordination among all levels of government and institutional regions, on both sides of the ocean. Public, private and civil society leaders are all involved in this trend toward decentralization. These different forms of cooperation and partnerships among these subnational public and private entities have emerged not only domestically but also transnationally (Andonova et al., 2009; VanDeveer, 2010). This is to say that the partnerships are part of a larger movement toward governing sustainability beyond the national and international arenas.

Despite the growing attention in the literature to new modes of climate and environmental governance, little attention has been given to the movement of transnational environmental cooperation among subnational and other actors or transnational 'regime' formation. Scholars typify three such transnational networks and/or partnerships: public, private and hybrid (Andonova et al., 2009; Bäckstrand, 2008): for example, ICLEI-Local Governments for Sustainability; World Business Council for Sustainable Development; and Renewable Energy and Energy Efficiency Partnership, respectively. Within the public, there are same-level and mixed-level partnerships, such as transnational city-to-city (for example, Chicago and Hamburg), state-to-country (for example, New Jersey and the Netherlands) and region-to-region (Northern Virginia Regional Commission and the Verband Region Stuttgart) (Knigge, 2005; Medearis and Swett, 2003).

As with the US–German state partnerships, much of this transnational environmental collaboration started to crop up in the 1990s parallel to the UNCED and the climate change regime. They can be viewed as an effort to find alternatives to more traditional international policymaking among states and as means to fill in gaps created by the absence of state or inter-national initiatives. There are also factors specific to the partners that can drive cooperative arrangements (Bäckstrand, 2008; Kern and Bulkeley, 2009; Schreurs et al., 2009; VanDeveer, 2010). Cities and states face similar problems and transnational learning is seen as an important strategy for them (Kern and Bulkeley, 2009). The climate change regime also lent itself easily to transnational governance because of the involvement of multiple sectors whose interests and activities transcend borders (Andonova et al., 2009). This adds more depth to the multi-level governance discussed above.

As these efforts continue to attract the attention of policymakers, private sector actors and scholars alike, the question remains: do such arrangements have an impact? And how do they function in relation to the traditional forms of government? Kern and Bulkeley (2009) ask if trans-national municipal networks make a difference at the European, national and local levels. They find that such networks only benefit the pioneer cities because they have the resources to compete for and undertake projects that attract other funds. This study raises the question about the governing capacity of such networks, as they are highly dependent on gov-ernmental and European funding, and because they lack authority to force members to apply specific strategies. The soft approaches reinforce leaders and laggards. Bäckstrand (2008) had similar findings regarding governing capacities, indicating that since power is dispersed among market, govern-ance and civil society actors, transnational public–private partnerships or network governance is limited to advocacy, service provisions and implementation, while standard setting remains in the hands of govern-mental actors. Others have found that the different forms of transnational governance steers constituents to achieve public goals (Andonova et al.,

2009; VanDeveer, 2010). But again, this is through soft approaches such as information sharing, capacity building and implementation. That said, these scholars found that some standard setting has occurred through networks such as the RGGI and the Chicago Climate Exchange, but these are primarily domestic networks.

The subnational partnerships between Germany and the United States are different from the traditional international friendship arrangements among cities and states or provinces (subnational governments) that began in earnest in the 1950s. They are more political, sovereign and issue- or project-centered compared to the twinning arrangements that generally centered on cultural, educational, professional and business exchanges that were set up to be long term (Clarke, 2010).[2] It is therefore not surprising that the US–German subnational environmental partnerships do not identify themselves as sister-state arrangements. The state of Maryland, for example, mentions that it has sister partnerships with 11 different regions from ten different countries (this is not counting the numerous sister cities), but it does not list its environmental partnership with Schleswig–Holstein among these arrangements. Furthermore, these partnerships also differ from the many cross-border environmental arrangements that form out of geographical necessity. They are not connected to the global organizations of subnational governments that are normally led by an international agency or based on a particular project or issue (Furmankiewicz, 2007).

While there are no complete data about exactly how many such partnerships exist, the trend between the United States and Germany has stood out. Yet, no study has comprehensively examined more than two partnerships (Wisconsin-Bavaria 1998, and Maryland-Schleswig–Holstein 2002) (Jörgensen, 2006; Knigge, 2005; Medearis and Swett, 2003). Even less has been written about how such arrangements fit into the overall picture of global governance for sustainable development in a multi-level international system (Jörgensen, 2006).

This increased role of US and German states in environmental policy and their cooperation is an important development in the called-for multi-actor, multi-level approach to achieving global sustainable development. This is particularly true in light of the lack of accord between the United States and the European Union on important issues such as climate change. Rabe (2009) and VanDeveer (2010) even go as far as to say that climate change policy development in the United States is comparable to that of the European policy, when these governance systems are examined as analogous types of federations. When comparing at these adjusted scales, one sees both leaders and laggards, similar policy choices that have prompted contacts between states and the European Union (EU) and other member states, and similar clusters of policy professionals that not only develop policy internally but look to other states and foreign governments to partner with. Furthermore, these parallels extend to other federal or multi-level governance systems, whether they ratified Kyoto or not, such as Canada and Australia (Rabe, 2008; Schreurs, 2010). And this is not limited to climate change, as Germany initially lagged in its sustainable development policies while the *Länder* took the lead. All of this suggests that climate change and sustainable development polices can no longer be framed simply as an issue among nation-states by way of an international regime. These issues should be approached through a lens of multi-level governance (Kern, 2008; Rabe, 2007, 2008, 2009; VanDeveer, 2010; Vogel and Swinnen, 2011).

This book aims to establish some generalizations about these partnerships based on the following four questions:

1. What are the common driving factors in which US and German states form innovative environmental partnerships?
2. What were the results of the arrangements?
3. What supports and hinders such partnerships in the implementation process?
4. What role do US and German innovative environmental partnerships at the subnational level have in global environmental governance for sustainable development in a multi-level system?

The value of such partnerships in a multi-level system and their effects or potential effects on policy is subject to their ability to function, that is, to be created and carried out.

The inductive, qualitative study compares five cases where Memoranda of Understanding (MoUs) have been established:

1. California–Bavaria (1995) – formed to mutually promote environmental and renewable energy technologies (Bavaria MRDEA and Cal/EPA, 1995).
2. Wisconsin–Bavaria (1998) – established to cooperate on environmental regulatory reform (Wisconsin DNR and MRDEA, 1998).
3. California–Bavaria (2000) – created for the purposes of environmental regulatory reform, specifically regarding environmental management systems (Bavaria MSDEA and Cal/EPA, 2000).
4. Maryland–Schleswig–Holstein (2002) – formed to collaborate in sustainable development, energy conservation, renewable energy, greenhouse gas emissions reductions, 'green' buildings and land management (MDE and MUNF, 2002).

5. California–North Rhine–Westphalia (2004) – established to work together in the field of clean energy technologies, particularly in hydrogen and fuel cells (CARB and MESP, 2004).

As for analytical tools, since not every state or *Land* has formed a partnership, yet enough have done so to make it a trend, both an agency and a structural approach are helpful. First, I turn to the theoretical concept of policy entrepreneurs, for example Kingdon (1984), Mintrom (1997), Mintrom and Vergari (1998), McCown (2005) and Schneider and Teske (1992). According to Kingdon (1984), policy entrepreneurs are 'advocates for proposals or for the prominence of an idea' (p. 122). Such advocates can be found in any location in the policy community, such as in government, interest groups or in other organizations. But while policy entrepreneurs may have diverse backgrounds, according to Kingdon (1984) they, like business entrepreneurs, have a defining characteristic: 'their willingness to invest their resources – time, energy, reputation and sometimes money – in the hope of a future return' (p. 122).

I employ the theoretical concept of multi-level governance (MLG), which characterizes the changing relationships between public and private actors situated at different territorial levels, thereby crossing the normally separate spheres of domestic and international politics. This concept may serve as a causal factor, as actors may feel the need to fill in a void left by the federal government. Hooghe and Marks (2003) outline two types of MLG, one which is characterized by flexible, task-specific, overlapping (intersecting) jurisdictions at an unlimited number of territorial scales; and the other as a limited number of non-overlapping (general-purpose) jurisdictions at a limited number of territorial levels with long life spans, which are nested within one another like a Russian doll, and that are more in line with the traditional federalism structures. The authors suggest that these two types co-exist; the first one is embedded in the legal structures of the more formal one.

In addition to this backdrop of multi-level governance, and adding an economic dimension, I apply the literatures on the diffusion of innovative environmental policy and ecological modernization. The concepts of policy transfer and policy diffusion (specifically innovative environmental policy diffusion and ecological modernization), which stem from the comparative politics literature, provide helpful lenses (in agency and macro structure, respectively) regarding the reasons for the spread of innovative policies and/or technologies and the characteristics of this process. Even though the literatures on the diffusion of innovative environmental policy and ecological modernization have based their characterizations on the nation-state, they can be applied for the most part to the subnational level as well. When it comes to vertical and horizontal diffusion, in a multi-level system vertical diffusion may span beyond the national and international levels to all levels of government and horizontal diffusion may occur across any level.

Policy transfer is concerned with the 'process by which knowledge about policies, administrative arrangements, institutions and ideas in one political system (past or present) is used in the development of policies, administrative arrangements, institutions and ideas in another political system' (Dolowitz and Marsh, 2000). Dolowitz and Marsh's (2000) policy transfer framework is useful for determining the motivation of actors to promote lesson-drawing. Their continuum is helpful for uncovering the degree of agent versus structural forces involved in the decision to transfer.

Policy diffusion, which 'asks for those conditions that favor or hinder the spread of policy innovations within the international system' (Tews, 2006), provides more of a macro-structural perspective for the spread of such policies. The literature on international environmental diffusion considers structural factors, which includes a globalization component. The works of Tews (analytical framework) (2006), Busch et al. (2006) and Kern et al. (2001) categorize three causal factors for the diffusion of innovative policy, namely the dynamics of the international system, national factors and the characteristics or type of the policy innovation. The literature on ecological modernization, which is the 'innovation and diffusion of environmental technologies' (Jänicke, 2006a, p. 12) looks at the factors 'influencing nation-states to promote the diffusion of such technologies. Jänicke (2006b) and Jacob and Volkery (2006) examine the characteristics of frontrunner countries. Furthermore, Jänicke (2006b) distinguishes why pioneering countries come and go. Jänicke and Jacob (2006) lay out the phases in which countries become lead markets.

Finally, I turn to the literature on 'new institutionalism', to answer the question: what supports and what hinders partnerships? In his book on institutional theory in political science, Peters (2005) argues that among the strands of institutionalism there is a central core that binds them all. The basic argument of new institutionalists is that not only do structures matter, but that they are a primary variable in explaining political behavior.

The potential usefulness of this work will include first and foremost a better understanding of how and why such transnational subnational horizontal cooperations came into being, their functionality and what the potential of such arrangements are. While some of the components will be distinct to the state-to-state partnerships, I suggest that their underlying driving factors and functionality will have a general applicability to other non-national transnational governance arrangements that have emerged around the same time and in conjunction to the same international pressures, as they face similar opportunities and obstacles. What are the required drivers, impacts, means of implementation and their relationship to institutional governmental structures? Do international subnational agreements really function? The study provides insight into the dynamics of global governance for sustainable development in a more inclusive multi-level system (international to subnational), and the potential role of the subnational level both in regime implementation and in the vertical and horizontal diffusion of policies. Finally, it will contribute to a better understanding of the coexistence of multi-level governance – that is, 'policy actors and stakeholders operating across horizontal and vertical levels of social organization and jurisdictional authority around a particular issue' (VanDeveer, 2010, p. 7) – within the traditional institutions of government.

This book is organized into nine chapters. Chapter 2 reviews relevant theoretical perspectives, that of policy entrepreneurs, multi-level governance, policy transfer and policy diffusion (specifically environmental policy diffusion and ecological modernization), and new institutionalism. Chapter 3 provides background into the evolving roles of US and German states in reference to the international agenda of the UNCED, the ISO's EMS standards and climate change (for example, the United Nations Framework Convention on Climate Change (UNFCCC) and the Kyoto Protocol) and to their respective federal governments throughout the 1990s and into the 2000s as the partnerships began to transpire. This includes a discussion of the respective federal systems and of state/*Land* capacities. In addition, it considers the internationalization of subnational (state/*Land*) politics in general, especially regarding their respective economies. Chapters 4–8 present the case studies in chronological order starting with the California–Bavaria partnership of 1995 and ending with the California–North Rhine–Westphalia partnership of 2004. Each case study is divided into four sections to examine the key components of the different stages related to the establishment of the partnership and its implementation: the MoU, driving forces, the process, and the implementation and overall results. Chapter 9 provides an analysis and discusses implications.

NOTES

1. The Conference of the Parties is the highest decision-making authority, consisting of representatives of all states that are parties to the climate convention, which meets annually to review and promote its effective implementation. The number represents which annual meeting.

2. Such arrangements can also have an environmental component. There is a 1997 sister-state partnership between South Carolina and Rhineland Palatinate, the primary focus of which is education.

2. Analyzing transnational partnerships: theoretical frameworks

This chapter explores both agency and structural theoretical perspectives for analyzing the trend of German and American (US) state-to-state environmental agreements. The first section looks at the theoretical concept of policy entrepreneurs, outlining how certain policy advocates shape ideas. The second section discusses the literature on the transfer and diffusion of innovative environmental policy, considering both rational and structural motivations behind the spread of ideas. The third and fourth sections add to the discussion on structural influences, examining the theoretical concepts of multi-level governance and the literature on new institutionalism.

POLICY ENTREPRENEURS

The environmental partnerships between US and German states are voluntary, yet extraordinary efforts of subnational governments in their pursuit of innovative policies. As mentioned in Chapter 1, they were officially created through Memoranda of Understanding (MoUs). They were created by people, as opposed to stemming from an institutional requirement, as a tool to realizing their aims, which was innovative in and of itself. The literature on policy entrepreneurs links the role of certain individuals to the advocacy of ideas.

Kingdon defines policy entrepreneurs as 'advocates for proposals or for the prominence of an idea' (1984, p. 122). Such advocates, Kingdon argues, can be found in any location in the policy community, such as in government, interest groups or in other organizations. But while policy entrepreneurs may have diverse backgrounds, according to Kingdon, they, like business entrepreneurs, have a defining characteristic: 'their willingness to invest their resources – time, energy, reputation and sometimes money – in the hope of a future return' (1984, p. 122).

Through his research, Kingdon (1984) compiled a list of qualities of policy entrepreneurs and sorted them into three categories. First, policy entrepreneurs have a certain societal position that allows them to be 'heard' (p. 180). These authorities include people who have (1) expertise; (2) the ability to speak for others such as the leader of a powerful interest group; and (3) an authority in a decision-making position such as a congressional chair. Second, they have political connections or negotiating abilities. And third, policy entrepreneurs are persistent. Kingdon puts forward several reasons why policy entrepreneurs advocate for a proposal or an idea, ranging from promoting personal interests to deriving pleasure in advocacy in the policy process. Despite these seemingly inherent characteristics of the policy entrepreneur, it should be noted that there are a couple of studies that indicate that the institutional environments impact whether there are policy entrepreneurs or not (Perkmann, 2005; Schneider and Teske, 1992).

In his book, Kingdon (1984) discusses some of the ways policy entrepreneurs push their ideas. One primary tactic is to 'soften up' both policy communities and larger publics – getting them used to new ideas and winning their support (p. 128). Examples of 'softening up' or 'paving the way', another term Kingdon uses, include through speeches, introducing bills, holding hearings, writing or issuing reports and studies, and floating trial balloons. This is necessary work, according to Kingdon, without which any proposal put forth, even at the right time, would not likely achieve acceptance.

Once the preliminary work is accomplished, Kingdon says that policy entrepreneurs must wait for a policy window to open – an 'opportunity for action of given initiatives', which presents itself for only short periods (p. 166). At the time of the opening, entrepreneurs either attach their solutions to a problem or connect their proposal to a new political situation, which Kingdon refers to as 'coupling' (p. 165). This coupling represents the moment when the normally separate process 'streams' in agenda setting – which Kingdon categorizes as problems, policies and politics – are brought together by the abilities of a policy entrepreneur at the moment a policy window opens.

Kingdon (1984) argues that a policy window opens when there is a change in the political stream, for example a change of administration, a shift in congressional make-up or a change in the national mood. Or it opens because a problem arises that officials feel they have to address. A change in administration, for example, opens up policy opportunities. The agenda is affected by the problems and political streams, while the alternatives are affected more by the policy stream. A window does not stay open for very long. It closes for several reasons; for example, participants may feel they have addressed the problem; participants may have failed in their endeavors; the triggering events may have passed; the personnel, which may have opened a window, may have changed again; or an alternative policy was not ready and presented (as discussed above). This is why many speak of the importance of timing when it comes to pushing a proposal or an idea.

In contrast to Kingdon, Brouwer et al. (2009), argue that the timing of the developing and coupling of the streams is less unpredictable than Kingdon assumes. These authors found that policy entrepreneurs can influence and steer the development of the streams and consequently their coupling. Brouwer et al. (2009) conducted a study on the actions that policy entrepreneurs can take to have such an influence. They found that entrepreneurs employ numerous strategies in their efforts to pursue policy change. They summed them up in four categories. First, policy entrepreneurs use attention- and support-seeking strategies. In this regard, the authors found that they use small-scale pilot projects, expert testimony and indicators (of the magnitude of the problem) as a strategy. In addition, they were found to present ideas as solutions and highlight focus events. In all of these strategies, though, the authors found that rhetorical persuasion was a key element, particularly the framing of the issue. For example, an entrepreneur may argue that a problem is shared. Second, policy entrepreneurs link strategies. Knowing they cannot accomplish their objectives alone, that they are dependent on the actions or resources of others, entrepreneurs tend to link individuals and groups in a coalition. This means that entrepreneurs actively select which actors are best to include. Because of this group formation, policy entrepreneurs must link their issue to that of one or two other issues, including the problem and the solution. Policy entrepreneurs link with other games of problem solving and policy change – for example supporting something they will not gain from with the hopes to receive support from others at a future time.

When it comes to relationships with others, policy entrepreneurs take a more human approach (Brouwer et al., 2009). They put a lot of effort into building relationships based on respect and mutual trust. In addition to the attitude of the entrepreneur, this relationship can be built through 'efforts of networking and repeated interactions of reciprocal, preferential and mutually supportive actions' (p. 13). This can be formal or informal, external or internal, talking and listening to a broad set of actors in a particular area. In addition to information gathering, helping to understand others, to discover ideas and fine-tune strategies, they help entrepreneurs find opportunities to build coalitions. Mintrom and Vegari (1998) emphasize the importance of using both external and internal policy networks. External networks serve to help generate new ideas and insights of how approaches used elsewhere can be applied, while a good understanding of the internal networks is critical for knowing how to get proper attention for the idea. According to Rose (1993), 'their concern with a special subject . . . leads them to build up a nationwide or international network of contacts that are a source of ideas for new programs' (p. 57). One way of furthering the acceptance of ideas is by lesson-drawing.

Networking and the promotion of lesson-drawing are often cited as important components of policy entrepreneurialism (Dolowitz and Marsh, 1996; Mintrom and Vergari, 1998; Rose, 1993). Mintrom (1997) found that policy entrepreneurs play a decisive role in the diffusion of innovative policies, concluding that their presence increased the chances that the policy be considered legislatively and approved. In addition, Mintrom and Vergari (1998) found that the more policy networks were involved in the diffusion of innovations the greater the chance that entrepreneurs achieve their legislative goals.

Finally, Brouwer et al. (2009) found that policy entrepreneurs participate in arena strategies such as timing. This means that entrepreneurs are not only aware of the right moment, but try to influence time. For example, they may try to create a sense of urgency. They may try to speed up or slow down the policymaking process, for example by asking for additional research or, conversely, setting a deadline. They try to find the right venue, such as a certain level of government or regulatory agency.

Policy entrepreneurialism, however, is not limited to early stages of the policymaking process (McCown, 2005). Policy entrepreneurs may play an important role in the other stages of the policymaking process, particularly the formulation and implementation phases. There is a gap in the literature regarding how policy entrepreneurs select their strategies to pursue this policy change (McCown, 2005).

McCown (2005) argues that in determining the most effective approach to changing policy, policy entrepreneurs take three major factors into account when considering their strategy. The first is the current status of the policy in the policymaking process; the second is the level of salience the issue is receiving; and the third is the position of those interested in the specific policy in relation to the policy entrepreneurs' ideas for change. Based on these components, McCown (2005) offers a model that theorizes what the likely strategy of a policy entrepreneur would be based on the stage and salience of the policy, ranging from conducting hearings to trying to keep an issue 'quiet' through, for example, adding an amendment.

With the understanding of these facets of policy entrepreneurs, one can make some assumptions in reference to the innovative partnerships. As stated in Chapter 1, the partnerships are efforts to draw lessons on cutting-edge policies and technologies or to even push for such transfers, which is a frequently cited action of policy entrepreneurs. From this, it can

be derived that the creation of partnerships not only requires policy entrepreneurs, but also necessitates entrepreneurs who are interested in policy
learning or policy diffusion. In addition, since there is a difference between
the initiation and later stages, and entrepreneurs may play an important
role at different stages, it can be concluded that their absence or presence
during implementation will be a key factor as to how well the partnership
is carried out.

TRANSFER AND DIFFUSION OF ENVIRONMENTAL POLICY INNOVATIONS AND TECHNOLOGIES

As discussed above, one of the tactics of policy entrepreneurs is lesson-
drawing. Entrepreneurs play an important role in the diffusion process.
Analytically, the literatures on policy transfer and policy diffusion (specifically innovative environmental policy diffusion and ecological modernization) provide helpful lenses for the reasons for the spread of innovative
policies and/or technologies (regarding agency and macro-structure,
respectively) and the characteristics of this process. While these literatures
have different focuses regarding the reasons for the spread of innovative
policies and/or technologies and the characteristics of this process, they
nonetheless all stem from comparative politics.

Policy Transfer

Most of the literature on policy transfer denotes transfer as a voluntary
act, in which political actors rationally examine policies implemented elsewhere with the idea of potentially using them in another system (Dolowitz
and Marsh, 1996; Stone, 2000a). A smaller amount of work has shown
the influence of a 'compulsion to conform' or of structural forces (Stone,
2000a, p. 5). Thus, around the turn of the century, this literature came
under criticism for being too micro or agency-centered and, accordingly,
for lacking more of a structural approach, particularly a macro or global
perspective (Evans and Davies, 1999; Ladi, 2001; Stone, 2000a).

Dolowitz and Marsh (2000) believe that globalization – that is, con-
formity pressures from the global economy and from supranational and
international institutions, together with the increase in ease and speed for
policymakers to communicate and the increase in available information
– is what is really behind the significant increase in the amount of policy
transfer throughout the 1990s. These pressures and the growth of all
forms of communication have meant that policymakers increasingly
look to other political systems for knowledge and ideas (Dolowitz and

Marsh, 2000). Thus, the authors say, politicians and bureaucrats meet more frequently in both bilateral and multilateral settings, while policy entrepreneurs 'sell' their policies around the world, and international policy networks, advocacy coalitions or epistemic communities develop and promote ideas.

Evans and Davies (1999), Ladi (2001) and Stone (2000a) find that while transfer may be facilitated by globalization (which may be measured by convergence and divergence; Ladi, 2001), it may in turn be considered a part of the process of globalization in that the dissemination of ideas, programs and the like may be contributing to the convergence of policies, which arguably may again, in turn, provide further opportunities for policy transfers resulting in a cycle of cause and effect. Evans and Davies (1999) point to some examples of opportunity structures caused by globalizing tendencies, for example global communications, international regimes and epistemic communities (exogenous structures), and new forms of governance, the European Union and the competition state (endogenous structures). Evans and Davies (1999) say that these endogenous and exogenous factors play off each other and with policy transfer at the micro level.

Stone (2000a) points to the new opportunities that 'knowledge organizations' (p. 24) (in other words, think tanks, consultancy firms, foundations and academia) have in policy transfer, particularly through network governance; such organizations, Stone says, have 'met the entrepreneurial opportunities afforded to them by the retreat of the state' (2000a, p. 19). In her work, specifically on the role of think tanks in policy transfer, Stone (2000b) concluded that such non-governmental entities can be best described as 'brokers' for or 'facilitators' of transfer (p. 51). They may act 'as a clearing-house for information' (p. 51), with all of their knowledge and expertise, and play the role of networkers, one aspect of which is providing fora for exchange, matching different governments and sectors (this facilitates the transmission of knowledge) (Stone, 2000b).

Dolowitz and Marsh (2000), who have drawn on the work of Rose (1991, 1993) and Bennett (1991a, 1991b, 1992), have created a useful framework that not only includes both agency and structural components but also outlines the characteristics of policy transfer. Dolowitz and Marsh look at policy transfer as something that needs to be explained, as the dependent variable. The main questions of the concept, which, as said, focuses on the characteristics and reasons for the transfer, are: who transfers, what is transferred, from where, why, to what degree, with which help or restrictions and with what success? These questions can only be answered satisfactorily by examining individual cases (Dolowitz and Marsh, 2000; Tews, 2006).

Concerning actors' motivations or the reasons for transfer, Dolowitz and Marsh (2000) have created a useful policy transfer continuum that helps to discern the agency and structural influences when seeking the answer as to why actors have engaged in policy transfer. The continuum, moving from left to right, distinguishes between voluntary lesson-drawing on the far left to coercive direct imposition on the far right. The most voluntary type of transfer, on the far left of the continuum, is rational lesson-drawing. A perfectly rational actor, however, is rare. Most lesson-drawing is 'bounded', characterized by limited information and by the actors' own subjective perceptions, which falls to the right of rational voluntary transfer. Most authors argue that the main reason for engaging in policy transfer is for lesson-learning, which indicates dissatisfaction with the status quo (Dolowitz and Marsh, 1996, 2000). Lessons can be used to gain support in the fight to get an idea accepted, to legitimize a decision made, and because of uncertainty (which is in the nature of interdependency) regarding the cause of problems, the effects of decisions already made or the future (international collaboration reduces this uncertainty) (Bennett, 1991a; Dolowitz and Marsh, 1996; Haas, 1989).

A little farther to the right on the continuum, there is voluntary lesson-drawing that starts to have elements of coercion – that which is perceived as a necessity (for example, to achieve international acceptance) (Dolowitz and Marsh, 2000). Indirect coercive transfer is about 'externalities' or 'functional interdependence', which have necessitated cooperation between countries (Dolowitz and Marsh, 1996, p. 348). While examples of indirect coercive transfer may be issue-specific, there are more abstract pushes behind it, such as: (1) technology (due to how fast it forces change and thus the need to deal with these changes); (2) the world economy (relying on certain markets may coerce a country to adopt similar policies); (3) fear of falling behind a neighbor or a competitor on an important issue (or being embarrassed); and (4) pressure from the international community (when an international consensus has emerged, and even more when a solution to that problem has been introduced by many countries) (Dolowitz and Marsh, 1996).

On the right half of the continuum, there is obligated (and negotiated) transfer, for example as a result of being a member of an international regime and structure (Dolowitz and Marsh, 2000). Then there is policy transfer that is used as a condition for getting something else. The best examples of this are the International Monetary Fund (IMF) or the World Bank, which require the implementation of certain economic policies in return for loans (Dolowitz and Marsh, 1996). The European Union and transnational corporations (TNCs) are other examples. A TNC, for example, can force a country to adopt a certain policy by threatening to move elsewhere. And finally, at the extreme end of the continuum is coercive transfer, the direct imposition of policy transfer or when one government forces another to adopt a certain policy. This, however, is rare; most cases lie somewhere between the two poles, involving different degrees of both voluntary and coercive elements (Dolowitz and Marsh, 1996, 2000).

Degrees of transfer range from the complete copying and transferring of an idea, to inspiration. Constraints may include how complex the policy is and structural and institutional feasibility between systems (political, bureaucratic and economic resources). This could include how confined policymakers are within already established programs and laws (Dolowitz and Marsh, 1996).

That there is a visible trend in the direction of partnerships implies that structural elements are involved. The desire to draw lessons or transfer policies suggests that motivations range from bounded rationality to some coercive elements. Since the partnerships are at the subnational level and since they are related to innovative ideas, this suggests that there is a combination of dissatisfaction with the status quo and the fight to get an idea accepted on the one hand, and the impact of international pressure for a standard or norm, or what the diffusion literature below refers to as 'ideational' and 'regulatory' competition, on the other hand. The next section touches more upon the globalization of environmental policy and causal factors for diffusion.

The Diffusion of Environmental Policy Innovations and Technologies

The causal factors for diffusion of innovations
The literature on the diffusion of environmental policy innovations arose in conjunction with the globalization of environmental problems (Biermann and Dingwerth, 2004) that captured the world's attention by the 1990s and has led to the globalization of environmental policy, defined as the 'global convergence of environmental policy regulatory patterns at a relatively high protective level' (Kern et al., 2001, p. 1). In this school of thought, several scholars, particularly Tews, Busch, Jörgens, Kern and Jänicke, have outlined some structural factors for the diffusion of environmental innovations. These scholars point to three categories of causal factors for diffusion: (1) dynamics of the international system; (2) national factors; (3) and the characteristics or type of the policy innovation (Busch et al., 2006; Kern et al., 2001; Tews, 2006). The first and third components, the most relevant for this study, will be discussed more in detail below.

In today's international system, the most common characteristic of which is globalization, the vertical and horizontal political and institutional interconnections among countries, and the increased economic and institutional interlinkages, has led to both 'rational' motivations or 'ideational competition', and 'regulatory competition' (Busch et al., 2006, pp. 127–128; Tews, 2006, pp. 102–104), which can be conceptualized on Dolowitz and Marsh's (2000) continuum. In the case of a rational motivation, a policymaker looks to other countries for solutions to problems, to draw lessons. When there is uncertainty regarding the results of such policies, policymakers may simply adopt a policy from a country that has a reputation of being successful (Busch et al., 2006).

Tews (2006) refers to these rational motivations or driving forces as ideational competition. This stimulus to learn or emulate, and/or the pressure not to look like a 'laggard' (p. 104), is the result of the institutionalization of environmental protection through international institutions and environmental regimes. These dense networks of transnational and international social relations have, in essence, institutionalized policy transfer through their diffusion and harmonization goals, information exchanges, publication and dissemination of best practices (in frontrunner countries) and comparisons of policies (Kern et al., 2001; Tews, 2006). This point has been proven by the fact that environmental policy innovations worldwide were the highest around the times of the 1972 and 1992 United Nations (UN) conferences (Tews, 2006). These complex social relations indicate another key structural factor in the international system: communication (Busch et al., 2006). And thus, it is necessary to identify such international or transnational channels and actors (for example, international organizations, transnational networks and non-governmental organizations, NGOs) that relay policy information (Busch et al., 2006; Tews, 2006). These actors and their activities are the link between the national, international and subnational levels (Tews, 2006).

Motivations caused by regulatory competition are more complex. There are two different points of view on this concept. The first assumes that the increasing international competition for goods and services and the increasing capital and labor mobility result in lower environmental regulations. The second assumes that taking up frontrunner roles in environmental policy, particularly in the European Union (EU), will hinder political and administrative adjustment costs (Busch et al., 2006).

Busch et al. (2006) explain that there are two different types of regulatory competition: political and economic. Political competition takes into account the effects of diffusion processes in a multi-level setting. While this was meant 'both horizontally to other countries and vertically to the international level' (Busch et al., 2006, p. 128), this could now be included in a deeper multi-level sense, as subnational governments are involved heavily in the competition (see Chapter 3 in this volume). It speaks to the second assumption on frontrunner roles. It is better to provide the model than have to adjust to one that may later be imposed (Busch et al., 2006; Jänicke and Jacob, 2006; Kern et al., 2001). The United Nations Conference on Environment and Development (UNCED) is considered as being the one major international event, 'with its regular follow-up conferences and reporting obligations', that has become a major instigator of regulatory competition (Kern et al., 2001, p. 5).

Jänicke (2006b), Jacob and Volkery (2006) have examined more closely the characteristics of the 'trendsetters' from which others copy. Such countries are those with 'stable factors' that include economic and fiscal resources, informational (knowledge) structures, the right political and institutional systems, and the existing strength of the green advocacy coalition of a country (a coalition for ecological modernization) (Jänicke, 2006b). But which countries end up as leaders in terms of innovativeness in a certain policy area is contingent more on 'unstable' factors. Jänicke (2006b) refers to these factors as 'situative factors' (policy windows) and 'strategic factors' (the ability to take advantage or make use of a policy window) (p. 53). Situative factors can be sudden economic changes such as recessions, high oil prices or new technologies, as well as political events or changes such as a government turnover or policy innovations in other countries (Jänicke, 2006b, p. 60). Regarding strategic factors, Jänicke points to two: a forerunner or a pusher (Jänicke, 2006b). A forerunner is 'reacting to domestic problems or certain market opportunities'; a 'pusher' transfers its policy innovation to the higher level, for example the EU (Jänicke, 2006b, p. 62).

Regarding economic competition, it has been predicted there would be a 'race to the bottom' for regulatory standards (Busch et al., 2006, p. 129); and in practice, many governments have attempted to change policy instruments, from legally binding regulations to softer approaches such as voluntary agreements, a sort of de facto weakening of standards, which is often justified as an emulation of other countries, especially their primary competitors, or as a response to concepts promoted by inter-national organizations (Busch et al., 2006). That said, some believe that this economic competition may have induced a 'race to the top', in which countries wish to emulate tougher standards in their early stages of diffu-sion (Busch et al., 2006, p. 129; Jänicke and Jacob, 2006; Kern et al., 2001, p. 1; Porter and van der Linde, 1995). The reasons for this are so that they can secure 'first-mover advantages' (Busch et al., 2006, p. 130; Jänicke and Jacob, 2006), and to act in accordance with domestic industry's desire to do so (because industries are obliged to raise their standards to that of the strictest market anyway if they want to sell their products in the country's market) (Busch et al., 2006, p. 130). Industries may be interested in a harmonization of standards (Busch et al., 2006). Stricter environmental policies may lead to innovation within the polluting industry, which gives an economic edge (Jänicke and Jacob, 2006).

In addition to a 'race to the top' for tougher standards, scholars have found that nation-states are increasingly strategically linking ecology and economy by deliberately promoting the 'innovation and diffusion of environmental technologies', or ecological modernization (Jänicke, 2006a, p. 12). In his study on ecological modernization, Jänicke (2006a) found the driving forces for nation-states to pursue such strategies akin to those prompting countries to become frontrunners or first-movers in the process of international diffusion of environmental policy innovations. But globalization has not only spurred regulatory and ideational competition as stated above; it has caused more economic insecurity for businesses because of the increased environmental pressures and obligations on polluters in the multi-level, multi-actor governance system, and made them more apt to innovate in environmental areas. Thus, globalization has prompted both the public and private sectors to the mutual aim of ecological modernization (Jänicke, 2006a).[1]

There are several major incentives for becoming a lead market in environmental innovations. A nation may: (1) secure first-mover advantages for domestic industry; (2) attract foreign investors; and (3) garner legitimization for national policymakers and even sometimes provide them with roles in the global arena. In addition to these national inducements and advantages, there is a benefit for the rest of the world as the lead market country provides 'marketable solutions for typical environmental problems', that is, the lead country pays for product development and demonstration of both the political and technical feasibility of the innovation (Jänicke and Jacob, 2006, p. 43).[2]

Jänicke and Jacob (2006) assert that the process to becoming a lead market occurs in two phases. First is the 'struggle for success on the national market'. Governments may use instruments such as 'standards, subsidies, charges, labels, public procurement, network management or EMAS [Eco-Management and Audit Scheme] (demand of firms)'. Second is governmental support for technology transfer, which may occur through actions 'within international organizations . . . bilateral actions with strategic countries, special international conferences, reporting by the international media, cooperation with international NGOs, etc.' (p. 42).

Policy characteristics help to answer why it is that some policies or instruments diffuse faster than others (Busch et al., 2006; Tews, 2006). The characteristics of the policy innovation include problem structure, compatibility and political feasibility. Under the heading of problem structure, certain policies related to long-term environmental problems or those for which technological solutions are not available diffuse slowly (Tews,

2006). Conversely, concerning compatibility, innovations that can easily be added to an existing structure and which are incremental in change (versus those that would pose massive change), diffuse faster (Kern et al., 2001; Tews, 2006). Finally, under political feasibility, the more a policy conflicts with powerful actor groups, the slower the rate of adoption (unless it is exposed to regulatory competition) (Tews, 2006). If a regulation is related to products (such as eco-labels), it is easier; but if it is linked to production (redistribution of) costs (such as energy or carbon taxes), the brakes are applied (Kern et al., 2001; Tews, 2006). Another important aspect is whether there are available models to copy; something already developed and tested (Kern et al., 2001).

In her work laying the foundation for an analytical framework on the diffusion of environmental policy innovations, Tews (2006) concludes that while the international and national factors influence diffusion, they are unable to explain particular diffusion patterns. The best approach, therefore, is to look at the characteristics of policy innovations. The characteristics of the innovation can reveal which mechanism is at work, for example whether it is regulatory competition (linked globally by trade, regional, political and economic integration) or ideational competition (global society – intergovernmental organizations – IGOs, NGOs, media, transnational advocacy networks and epistemic communities). Moreover, these mechanisms help point to the different success rates (for example, if a policy is adopted for legitimization purposes, it may not be substantive). In this regard, it helps to know the motivations for adoption, which is where including policy transfer analysis is helpful, and the conditions for diffusion success. Furthermore, incorporating the more micro aspects helps determine which institutional actors, agents and strategic approaches are the most relevant (Tews, 2006).

While the diffusion literature provides many details, one is struck from the start by the clear parallel between the observed increase in the diffusion of environmental policy innovations that rose with the globalization of environmental problems and the emergence of the trend of innovative environmental partnerships between US and German subnational governments. The aims of the partnerships range from lesson-drawing to trying to push transfer or initiate diffusion, while the content of the partnerships relates to global governance for sustainable development and all that this encompasses. Considering the discussed interlinkages that today's international system has prompted at all levels, one can assume that one of the causal factors for the partnerships was ideational or regulatory competition as triggered by pressure caused by different approaches and processes stemming from the UNCED. This will be shown when looking at the characteristics and type of policy innovations of the partnerships, which according to the literature reveals which diffusion mechanism is at work.

Literature overstresses the nation-state
Even though the literature on the diffusion of innovative environmental policy, including the characteristics of the trendsetters and of lead market states, are nation-state based, as analytical tools they can be applied, for the most part, to the subnational level as well. That said, when it comes to the philosophy regarding global governance as is discussed in the next chapter, the nation-state centeredness of these literatures is problematic. Vertical diffusion refers to transfers from the national to the international levels, while horizontal diffusion primarily focuses on transfers from nation-state to nation-state. Thus, the aforementioned scholars do not properly take into account the role of subnational-level governments as political actors in the multi-level international system regarding environmental policy and especially the economy and consequently ecological modernization, which is demonstrated in the next chapter. The literature on multi-level governance (MLG), however, provides a deeper dimension to the international system in a globalized world, characterizing the changing relationships between public and private actors situated at different territorial levels, thereby crossing the normally separate spheres of domestic and international politics.

MULTI-LEVEL GOVERNANCE

The theoretical concept of MLG developed as a way to describe a reallocation of authority from the central state 'upwards, downwards and sideways' (Hooghe and Marks, 2003, p. 233). According to VanDeveer (2010), multi-level governance can be defined as: 'policy actors and stakeholders operating across horizontal and vertical levels of social organization and jurisdictional authority around a particular issue' (p. 7). Unlike the diffusion literature, which saw multi-level as national and international, this literature includes the subnational in such governance. One relevant study on energy and climate change policy in Europe unveiled three MLG modes, two of which provide new opportunities for subnational actors independent of national boundaries: 'hierarchical Europeanization', in which subnational authorities implement EU and national legislation; 'cooperative Europeanization', in which cities and regions are directly involved at the European level; and 'horizontal Europeanization', in which subnational actors in different countries, absent EU involvement, transfer best practices (Kern and Monstadt, 2008, p. 4).

Some scholars have branched out beyond the European Union to include the international level as another level (for example, the UN and the World Trade Organization, WTO) (Hooghe and Marks, 2003; Kern et al., 2007; Knodt, 2004; VanDeveer, 2010). A study by Kern et al. (2007), showed a two-way vertical and horizontal multi-level diffusion process of local Agenda 21 in Germany. VanDeveer (2010) also described extensive horizontal and vertical interaction among representatives from all societal sectors from the federal to the municipal levels in Europe and North America regarding climate change governance, as authorities operate across all levels, even continentally and globally. Another study on sustainable development implementation in Germany found that most *Länder* undertook sustainable development initiatives on their own, within the context of the German and European multi-level system, especially in the areas that were lagging federally (Kern, 2008). Others have looked at the international as configurations beyond national boundaries – for example region-to-region collaborations and governance by networks – and how they affect policy outcomes in an MLG system (Blatter, 2001; Gunnarsson, 2003; Hooghe and Marks, 2003). The concept has been extended to other continents, such as North America (Blatter, 2001; Hooghe and Marks, 2003; Kaiser, 2005; VanDeveer, 2010).

A recent study even examined the possibilities for a transatlantic MLG. Vogel and Swinnen (2011) believe that the best way to improve environmental protection and policy globally is through cooperation between California and the EU because of the influence these governing bodies have (California nationally and the EU globally). In looking for ways in which these non-sovereign bodies can cooperate, the book argues that MoUs are the best way. This type of cooperation would fall under the categorization of Type II MLG.

This characterization of the two types of MLG came from Hooghe and Marks (2003). Type I MLG is characterized by a limited number of non-overlapping (general-purpose) jurisdictions at a limited number of territorial levels, such as a 'local', 'intermediate' and a 'central level' (although it can extend into the international level as stated above), which are nested within one another like a Russian doll (pp. 236–237). It is characterized by long life spans. The jurisdictions usually have a legislature, executive and judicial system. The intellectual underpinning is federalism, which analyses the specific government versus the policy, and in consequence 'extends the Westphalian principle of exclusivity into the domestic arena' (Hooghe and Marks, 2003, p. 237).

Type II is characterized by having many overlapping jurisdictions, which operate on numerous territorial scales as opposed to just a few (Hooghe and Marks, 2003, p. 237). The argument is that a public good or service should be in the jurisdiction where it can be best provided, resulting in 'jurisdictions at diverse scales', which would look like a 'marble-cake' (p. 238). The jurisdictions are made to be flexible, they exist only as needed, as opposed to lasting, and they are task-specific, instead of general-purpose (p. 237). Type II governance is intersecting as opposed to nested. This concept stems from neoclassical political economists and public-choice theorists, as well as federalism, local government, international relations and European studies (Hooghe and Marks, 2003). This type of governance is prevalent at the local level.

These two types of multi-level governance are based on fundamentally different concepts of community. Type I governance is territorial, or religious or ethnic, based on citizens' preferences to unite based on common factors and to have a common identity. It is not possible to leave Type I unless one moves from the region or country, or changes one's identity. Type II governance is based on solving a particular problem, such as managing a common pool resource, establishing a technical standard or transporting hazardous waste. It is based on people who share a common geography or function, or who have a common need to work together. Type II is voluntary and it is easy to enter and exit. It represents only one part of a person's identity (Hooghe and Marks, 2003).

While each type of MLG is based on these different concepts of community, one of the most important points about these types of MLG is that they can exist together because they complement one another. Hooghe and Marks (2003) suggest, on the one hand, that Type II jurisdictions function 'alongside' those of the nested Type I, and on the other hand, that Type II MLG is usually embedded in Type I MLG (p. 240). There is, however, no particular way as to how. In one case cited by Hooghe and Marks, Type II structures were formed within the legal structures of Type I. This implies that Type II is bound by the legal structures of Type I. Indeed, a recent study by Kern and Bulkeley (2009) showed, in effect, that there was a certain impotency of policymakers in Type II governance because of the lack certain legal governing capabilities – that is, mandate or enforcement capabilities, or 'teeth' – in such governance. More needs to be studied on this point, however.

The literature on MLG adds the missing depth to the concept of multi-level that is lacking in the diffusion literature. What is more, it demonstrates the noteworthy role of the subnational government amidst all the horizontal and vertical activities that are transpiring across these many jurisdictions. More specifically, it suggests that the partnerships represent Type II multi-level governance as they are voluntary, overlapping jurisdictions (territories), based on a common need to work together, and are task-specific and easy to enter and exit. The literature makes clear, however, that Type II fits into Type I. It can be assumed that to be implemented, the partnerships have to fit into the legal systems of Type I as well. The literature on new institutionalism serves as an analytical tool for understanding when something is institutionalized.

NEW INSTITUTIONALISM

The concept that has come to be known as 'new institutionalism' was an effort to bring back the role of the institution in analyzing politics, which had lost authority to behavioral and rational-choice perspectives in the 1960s and 1970s. In an exhaustive effort to tackle the issue of ambiguities as to what new institutionalism is about, Peters (2005) finds a nucleus to new institutionalism. In his book on institutional theory in political science, Peters (2005) first points out that there are at least seven strands of institutionalism, beginning with March and Olsen's 'normative insti- tutionalism' and including 'rational choice institutionalists', 'historical institutionalism', 'empirical institutionalists', 'sociological institutional- ism', 'interest representation' and 'international institutionalism'. But after having examined each approach, Peters found that there is one central core that equates to 'a' new institutionalism. While the reality of the structure–agency debate is that both factors are almost always in operation (Giddens, 1981), all the scholars in these different schools find that they have greater analytical force by starting with institutions instead of individuals. According to Peters (2005):

> Individuals remain as important actors in most of these theories, but . . . there is a substantially greater leverage to be gained through understanding the institu- tional frameworks within which they operate. Perhaps more than anything else, the individual element of policy-making comes into play as the members of the institution interpret what the rules and values of their institutions are. (p. 164)

They all indicate the role of structure in determining behavior and the out- comes of political processes. Of all the schools, the normative approach (not rational-choice institutionalism) gives the most latitude for human agency.

Moreover, according to Peters (2005), these versions of institutionalism find that institutions cause regularity in behavior. This is to say, if there were a great capacity for human agency, there would be less regularity. In addition, institutions may allow for the occasional irregularity of a person. Thus institutions mold individual behavior and reduce the uncertainty that is prevalent in social life, making prediction easier. Finally, institu- tions are understood as being creations of human action which, after creation, constrains them. Some explain this paradox by saying that they do it to restrict adversaries, while others provide a normative explanation, arguing that it is so that the institution provides values and roles. This also applies to the role of regimes in international relations theory, as it constrains the sovereign states which choose to be members. The reason for having things institutionalized and ritualized is because they matter (Stinchcombe, 1997). This formality and ritualization subsequently increases with the importance of the issue.

Hira and Hira (2000), however, argue that new institutionalism ignores changes that come from outside the system. They point out how marginalized groups can make claims upon institutions through efforts ranging from lobbying to plain resistance. They also point to factors such as technology, culture, ideology, irrationality, history and economic shocks. Finally, Hira and Hira (2000) argue that people learn how to maximize their opportunities within an institutional framework (those who do it best are the entrepreneurs), which, in turn, alters the institutional framework.

Among the differences that Peters encountered was how constraint is exercised. Some say that this constraint is through values and norms, while others say it occurs through rules. Scholars also differ on whether institutions are more fixed or have a capacity for change, planned or unplanned (Peters, 2005, p. 156). And there is debate as to whether institutions are tangible objects or intangible norms and values, the strength of which is based on the perception of the members of the institution.

The basic argument of new institutionalists is that not only do structures matter, but that they are also a primary variable in explaining political behavior (Peters, 2005). 'In all the approaches, something about institutions – their values, their rules, their incentives or the pattern of interactions of the individuals within them – explains the decisions that governments make' (Peters, 2005, p. 164). The common core of the scholarly works of institutionalism that binds the approaches together is the understanding of what an institution is (Peters, 2005). As such, Peters (2005) argues that institutions can be characterized by: (1) formal (a legislature, an agency in the public bureaucracy or a legal framework) or informal (a network of interacting organizations or a set of shared norms) structures (as such institutions involve patterned interactions among groups of individuals that are predictable; in accord with the institution – such as a university versus a prison); (2) the existence of some stability over time (in other words, according to Peters if a group of people meet once for coffee, that is not an institution, but if they were to meet every week at the same time and at the same place, that would be the beginnings of an institutional feature); (3) the ability to affect the behavior of their members, thus constrain them (this could be formally or informally), in that there is some level of importance placed on the institution; and (4) some sense of shared values and meaning among the members of the institutions.

Based on this literature, if institutions are a major variable in explaining the decisions that governments make then they will have an important role regarding the partnerships. While it is clear that state institutions allow public officials to initiate partnerships, by way of MoUs, it is unclear – yet no less important – what the role of the institution is at later stages, such as at the implementation stage. This is to say that if an MoU is important for the creation of the partnership, further institutionalization is necessary to execute it. Put another way, a policy entrepreneur can initiate a partnership but will have difficulty sustaining it without formal institutionalization. Formal institutionalization requires more than an MoU. Interestingly, these correlations correspond to those from the MLG literature, in that the partnerships, representing Type II MLG, have to fit into the system of Type I MLG, which in this case is the state institution. The next chapter provides a historical background, setting the stage for the case studies.

NOTES

1. Jänicke (2006a) lists several specific economic, political and societal pressures on businesses for ecological modernization. One economic factor is the EMS certification for competitors (EMAS and ISO 14001); political factors include strict regulation of important markets (for example, the EU) and international environmental regimes; and one societal factor includes 'green' consumerism of the growing global middle class (p. 21).
2. Historic examples include mobile phones in Finland, the fax in Japan and the Internet in the United States. Examples of environmental innovations include the catalytic converter in the United States, CFC-free refrigerators in Germany and support for wind energy in Denmark (Jänicke and Jacob, 2006).

3. The road to the partnerships: a historical background

This chapter looks at the larger context in which the German–US subnational environmental partnerships began to emerge. To this end, it examines how governance for sustainable development had been playing out in a multi-level international system at the time. The international level is first examined, covering the 1992 United Nations Conference on Environment and Development (UNCED), the International Organization for Standardization's (ISO) 1996 environmental management system (EMS) standards, and the ongoing political developments related to climate change – the 1992 United Nations Framework Convention on Climate Change (UNFCCC) and the 1997 Kyoto Protocol. The chapter then considers first how the European Union (EU) responded to this international agenda, followed by the US and German federal and subnational governments. Furthermore, it examines the changing dynamics among the levels of government, including the federal enabling roles, the federal systems in general, state/*Land* capacities and decentralization. It also considers the larger trends of devolution and the internationalization of subnational politics and the pursuance of economic growth. Finally, the chapter concludes with a look at the first observations of subnational transatlantic environmental partnerships.

RELEVANT INTERNATIONAL TREATIES AND ACTIVITIES

UNCED

The quintessential intergovernmental initiative regarding global governance for sustainable development was the 1992 UNCED in Rio de Janeiro. It was at this summit, where the emerging principle of sustainable development that would set the stage for the twenty-first century became solidified.[1] There, governments agreed that it was necessary to rethink economic development at the price of detrimental damage to the environment and natural resources (UN, 1997); that the two aspects must always be considered together to achieve 'sustainable development'. As an approach, this would mean integrating the relevant sectors that impact the environment and the different environmental media into environmental policymaking that is based on a long-term strategic plan at all levels of government with the emphasis on the most relevant level. In other words, it was a multi-actor, multi-level governance approach.

Agenda 21 was the largest product of the conference, providing a non-binding international plan of action for achieving sustainable development. It asks countries to create a long-term national strategy for sustainable development that integrates policy and is in cooperation with the private sector (Jörgensen, 2002). It recommends an increased role for other major groups in environmental policymaking including local authorities, businesses, trade unions, non-governmental organizations (NGOs), women and youth, the scientific community and farmers. Finally, it proposes means of implementation, which include environmental technology transfer and public outreach (UN, 1997). In brief, it set up 'a multi-level governance ranging from the global to the local and a multi-actor governance approach including economic and societal sectors' (Jörgensen, 2006, p. 151). Since this document was created, scholars have increasingly examined local-level efforts to implement sustainability including climate change (for example, Betsill and Bulkeley, 2004; Bulkeley and Betsill, 2003; Kern and Bulkeley, 2009; Lafferty and Eckerberg, 2009; Owens and Cowell, 2011).

ISO EMS Standards

Another very important milestone in global governance for sustainability occurred at the UNCED. The ISO was successful in getting the concept of uniform international EMS standards solidified so that it could further develop them. The United States Environmental Protection Agency (EPA) defines an EMS as: 'a set of processes and practices that enable an organization to reduce its environmental impacts and increase its operating efficiency' (US EPA, 2008).

Actually, it was the UNCED that stimulated these developments, as the private sector was concerned about the repercussions that the upcoming conference would have on business. With globalization on its steep ascent, the private sector could see the detrimental trade barriers if it had to contend with individual EMSs worldwide; so it became determined to secure uniform global standards. Consequently, in 1991, the Geneva-based ISO, led by the private sector, set up an advisory group to recommend standards at the UNCED (Clapp, 2005). As the movement to create EMSs was underway at the ISO, there were simultaneous national efforts to do the same. The United Kingdom (spurred on by Europe's Eco-Management and Audit Scheme, EMAS) led the way and established a national EMS by 1992. This model, in addition to some developed by other countries, later became the foundation for what became the 1996 ISO 14001 series (Natural Resources Conservation Authority – NRCA, n.d.). Today, the number of companies that are becoming certified to these standards is growing rapidly.

Climate Change

The UNCED was not the only major international environmental achievement at that time. It served as a forum that marked another milestone in international action on an emerging global environmental problem: climate change. There, the UNFCCC, a legally non-binding, voluntary agreement calling for developed countries to reduce their greenhouse gas (GHG) emissions to 1990 levels by 2000, was signed by 154 countries and the European Community, including the United States, making it a treaty by 1994 (UNFCCC, 2004).

In December 1997, after having concluded that reductions needed to be legally binding, the signatories drafted the Kyoto Protocol, requiring developed countries to reduce their GHG emissions to at least 5 percent below 1990 levels by 2008–2012 (UNFCCC, 2004). But several months before the protocol was put forth, the US Senate voted unanimously against ratifying any treaty that does not include binding emission reductions for developing countries. The Clinton administration thus only symbolically signed the protocol in 1998, saying afterward that it did not plan to submit it to the Senate for ratification until developing countries were included ('US Signs', 1998). But in March 2001, only a couple of months after entering office, the Bush administration made it clear that there was no hope for ratification (Borger, 2001). The protocol, however, was ultimately ratified by enough countries to make it a treaty in 2005. The meaning of the United States' lack of participation, however, was well known since it contributed 25 percent of the world's emissions, the most of any country at the time, while totaling about 5 percent of the global population. So, if climate change were to be addressed effectively, it was understood that the United States would still have to be a part of the effort.

EUROPEAN POLICY

In addition to these international pressures, the 1990s saw a push from the European level that was inspired by and in accordance with the new integrative approaches of Rio and which served as a driving force for the establishment of successful sustainable development policies. The EU set forth, for instance, the target-oriented (1993) Fifth Environmental Action Program 'For Sustainable and Ecological Development', which said that self-regulatory and market-based instruments should be used in sustainable policy approaches in the sectors of industry, energy, transportation, agriculture and tourism, as opposed to the customary top-down methods (Jörgensen, 2002). The EU also created its EMAS as a model for collaboration between state and industry in 1993 (drafted in 1990), in effect by 1995 (EC, 2009a). This was a way to integrate business into environmental policymaking. Finally, the Amsterdam Treaty (1997) strengthened the legal basis for environmental protection and sustainable development, requiring the integration of environmental interests that are not already under given rules and standards (Jörgensen, 2002). Likewise, the 1998 Cardiff Process required that the Council of Ministers in all areas integrate sustainable development into their policies (Bomberg, 2009).

With climate change, there were both EU- and some national-level efforts that led to two-way influencing. The forerunners in the early 1990s were Germany, Denmark, the Netherlands and Sweden. The EU itself adopted an emissions target, to stabilize emissions at 1990 levels by 2000. In 1991, the Commission proposed a strategy on carbon dioxide (CO_2) emissions reductions. In this decade, it played a large role in working out an EU negotiating strategy for Kyoto and in creating the burden-sharing agreement for the member states with different targets for each country but with the collective goal of reaching an 8 percent emissions reduction from 1990s levels by 2008–2012 (Schreurs et al., 2009). In terms of renewable energies, high-level attention did not happen until the mid-1990s. By October 2001, the first Directive entered into force that required member states to increase their share of renewable energy into the electricity supply, with the collective objective of reaching 22 percent by 2010 (Rowlands, 2009). Today, environmental policy in the EU, from the '"top-down" vantage point' alone, has become 'one of the most integrated and centralized policy areas' of this supranational body (Wälti, 2009, p. 44).

DOMESTIC ACTIVITIES – FEDERAL AND SUBNATIONAL

The German and US Federal Governments

While both Germany and the United States have been pioneers in different environmental areas over the years, neither has led in the coordination of the national sustainability processes; on the contrary, according to an international comparative study, Germany was described as 'cautiously supportive', and the United States was deemed 'disinterested' (Lafferty and Meadowcroft, 2000, pp. 416–417). This seems to be in line with an overall pattern among European countries, as the period after the UNCED was curiously that of 'a downward cycle of environmental policies' in EU member countries (Hey, 2005, p. 23). 'Shortly after the UNCED conference a new agenda was promoted by several Member States, which concentrated mainly on the competitiveness of industries and the decentralization of environmental policies' (Hey, 2005, p. 23).

In Germany, implementation of sustainable development at the federal level even lagged behind that of other Organisation for Economic Co-operation and Development (OECD) countries (Jörgensen, 2006); two-thirds of OECD countries developed a sustainable development plan between the late 1980s and late 1990s (Kern, 2008). It was not until April 2002 that Germany adopted its National Sustainability Strategy, which was an effort to bring together ecological, economic and social goals, and include all groups in society for its implementation (UN, n.d.). The National Service Agency for Local Agenda 21 was also not established until 2002 (Kern, 2008). Prior to that there were a couple of tentative steps including federal government deliberations (in the late 1980s) and dialogs with stakeholders and studies on the matter. In 1998, when the Social Democrats and the Greens formed a coalition government (after 16 years of a conservative government), the new government decided to use sustainability as the 'guiding principle' for all of its policies (UN, n.d., p. 3).

Climate efforts were a different story, as Germany was among those at the forefront (Hatch, 2007). In 1990, the federal cabinet agreed to a non-binding goal to reduce its CO_2 emissions by 25 percent by 2005 (Treber, Bals and Kier, n.d.). Policy instruments included: (1) the 1991 Electricity Feed Act, subsidizing utilities to buy electricity from renewable energy sources; (2) the Waste Avoidance and Waste Management Act; and (3) the Ordinance on Heat Insulation, requiring insulation standards for new buildings. Government and industry also agreed in 1995 to cooperate to limit CO_2 emissions. Industry agreed to use 'special efforts' to reduce CO_2 emissions by 20 percent by 2005, while the government agreed to hold back on additional regulatory measures such as the Heat Utilization Ordinance and CO_2 energy tax (Hatch, 2007, p. 14).

Climate efforts got a boost in 1998 under the new government. In 2000, it issued its climate protection program confirming the stated goals (Kern, 2008). Over the next years, it established measures to achieve these obligations, including: (1) the Renewable Energy Sources Act (2000), promoting renewable energy through compulsory minimum prices; (2) the market launch program for renewable energy sources (1999), providing benefits for their usage; (3) the ecological tax reform (1999–2003), gradually raising taxes on fuels and electricity; (4) an ordinance to save energy in buildings (2002); (5) financial support for building modernization (2000); (6) the expansion of combined heat and power generation (2001 and 2002); (7) a consensus to shut down nuclear energy plants (2002); and (8) the promotion of research and development (K. Müller, 2005).

In the United States, the 'disinterested' label was partly a misunderstanding. While not couched in relation to the UNCED or its Agenda 21, the federal government, indeed, made efforts to achieve these ends. And this does not include the sustainable development efforts that were made prior to the 1990s. Sustainable development principles, practices and politics have existed for quite some time in the United States, albeit under different terms. Furthermore, principles such as precaution, policy integration and corporate social responsibility began in the United States. During the 1970s environmental movement, there were references to a more comprehensive, integrative approach (Bomberg, 2009).

But subsequent to the UNCED, in 1993, President Clinton created the President's Council on Sustainable Development to bring together different government agencies and societal sectors to help develop approaches to realize these goals. Likewise, the EPA commenced its 'Reinventing Environmental Regulation', part of what came to be known as New Environmentalism, which was clearly reflective of the international agenda as illustrated in the programs Common Sense Initiative, Project XL and National Environmental Performance Partnership System (Kraft and Scheberle, 1998). These programs contained components including stakeholder inclusion, cross-media assessments, flexibility, performance goals, environmental management and cost-effective strategies, regulatory relief, public–private cooperation and federal–state partnerships.

Another endeavor in line with the international agenda was the EPA's first Strategic Plan (1997), a five-year blueprint on how it was preparing for a new era of environmental protection. The document lays out its mission, goals and principles. It outlines its approaches to achieving these goals; the benefits and costs of its activities; how it connects to other agency plans; and its consultations with stakeholders (US EPA, 1997).

But regarding climate change, as discussed above, it was pronounced dead by the administration by 2001. That said, one must not forget that the United States is a federalist system and that states have certain degrees of autonomy. Accordingly, this issue was taken up at the state level, both in the number of activities and in innovative policies. This is not to say that there were no relevant federal actions that contributed to state activities or that the federal dynamic itself did not play any role, as one must not forget that the federal system is interlocking. These issues will be discussed in the following section.

States and *Länder*

By 2001, representatives of environmental departments from both US states and German *Länder* deemed their respective federal governments' efforts on sustainable development to be lacking (Jörgensen, 2006). In contrast, many *Länder* and states were more active in these areas than the federal level was for much of the time. Moreover, in many ways they served and in many instances continue to serve as 'laboratories for experimentation' or frontrunners in designing and implementing policies related to sustainable development and climate change, including those that promote renewable energy (Berthold, 2004; Jörgensen, 2006; Kraemer, 2003; Rabe, 2002).[2]

In Germany, in the first half of the 1990s, it was the *Länder* that pushed for improvements in federal policy drafts and initiated policies in environmental liability, waste management and climate protection. Furthermore, in implementing federal law, some created model programs (for example, Hesse's target-oriented management approach for the Emission Protection Act) that diffused to the other *Länder* (Jörgensen, 2002). Specific to sustainable development, by 1994, the *Länder* minister-presidents declared their support for the development and implementation of the Rio principles (UN, n.d.) and by the mid-1990s, all of them had introduced related policies (Jörgensen, 2006). Within these policies, there were novel approaches of all types (Jörgensen, 2002). By 2002, all of the 16 German states, together with business, had either adopted or were in the process of setting up their own regional sustainability strategies, programs on sustainable development or implementation strategies for Agenda 21. Moreover, 12 *Länder* had established voluntary or cooperative agreements by 2003; the first was Bavaria in 1995. By 2002, when the federal government set up the National Service Agency for Local Agenda 21, all the *Länder* had created some support initiatives of local sustainable development, which resulted in more than 2000 municipalities with Agenda 21s (Kern, 2008; UN, n.d.). The federal government's efforts were modeled after North Rhine–Westphalia (NRW) (Kern, 2008).

As for climate change, Jörgensen (2002) reported that 13 *Länder* had put forth climate protection plans and relevant energy programs outside of federal mandates. This is noteworthy since *Länder* have almost no implementation responsibilities in this area (Weidner and Mez, 2008). Any measures in this regard are additional. Nine of these had measurable targets in GHG emissions, energy efficiency enhancements and renewable energy requirements (Jörgensen, 2002).

Since the late 1990s, it has been primarily the federal government that has been the driver in climate change policy (Weidner and Mez, 2008). But this is not to say that no *Länder* have been proactive or even influential in policy development, particularly in renewable energy. NRW, for example, set a goal 'to make the region number one for future energies' (EnergieAgenturNRW, n.d.-a). And even with strong federal action, the *Länder* continued to create their own climate protection strategies. By 2000, the year the federal government released its climate protection program, 12 *Länder* had established such programs.

The US states have also broken new ground (absent the federal government) in developing programs that correspond to the new approach to environmental protection – for example, allowing for industry-wide instead of source-by-source permits, requiring performance indicators and/or cooperating with the private sector (Jörgensen, 2002). Different studies have provided examples of states' pioneering efforts. Jörgensen (2006) pointed to cutting-edge efforts regarding environmental planning strategies. Likewise, Rabe (2000) provided some examples of innovative programs on the prevention of pollution instead of pollution control (for example, in Minnesota, with the 1990 passage of its Minnesota Toxic Pollution Prevention Act and later its Interagency Pollution Prevention Advisory Team) and the integration of regulations to minimize pollutant transfer across mediums (for example, New Jersey and Minnesota, and their approaches to permitting). Rabe also identified states with innovative activities involving economic incentives (for example, some states have implemented different types of 'green taxes'), disclosure mandates (Rabe, 2000), technology sharing, and cross-boundary collaboration and agreements with other national and subnational governments (Rabe, 2002), as is discussed below.

US States and Climate Change

Regarding climate change, the level and diversity of innovative activities that states have taken on their own initiative is remarkable. Many of these approaches, which were controversial at the federal level (for example, Renewable Portfolio Standards, RPSs; and mandatory GHG reporting), have already been diffusing across the states (Rabe, 2002). Efforts have ranged from creating inventory-type plans of GHGs to cap-and-trade programs and lawsuits against the federal government.

For starters, more than half of the states have developed 'Climate Action Plans' (US EPA, 2007).[3] Many states, however, have taken more serious pains to address climate change, including the establishment of target levels and dates for reducing GHG emissions.[4] Other efforts have included goals to offset emissions.[5]

One of the most significant and controversial measures occurred in one state alone, California, but with implications for the rest of the 49 states. In 2002, it enacted the first law of its kind in the nation, requiring a reduction of GHG emissions from cars and light trucks manufactured from 2009 onwards that would translate to a 22 percent reduction in emissions by 2012 models, and 30 percent by the 2016 model year (CARB, 2004).[6] In terms of GHG emissions alone, this standard would have global importance. California is the fifth-largest economy in the world and the thirteenth-largest GHG emitter. Moreover, the transportation sector in California contributes to almost 60 percent of the state's total emissions (measured in 1999) (Pew Center, n.d.-b). Nationwide, this sector accounts for about 27 percent of total emissions (measured in 2003) (US EPA, 2006).

Other significant efforts include emissions trading. Beginning in April 2003, several New England and Mid-Atlantic states began discussions to create the Regional Greenhouse Gas Initiative (RGGI), a regional market for a CO_2 cap-and-trade program (a Memorandum of Understanding, MoU, was signed in December 2005) – the first mandatory program in the United States (RGGI, n.d.). Meanwhile, numerous states began promoting renewable energy such as renewable energy mandates requiring electric utilities to generate a specified amount of electricity from renewable sources; most of these take the form of RPSs (Pew Center, n.d.-c).[7] Likewise, many states have established funds, often called 'public benefit funds' to provide subsidies for energy efficiency and renewable energy projects (Pew Center, 2006, p. 5).

In addition to the unprecedented state-level legislative and executive actions, many states utilized their legal options as a way to get climate change addressed in the country. For instance, several states sued the EPA, in 2003, for its decision not to regulate CO_2 as a pollutant (in vehicle emissions) under the Clean Air Act (CAA) (NYAG, 2003).[8] Other first-time lawsuits included one in 2004, when several states filed a lawsuit against five power producers for emitting 10 percent of the nation's GHG total (CAG, 2004).[9] Moreover, in 2006, California filed a lawsuit against the world's six largest automakers for their contribution to global warming (Bunkley, 2006).[10]

These state actions, while not the same as federal government mandates, are nonetheless not insignificant in the greater context. As shown with California, many states have high-level economies and emission levels compared to other countries. The combined emission levels of several of the states making targeted efforts are on a par with the emissions of other developed and developing countries (CCAP, 2002). Indeed, in 2002, a report comparing all efforts in the United States and Canada revealed this trend, declaring that Canada was actually lagging behind the US because of the states' activities (Pembina, 2002).

Another notable approach that the states have taken, but more in the realm of the system of governance, is that they have reached out beyond the country's borders and have sought out an international role. For example, as early as June 1998, New Jersey formed a climate change partnership with the Netherlands in accordance with the UNFCCC (NJDEP, 1998b). This unprecedented cooperation included efforts to identify and design a prototype GHG emissions trading system. Likewise, in 2001, the New England states and five eastern Canadian provinces teamed up to reduce their emissions to 1990 levels by 2010, followed by an additional 10 percent by 2020 (NYSERDA, 2002). Some states also went to international conferences and negotiations, for example seeking transatlantic partners to create markets for renewable energy technologies and linking up with Europeans to create a backdoor emissions trading scheme (CESA, 2004; 'Some States', 2004).

CHANGING DYNAMICS AMONG LEVELS OF GOVERNMENT

Federal Governments and Enabling Roles

Here it must be said that although many of these state and *Land* initiatives occurred absent federal-level mandates, one cannot exclude the role of the federal level in these federal systems. Moreover, in Germany, one must consider the role of the European Union (EU), as environmental policy has mostly shifted upwards (Kern, 2008). In looking at sustainable development, some of the local Agenda 21 programs the *Land* helped establish were aided through their use of European funds and indirectly though federal monies (Kern et al., 2007). Moreover, while the federal level was lagging in reference to sustainable development, there were some definitive actions taken at the EU level with direct impact on the *Länder*. The most obvious example is the establishment of the EMAS system, which Bavaria became a leader in implementing. And the federal government encouraged such voluntary public–private cooperation, the first of which was in the late 1980s (Kern, 2008). Arguably, the most prominent of such agreements was the 1995 government–industry climate change agreement. Thus, regarding sustainable development, there was at least an EU-level agenda for this. And concerning climate change, there was a clear national-level agenda that also set a certain tone.

In the United States, many of the states' innovative programs were partially stimulated and underwritten through federal grants. In the 1990s, more than a third of all state spending on pollution prevention was from federal coffers. Moreover, certain federal programs have provided the basis for state advancements. The federal Toxics Release Inventory (modeled in 1986 after a New Jersey program), for example, was essential in many of the states' pollution prevention and cross-media integration efforts. Furthermore, much of the knowledge and insights came out of federal money spent on research and development. Finally, the federal role in the coordinative efforts between federal and state were many times essential for the ensuing innovative state program (Rabe, 2000).

There were also some relevant indirect federal incentives for climate change. The 1992 Energy Policy Act gave states the freedom to redesign their electricity markets (prompting electricity deregulation) and consider alternatives to fossil fuels (Rabe, 2002). Also included in this Act was the renewable energy Production Tax Credit, which subsidizes renewable energy facilities for the first ten years (UCS, n.d.). In addition, the 1990 CAA Amendments introduced states to the emissions trading idea – the sulfur dioxide emission trading program originally diffused from Wisconsin, and in turn was influential in the Kyoto Protocol – which is diffusing back to the states (Rabe, 2002).

Likewise, the Climate Action Plans were advocated by the EPA through its State and Local Climate Change Program when it appeared that the United States would be participating in an international agreement in the 1990s (D. Mulholland, pers. comm., 19 September 2006). This program was created as a result of Clinton's 1993 Climate Change Action Plan, which was designed to reduce GHG emissions mostly through voluntary efforts by companies, state and local governments, and other organizations (USGAO, 1997). Finally, the federal government has been providing support for research and development of new climate-friendly technologies (Pew Center, 2004).

Thus, in both cases, while the states/*Länder* have clearly taken the initiative in many environmental and energy matters, the federal governments cannot be ignored. It is more of a question of changing roles and dynamics between and among levels of government, as discussed in the previous chapter regarding multi-level governance, and which is touched upon below. These changed roles for subnational governments in the international system also explain why many of the innovative ones (not only at the state/*Land* level but also at the local level, and in all OECD countries) have been turning to their counterparts beyond their nation's borders to cooperate on environmental policy.

Federal Systems, State/*Land* Capacities and Decentralization

US and German subnational-level governments are responsible for policy-making in many of the key areas that the international level is addressing. States play a large role in implementing and enforcing federal regulations. They also predominantly manage several areas of environmental concern including waste management, groundwater protection, coastal zone management, transportation, building and land use; and they oversee areas of energy production and distribution (Knigge, 2005; Rabe, 2000, 2006).

Regarding federal-level laws, the EPA delegates most of its authority to state programs that are operating in accordance with national standards. While the EPA maintains a parallel implementation and enforcement presence through its regional offices to ensure national laws are being executed evenly throughout the states, most enforcement and implementation activities occur at the state level; in reality, for about 80 percent of the federal programs, states exercise the primary authority (Brown, 1999; UNEP, n.d.-a, n.d.-b). Generally, states may also enact tougher laws than the minimum standard that was established federally (unless the law was intended to pre-empt more strict state laws). In actuality, there is a 'long-standing tradition in American governance whereby states serve as laboratories for subsequent federal policy' (Rabe, 2002, p. iv).

As discussed above, this relationship has grown even more decentralized. The delegation of programs has dramatically increased. And the states themselves have been some of the biggest advocates for decentralization and the New Environmentalism approach as they have significantly built up their institutional capacities since the adoption of modern environmental protection policies in 1970s. By 1996, only a little more than 20 percent of the funding that the states spent on environmental and natural resource concerns was from the federal government (Brown, 1999). Moreover, about 70 percent of their policies had nothing to do with federal legislation (Rabe, 2000).

As such, state-based institutions have emerged in line with this empowerment, such as the Environmental Council of the States and the Multi-State Working Group on Environmental Performance (MSWG), which help states exchange ideas and experiences, and have become a force in regulatory reform efforts. The MSWG is an example of multi-level governance (MLG) in action. It started out as a small group of innovative states (along with a few officials from the EPA, the private sector, NGOs and academia) in late 1996 that were determined not only to reconcile international and national (state and local) environmental policies, particularly EMSs (and government's relationship to the business community), but also to take an active part in the molding of such policy.[11] Today it is an epistemic community consisting of a network of about 1000 participants in 30 states and 20 countries from all governmental levels and societal sectors (MSWG, 2007).

Another aspect of the US federal system is the dual court system. This system provides states with the possibility to challenge the federal government's regulations, or failures to regulate, as discussed in the aforementioned cases. That said, there is also a great deal of opportunities in this system for environmental groups to address environmental policy at the state level (Wälti, 2009).

In Germany, both the federal and *Länder* levels have legislative and executive responsibilities. Generally, the federal government has a larger legislative role and the Länder have a greater administrative role (Donfried, 1996). In these divisions of powers, legislation is divided among the federal parliament (Bundestag) and the second chamber representing the *Länder* (Bundesrat) and the *Länder* parliaments (Kraemer, 2007). There are select areas that are the sole purview of the federal government (for example, defense, foreign affairs, immigration and currency) and some that are the responsibilities of the *Länder* (for example, education and law enforcement) (Donfried, 1996). Then there are other federal legislative areas in which the *Länder* may enact their own laws with varying degrees of liberty: 'concurrent competence', in which there are parallel responsibilities where the *Länder* may pass laws that were not touched upon by the federal government (Kraemer, 2007); and 'framework competence', in which the federal government provides policy guidelines and the *Länder* develop detailed legislation. These competences contain environmental policy areas that include land management, housing, shipping, road transportation, waste disposal, air pollution, nature conservation, landscape management, regional planning and water management. Other areas of joint responsibility were added in 1969 including regional economic development and agricultural reform (Donfried, 1996).

The *Länder*'s greater administrative role means they are primarily responsible for implementation, monitoring and enforcement of environmental policy and law (Kraemer, 2007). This means that the success of any one policy objective depends on them (Jörgensen, 2002) and that they 'act as laboratories for solution in policy instrument design and implementation, and provide a competitive setting for innovations in environmental policy' (Kraemer, 2003, p. 3). NRW and Bavaria have a history of being environmental policy pioneers and exporters (Kern, 2008; Kraemer, 2007). The first air pollution laws were enacted in NRW (1962),

Baden-Württemberg (1964), Lower Saxony (1966) and Bavaria (1966), the experiences of which were drawn upon by the federal government in the creation of its first federal air pollution law in 1974 (Kern, 2008).

While most talk about the EU in terms of an MLG system, there are good reasons for comparing US federalism with EU MLG, at which the *Länder* also have a place at the table. The European Community (EC) can create environmental legislation and take measures to ensure compliance with the law. Because EU law is domestic (federal/state/municipal) law, *Länder* have become more active in European affairs, mainly to ensure *Länder* autonomy and for feedback to the EU on implementation. Since the formation of the European Union in 1992, Germany passed a law making sure the *Länder* would be consulted in EU affairs through the Bundesrat when it comes to their areas of interest. In addition to their role through the German federal system, they also have a place at the European level through the Committee of the Regions. The *Länder* also gained more rights to diverge from federal laws in 2006 through federal reform (Kraemer, 2007).

In addition to this decentralization of certain environmental policy areas, another trend occurring over the years has been more coordination among the *Länder* and including the federal government. For instance, the ministers of the *Land*-level environmental ministries and of the federal level have established the Conference of Environment Ministers, which meets twice a year to coordinate on environmental policy. The *Länder* also work on harmonization efforts regarding EC law and coordinate reporting on their implementation experience to ultimately bring it to the attention of the appropriate officials at the EU level; thus policy learning plays a prominent role in the implementation of European legislation (Kraemer, 2003, 2007).

THE INTERNATIONALIZATION OF SUBNATIONAL (STATE/*LAND*) POLITICS

These increased state and *Land* actions and changing federal dynamics have not been happening in a vacuum. As of the turn of the century, many scholars began noticing that a widespread movement towards devolution was underway (Canaleta et al., 2004; Lecours, 2002; Ohmae, 1993; Richards, 2004). By the year 2000, 95 percent of democratic countries had elected subnational levels of government (Canaleta et al., 2004). And as for federal systems, the movement has been for a stronger subnational role. Among such increased state-level roles, environmental innovativeness has been particularly strong from OECD member countries such as

Germany, the Netherlands, Sweden, Denmark and Australia (Medearis and Swett, 2003).

Starting in the late 1990s, numerous scholars wrote of their observations on the increasing role of subnational governments in 'foreign affairs', 'international relations' or 'international arenas' (Aldecoa and Keating, 1999; Fry, 1998; Kaiser, 2002, 2005; Lecours, 2002). These augmented roles were linked to globalization in general (Chernotsky and Hobbs, 2001; Deeg, 1996; Fry, 1998; Gress and Lehne, 1999; Kaiser, 2002), but particularly to economic globalization, 'the liberalized movement of capital and goods across borders' (Jänicke and Jacob, 2006, p. 34). Other scholars connected the internationalization of subnational politics to specific components of globalization such as supranational integration, for example European integration (Goetz, 1995; Jeffery, 1996; Kaiser, 1999, 2002, 2005) and North American economic integration (the North American Free Trade Agreement, NAFTA) (de Boer, 2002; Fry, 2004; Kaiser, 1999, 2002, 2005).

The evidence of the internationalization of subnational-level politics can be seen through their representation abroad; leading of trade missions; participation in regional and international organizations; entering into relations with other subnational governments; and their signing of agreements (Lecours, 2002). Subnational entities seek an international presence for practical, cultural, political and economic reasons; many times the reasons interchange in one form or another (Lecours, 2002; Richards, 2004). When it comes to environmental issues, many subnational governments are looking beyond their national borders to learn how others are successfully dealing with similar problems. Arguably, the primary activity of states/*Länder* in the international arena is in the economic field. Due to the decrease in national governments' abilities to pursue macroeconomic policy and to the transferal of competences to supranational (EU/NAFTA) and international bodies (World Trade Organization, WTO), states and *Länder* have been pressured into and are thus doing more to promote their economies (Deeg, 1996). An example of this can be seen in their growing number of trade offices in foreign countries; by the turn of the century, states had established 240 trade offices abroad, up from three in 1970; accordingly, *Länder* had set up 130 offices since that time (Kaiser, 2005).

As the true nature of economic boundaries has become regional through economic globalization (Ohmae, 1993), and as region-oriented multinational corporations (MNCs) have grown exponentially, subnational-level governments have found themselves in competition (not only with each other domestically but also with their foreign counterparts) for international direct investments and to secure companies within their borders for jobs (Fry, 1998). This increased regional economic activity would be one component in what Cerny (1996, 1997) refers to as the 'competition state'. Cerny (1996) points out that rather than leading to a homogeneous marketplace, economic globalization expands the playing field for different market actors and interactions, which includes (in addition to different territorial and 'quasi-territorial' levels) different corporate forms and scales of economy in different industrial sectors.

Accordingly, another rising market actor, which is naturally linked to the subnational government, is the small business; according to Fry (1998), whereas MNCs currently are the biggest exporters, small businesses may account for a larger share in the future. In Germany, the federal government and the *Länder* have grasped this and for some time now have been consciously focusing their support efforts on small businesses or '*Mittelstand*' policies. Such microeconomic policies ('aimed to benefit the competitiveness of specific firms or sectors of the economy'), known in Germany as structural policy, have become really the only instrument they have because of globalization (as 'the increased mobility of investment capital narrows the range of policy strategies that governments may use effectively') (Deeg, 1996, p. 27). In addition to the *Mittelstand* policies, the other prominent structural policy instruments in Germany have been sectoral policies and regional policies. The aim of sectoral policies is to promote 'the growth of "knowledge intensive" industries and manag[e] the decline of old industries' (Deeg, 1996). Regional policy, which is intended to reduce regional economic disparities by inducing investment in economically weaker regions, has not only not noticeably achieved its goal, but has become a resource for which *Länder* compete for investment. It is thus not surprising why these governments are pursuing, as Deeg (1996) articulated, their 'own foreign economic policy with the aim of cultivating direct economic links between their regional economies and foreign markets'.

In terms of structural transformations in the international system, the main point is that globalization also simultaneously provoked a decentralization movement, an empowerment of lower levels of government, which together affected traditional federalism boundaries, causing them to 'shift' (Deeg, 1996) or 'structurally transform' (Chernotsky and Hobbs, 2001). But within this larger structural transformation are smaller nuances. In the case of German *Länder* and US states, one of the structural changes was the strengthening of the state/*Land* executive role when it comes to international activities (Goetz, 1995; Gress and Lehne, 1999; Kaiser, 1999). It is normally the executive that embarks on trade missions or receives delegations, or that signs agreements or involves itself in any way internationally. Furthermore, the subnational executive branch has also gained a larger say at the federal level when it comes to certain international activities. It was the Bundesrat (which is exclusively the executives), for example, that won a constitutionally sanctioned role in the conduct of European affairs (Gress and Lehne, 1999). US governors have also gained a consultative role when it comes to issues of NAFTA and the World Trade Organization (WTO) (Kaiser, 1999).

THE EMERGENCE OF SUBNATIONAL TRANSATLANTIC ENVIRONMENTAL PARTNERSHIPS

In this context, US and German subnational governments began forming partnerships. Not much has been written on this, however. Medearis and Swett (2003) discuss the broader phenomenon of subnational partnerships that took off in earnest around the mid-1990s particularly between Europe and the United States, which includes the local level and refers mostly to mixed-level partnerships. Medearis and Swett (2003) saw this trend as representative of a 'paradigm shift' in 'international environmental activities' (p. 4). From the reference point of the United States, these two federal EPA officials argued that the transformation was 'from one of exporting environmental expertise and dollars, to one of importing best practices from around the globe' (p. 4).

In examining why states and cities draw lessons from innovative environmental policies in the EU and OECD member countries, Medearis and Swett (2003) argued that it was because of: (1) the socio-economic similarities; (2) the same international pressure to develop sustainable policies; and (3) the more efficient use of environmental resources in many of these countries. The authors also pointed to some different types of institutional support that has emerged at the supranational and international levels to encourage best practice exchanges among subnational governments around the world, ranging from international associations formed by lower-level governments (for example, the Local Governments for Sustainability), to supranational programs and international databases (for example, the UN-Habitat's Best Practices Database), which can be also considered as part of the driving force for such partnerships.

Another study examined five different types of transatlantic partnerships – city-to-city, state-to-state, state-to-country and region-to-region – four of which were between subnational authorities in the United States and Germany (including the partnerships of Maryland–Schleswig–Holstein and Wisconsin–Bavaria) and one of which was between a US state and the Netherlands (Knigge, 2005). The author began by pointing to the multi-level complexities in dealing with environmental policy, including: (1) the global nature of many environmental problems and the corresponding number of international agreements; (2) the transatlantic tensions on issues including climate change and genetically modified organisms; and (3) the fact that the subnational governments are responsible for policymaking in many key areas that the international level is addressing, for example transportation, building and land use. With the assertion that subnational policies are more influential to the federal level than widely understood, Knigge's goal was to ascertain how these growing types of cooperation function, and what their contribution to environmental policymaking is.

Regarding the framework of cooperation, Knigge (2005) found that the partnerships varied mostly in level of formality and scope of geography. Cooperation between transatlantic governmental officials is formalized by documents such as MoUs or letters of intent, while partnerships between non-state actors such as NGOs, research institutes or individuals within local authorities are informal. Regarding geographical scope, these types of arrangements occurred between both same-level counterparts in addition to mixed levels as shown above. The formal partnerships usually concentrated on the geographic region the officials were representing. In a couple of instances, the partners looked at best practices examples from beyond the immediate vicinity of their counterpart. Conversely, informal partnerships generally do not seem to restrict themselves to a pre-prescribed geographical location. Concerning their contribution to environmental policymaking, Knigge (2005) found numerous impacts 'ranging from new ideas for projects, to the adoption of new legislation, to reflecting on existing environmental policies, to increased effectiveness and enhanced self-esteem' (p. 17).

Jörgensen (2006) also examined the general movement of subnational transatlantic lesson-drawing, in particular the state-to-state partnerships of Maryland–Schleswig–Holstein and Wisconsin–Bavaria, but in specific relation to global governance for sustainable development. The author links these arrangements to such governance because they are concerned with international agendas such as Agenda 21 and climate change, the successful implementation of which 'depends on governance by diffusion, including lesson-drawing and policy transfer' as underlined in this agenda (Jörgensen, 2006, p. 146).

Jörgensen (2006) sees the transatlantic lesson-drawing as a natural extension of the growing state/*Länder* roles regarding the creation of innovative polices in their respective countries, a topic that the author had previously studied extensively (Jörgensen, 2002). The author recapitulates how many states and Bundesländer have been making policies to address sustainable development and climate change absent federal leadership, demonstrating that innovations must not happen from the top down, but can also happen from the bottom up. Furthermore, despite existing within different types of federal systems, where it is easier in the United States to achieve decentralized policy innovations and regulatory policies, the *Länder* have been increasingly experimenting with policy, and the federal system has become more competitive. Thus, while diffusion mechanisms are much more advanced in the United States even that has changed a little in Germany with the Quandt and Böll foundations. In sum, Jörgensen says the role of subnational governments in the US and Germany is getting more important. They can act as laboratories of democracy (though not all do), and since they are strongly tied to implementation can be innovative and combine both hierarchical and horizontal governance (Jörgensen, 2006). In other words they have the capacity to serve as a mechanism in global governance for sustainable development.

ANALYSIS

This chapter has provided background about what was transpiring in the world in terms of global governance for sustainable development around the time in which subnational governments, specifically US states and German *Länder*, began to form partnerships. It has shown that the environmental agenda as established at the international level was not only taken up in many instances by subnational governments, but that many states and *Länder* took on frontrunner roles in designing and implementing policies related to sustainable development and climate change, including those that promote renewable energy. What is more, these activities were done either absent federal policies or as an enhancement to policies. Particularly striking were the states' climate change efforts in spite of the federal-level rejection of the Kyoto Protocol. Furthermore, the chapter has shown the importance of such subnational activities when it comes to implementing the sustainable development agenda, which is often overlooked, as both states and *Länder* are responsible for policymaking in many of the key areas that the international level is addressing.

Not only do these facts in and of themselves indicate a new trend in environmental governance, but other structural changes as discussed in this chapter point to this fact as well. State and *Land* roles have also been enhanced because of changes in their respective federal systems, for instance as caused by the emergence of the European Union. Among the upshots of these alterations is more horizontal and sometimes vertical coordination. These changes also seem to be part of larger structural transformations such as the worldwide movement towards devolution and a movement of increased subnational involvement in the international arena, particularly when it comes to economic promotion. Not only have subnational governments come to be seen as indispensable actors in sustainable development policies but this level is believed to be the more suitable governmental level when it comes to cooperation with target groups such as businesses and society.

This chapter has revealed a multi-level dimension to the issue of global governance for sustainable development, in which states and *Länder* have played a prominent role. It suggests some initial structural reasons why subnational governments such as states and *Länder* may be reaching out to one another to collaborate on and/or learn about innovative policies both nationally and internationally. The case studies will verify and uncover more of the causal factors of this phenomenon.

NOTES

1. The process leading to this culmination reaches back to the 1972 United Nations Conference on the Human Environment in Stockholm. This conference prompted the 1987 report *Our Common Future*, which contained the first reference to the sustainable development concept (NRCA). Most recently, the 20-year Rio Plus conference was held in June 2012.
2. This is not to say that every state and *Land* chose this frontrunner path. Indeed, some states and *Länder* have gone in the other direction and done the minimum or even less than was required at the federal level (Herbert and Blechschmidt, 2001; Rabe, 2000, 2002).
3. While the content of the plans vary from state to state, components include: taking inventory of greenhouse gas emissions; making projections of greenhouse gas emission levels; identifying areas where greenhouse gas reductions are feasible and cost-effective; and implementation plans.
4. New Jersey, for example, declared in 1998 that it would reduce its GHG emission levels to 3.5 percent below 1990 levels by 2005 (NJDEP, 1998a). Likewise, New England and five eastern Canadian provinces agreed, in 2001, to reduce their emissions to 1990 levels by 2010, followed by another 10 percent by 2020 (NEP/ECP, 2001). Additionally, New York, in 2002, vowed to reduce the state's emission levels to 5 percent below 1990 levels by 2010, followed by another 10 percent by 2020 (NYSERDA, 2002).
5. In 1997, for example, Oregon required new power plants to offset 17 percent of their CO_2 emissions through new technology or by funding climate-change projects worldwide (Pew Center, 2004). Likewise, in 2004, the state of Washington ordered new power plants to offset 20 percent of their CO_2 emissions including by investing in projects such as planting trees or by converting transit buses from diesel to cleaner-burning natural gas (WSDNR, 2004).
6. This is a powerful law for two reasons: first, because until now policy efforts to get low-level GHG-emitting vehicles onto the market have not been very successful despite the significant technological advancements in the development of such vehicles (CCAP, 2003); and second, because it would in effect supersede federal law, which had not ventured to lower vehicle GHG emissions, while simultaneously providing this same right to the other states if they so choose. Under the federal CAA, California alone

among the states has the unique right to establish vehicle emission standards that are stricter than the federal government's. What is more, the rest of the 49 states then have the option of either adopting California's more stringent law (which could mean even more emissions reductions throughout the country) or continuing to adhere to the federal standards. Since California enacted this law, a dozen other states have adopted its standards (Barringer, 2007; CCAP, 2002), while others have expressed an interest in doing so (Pew Center, 2006). This advancement in environmental protection, however, has not come without dissent by the auto industry. It took until 2009 to resolve the ongoing lawsuits in favor of the state (Barringer, 2007, 2009). Meanwhile, the state moved forward with its law and the first fleet in compliance was on the road in 2009. Furthermore, the Obama administration announced similar standards in May 2009 to be established for the nation (Barringer, 2009).

7. Iowa was the first state to enact such a law in 1991 (Rabe, 2006).
8. After several years of appeals and corresponding lawsuits that included other states, NGOs and interested parties, the Supreme Court, in a landmark decision, ruled on the side of the states in April 2007, saying that the EPA does have the authority to regulate GHGs under the CAA (Barringer, 2007; Greenhouse, 2006).
9. In June 2011, the Supreme Court ruled that this issue must be resolved by the EPA. This decision was in reference to the above-mentioned 2007 Supreme Court decision that ruled that the EPA does have the authority to regulate GHGs ('Justices', 2011).
10. On 17 September 2007, a federal judge in San Francisco dismissed the suit, saying that courts do not have the authority or expertise to decide injury lawsuits regarding global warming (Liptak, 2007).
11. The determination of these states came on the heels of the ISO's publishing of its first round of EMS standards in September of that year. Meanwhile, domestically, the New Environmentalism reforms were barely under way. Thus, on the one hand, the aim of the MSWG was to 'determine the effectiveness' of EMSs (particularly ISO 14001 systems) as a policy tool to improve both the environment and the economy. On the other hand, the focus was on changing policies in the country (R. Stephens, personal communication, 14 February 2006). And earlier on, since it found some deficiencies in the ISO standards, it endeavored to try to influence those standards.

4. California and Bavaria (1995)

THE MEMORANDUM

On 26 April 1995, at the German Consulate General in San Francisco, the California Environmental Protection Agency (Cal/EPA) Secretary, James M. Strock, and the Bavarian State Ministry for Regional Development and Environmental Affairs State Minister, Dr Thomas Goppel, signed a Memorandum of Understanding (MoU) 'To Create the Bavaria–California Clean Technologies Working Group' (Bavaria MRDEA and Cal/EPA, 1995). The objective, as formally stated, was 'to promote environmental and renewable energy technologies' (Bavaria MRDEA and Cal/EPA, 1995). The mechanisms chosen to realize this end included:

- 'to establish joint projects to promote the commercial viability of technologies such as renewable energy, efficient energy and clean vehicles';
- 'to work to mutually accept the environmental technology evaluations and certifications of . . . [the] respective agencies';
- 'to implement a professional exchange of experts between Cal/EPA, the Bavarian Ministry for Regional Development and Environmental Affairs and other appropriate agencies for the purposes of promoting sustainable development'; and
- 'to support joint environmental and energy trade missions, conferences and exhibitions to other regions' (Bavaria MRDEA and Cal/EPA, 1995).

To monitor the advancements made on the agreement, the parties also stated that they would meet one year later at an environmental technology fair in Bavaria (Bavaria MRDEA and Cal/EPA, 1995).

The MoU lists three reasons for the bilateral cooperation. First, both governments had set 'the development and commercialization of environmental and renewable energy technologies' as a top priority. Second, accordingly, these industries represented 'significant sectors' of both economies. And third, the two parties, likewise, saw these industries as growing in importance to both 'the environment and economy' (Bavaria MRDEA and Cal/EPA, 1995).

The document alone indicates that the partnership was part of a deliberate attempt at ecological modernization. It is a joint promotion of their respective environmental technology industries, specifically the bur-geoning technologies. Moreover, the goal of making their environmental certification programs compatible would be to extend the market for their environmental technology industries (a strategy of ecological moderniza-tion). The specific mention of the term 'sustainable development' (which was relatively new at the time), moreover, reveals another mechanism that inspired the two parties, the 1992 United Nations Conference on Environment and Development (UNCED), known to have served as a trigger for worldwide regulatory competition for first-mover advantages, which increasingly includes environmental technologies, thereby adding a vertical international dimension to the partnership. To gain more of a comprehensive understanding of the motivations for this partnership, however, it is essential to look at the driving forces that led to the idea to collaborate, the key components in the process that took the idea to work together to a successful MoU signing, how it was implemented and the overall results.

THE DRIVING FORCES

California and Bavaria Challenge Status Quo

Because of the structural changes that resulted from the end of the Cold War and the rise of globalization, and in the midst of new and developing international agendas (in other words, the UNCED, the United Nations Framework Convention on Climate Change (UNFCCC), the environ-mental management system (EMS) standards; and the European Union's agenda in this regard) as discussed in Chapters 2 and 3, both California and Bavaria found the status quo to be no longer acceptable. At issue for these states was how environmental protection and economic growth were treated as conflicting problems. Both states embarked on reform efforts to reconcile these opposing demands.

Bavaria's Reform Efforts

In his government policy statement in 1994, Minister-President Stoiber (1994a) cited many of these aforementioned points as having posed new challenges to Bavaria – the fall of the Berlin Wall and the rise of globalization, as well as the political and economic developments in Europe – and having instigated fundamental changes to the economy and society. Specifically, the minister-president went on to say, the state was confronted with increasing competition from among the developed countries, challenges to traditional markets by the rapidly rising Asian countries and competition from the countries that are able to provide cheaper labor. Moreover, Bavaria was faced with the escalating pace of scientific and technological advancements (Stoiber, 1994a).

Bavaria believed that the only way to create jobs, ensure its highly competitive areas of competence and its economic level (let alone its survival), and the only way to maintain its high level of social and environmental standards, was through the promotion of strategic, specialized, innovative areas and technological advancement (Stoiber, 1994a, 1994b). To that end, the state pinpointed traffic technology, communications technology, materials sciences, environmental technology and gene and biotechnology as the areas in which it needed to excel to stay ahead in the global economy. This strategy included getting many of such areas onto the global market, as one-third of the state's jobs and a great deal of its prosperity comes from its exports (Stoiber, 1994b).

In environmental technology alone, Bavaria saw its potential for becoming a top exporter in this field. Already, in 1995, Germany was producing more global environmental products than any other country, at 21 percent, employing more than 0.5 million people, with a major increase in that amount expected in the future (Stoiber, 1995). On the global scale (in 1991), environmental technologies accounted for $270 billion in business, with an expected annual growth of $25 billion in the next decade (State of California, 1993). By 2010, it was expected that 40 percent of all innovations would be related to environmental protection (Jänicke and Jacob, 2004).

Thus, to make the state a more attractive location for environmental technology businesses and to help give new ideas and new companies a better start, Bavaria decided to establish what Jänicke and Jacob (2006) refer to as lead-market strategies including centers for technology and environmental technology (Stoiber, 1994b, 1995). For instance, the state put forth concrete plans for the establishment of an environmental technology founders' center to encourage the creation of new companies in this field. Other state initiatives included: the setting up of centers for founders of new businesses to help young businesses get off the ground; the providing of funds for venture capital to give young and small technology businesses some capital for the development and marketing of new products (Stoiber, 1994b); the promotion of specific future-oriented technologies, such as new energy technologies (biomass, geothermal drilling, photovoltaic and hydrogen technology), among others; the establishment of an organization for innovation and technology transfer (Stoiber, 1995); and the allocation of finances for the establishment of an organization for international economic relations that would support companies in developing new markets and exports (Stoiber, 1994b).

Bavaria's ambitious efforts for its environmental technology industry were not created in a vacuum. These goals were tied to its environmental protection policy plans with the understanding that environmental protection can also mean economic prosperity as markets are developed for environmentally friendlier products, production methods and technology, which in turn is also a key to sustainable development – hence, a win–win scenario for both the environment and the economy (Stoiber, 1995). Accordingly, Bavaria's goals and approaches for its environmental protection policies were equally proactive. By the end of 1994, the state government said that its goal was to be on top, to be a pioneer in this area and establish innovative policies.

On 19 July 1995, the state government presented the Bavarian Environmental Initiative: Cooperative Environmental Protection, Sustainable Development, Ecological Prosperity (Stoiber, 1995). This policy embraced four of what the state believed to be the best means of addressing the environmental protection challenges of the day. For starters, Bavaria selected the then burgeoning sustainable development approach, and, correspondingly, the promotion of environmental technology, as outlined above (Stoiber, 1995). It also advocated a cross-sectoral course to environmental protection: that it include sectors such as economic, financial, energy, agriculture, forest, transportation, health, education, local, construction, environmental planning and rural development policies that are also relevant to environmental protection. Finally, Bavaria supported the social market economy, because it believed it to be the most conducive to realizing environmental awareness, or an environmental economic system (Stoiber, 1995).[1]

To assume these changes, the state government also put forth efforts to reform itself. These internal structural transformations resemble what Cerny (1997) refers to as the 'competition state' and included privatization and deregulation (Stoiber, 1994a, 1994b). According to Bavarian officials, the number of environmental laws and regulations (4690 administrative regulations, 2770 orders and over 800 laws) was climbing too high, making for a confusing, costly and ineffective system. Bavaria believed that it was not enough just to regulate the environment. One of the *Land*'s restructuring efforts was to promote more cooperation with business (Stoiber, 1995). One major endeavor to materialize these reform ideas was the creation of the Environmental Pact of Bavaria, the first of its kind to be achieved in Germany (STMUGV, 2000).

Completed on 23 October 1995, and intended to last for five years, the pact was created as a voluntary agreement, or collaborative partnership, of joint responsibility between the government and industry to work together to protect the environment versus functioning as adversaries in the traditional, hierarchical, top-down command-and-control fashion. Its focus was on prevention, establishing performance-oriented goals and processes that would allow industry to come up with the best, innovative ways to curb the pollution, instead of prescribing, through regulations, the so-called 'end-of-pipe' environmental technologies (Smoller; STMUGV, 2000; Weissbach, 2000).

The instruments set up to achieve the desired environmental ends were economic incentives, such as taxes and fees, and subsidies and self-responsibility (Stoiber, 1995). Through the use of the then new Eco-Management and Audit Scheme (EMAS) (which was in line with the UNCED goals and preceding the ISO's EMS standards), businesses would undergo a voluntary comprehensive systematic environmental inspection and commit themselves to the improvement of environmental protection. The use of EMAS is one of the incentives (the first phase) to create lead-markets (Jänicke and Jacob, 2006). The idea was that the more self-responsibility firms took, the less they would be regulated. This, in turn, would pave the way to a less complicated bureaucracy and to deregulation (Stoiber, 1995). As companies would be looking at innovative ways to reduce their pollution instead of administering a prescribed end-of-pipe technology, they would opportunely have all of the incentives from the state's simultaneous promotion of environmental technology. So, in essence, the pact was in part intended to help facilitate environmental technology and environmental services (Bavarian MEAITT, 2005; Wisconsin DNR, n.d.-a).

Bavaria's plans for its innovative policies and reforms did not stop at state lines. These reforms were incorporated into an international plan of action as well. While Bavarian officials frequently cite the Rio conference as a major impetus for its promotion of the international convergence of environmental policy, other statements indicate its goal of being a frontrunner in this realm (STMUGV, 2000; Stoiber, 2003). Statements in the Environmental Pact, for instance, talk about its aim of achieving a worldwide 'spread' of environmental protection together with the dissemination of the awareness of Bavaria's already achieved high levels of environmental protection and its goals of increasing its 'exports' in environmental technology and its cooperation model. Such international efforts belong to the second phase in creating a lead market. This is also relevant in relation to the emerging market countries that have a lot of catching up to do in environmental protection, such as the Eastern European countries and the rising powers of the East, such as China, that will need to concentrate more on environmental protection in the future (Stoiber, 2003). Bavaria also gets specific regarding the vertical dynamics of its cooperation with business – that they share information regarding developments on the European and international levels and, correspondingly, that they coordinate concepts and activities for policy at these levels (STMUGV, 2000).

Bavaria's goals of being a frontrunner in environmental protection and of being a leading global economic competitor, together with its resultant approach of promoting its environmental policies at the European and international levels (policy pushing), could only be realized if other competing countries would agree to or adopt the same policies, to help toward the establishment of 'a globalization of knowledge and experience, and ultimately, a globalization of approaches and standards' (Schnappauf, 1999). In its push for a minimum of global environmental standards, Bavaria's strategy was to do 'convincing work' at 'all international levels' through the exchange of experiences (Schnappauf, 1999; Stoiber, 1995).

One can see Bavaria's modus operandi through its efforts to secure international environmental partnerships over the years with both subnations and nations. While one joint collaboration can be found as early as 1975 (with Slovenia), most of them occurred in the 1990s, particularly the late 1990s, and in the early 2000s, such as the Brazilian states of São Paulo and Rio Grande do Sul (1997 and 1999) and the province of Quebec (2000) (Office of the Premier, 2001; Schnappauf, 1999; State of Bavaria, n.d; STMUGV, n.d.-b; Western Cape Government, 2004). Bavaria's 1995 partnership with California was simply one of the earlier ones.

California's Reform Efforts

California, like Bavaria, was pressed to promote environmental protection while keeping its businesses competitive. Moreover, the environmental reforms in California were also linked to a state-wide comprehensive reform, albeit not as directly as in Bavaria. Like Stoiber, Secretary Strock also mentioned similar instigating factors for reform, namely the end of the Cold War and the resultant changes on society.

In 1990, at the time of the gubernatorial elections in California, the state's biggest challenge was the budget deficit – the 'largest . . . ever faced by a state' (Reinhold, 1991) – and the state-wide recession (the worst since the Great Depression) (Purdum, 1999), which was prompted by cuts in aerospace and defense spending caused by the end of the Cold War. This decline in the economy provoked the other major theme of the elections – environmental protection (J. Strock, pers. comm., 14 November 2005); specifically, it triggered the debate regarding 'conservation versus development' (Bonfante and Seidman, 1990). There was tremendous controversy surrounding the subject: the one side argued that the best way to stimulate the economy was to cut regulations wholescale, including environmental rules, while the other side maintained that environmental regulations had no economic impact and should be left alone (J. Strock, pers. comm., 14 November 2005).

Upon taking office in 1991, Governor Pete Wilson pushed through structural changes to deal with the budget deficit. These changes included a $7.3 million tax increase (the largest in Californian history) and a $5.1 billion cut in state programs and services, including state employee layoffs (Reinhold, 1991). Concerning the issue of environmental protection, Wilson, under his reorganization authority, pushed through the establishment of a cabinet-level Cal/EPA. The reorganization authority allows the governor to reorganize state agencies, in other words, to consolidate, transfer, coordinate or abolish agencies; it does not allow the creation of new functions (requiring more money and staff). But Wilson's reorganization was an effort to establish a more efficient authority on environmental protection, for example the incorporation and coordination of programs that were under different agencies but that were essential to environmental protection, to reduce overlapping and redundant bureaucracies and provide a single point of accountability (a non-scattered administration of environmental laws) (Cal/EPA, 2006b).

Strock, who was named the state's first Cal/EPA secretary in 1991, was thus put in the difficult situation with how to deal with environmental protection during a recession. As secretary, Strock did not find either side of the debate satisfactory. Strock concluded that he would work to redefine the problem, to 'reconcile an environmental economy', or more specifically, to promote sustainable development, which was a new concept at that time. The critical insight, as Strock pointed out, was 'an actionable combination of a regulatory regime based on strict standards and flexible process' (pers. comm., 14 November 2005).

In 1994, the agency took a step in the direction of its objective of linking environmental improvement and economic progress (CARB, 1997): it created the Environmental Technology Certification Program (CalCert), which was the first program of its kind in the nation. The program was the outgrowth of the work of a 1993 partnership that Cal/EPA, together with the state's Trade and Commerce Agency, forged with environmental technology stakeholders, which included representatives from the environmental technology industries, all levels of government, academia, research institutes, national laboratories, the legal community, civil society groups and financial institutions, to define the barriers to environmental technology and devise ways to overcome them (CARB, 1997).

The obstacles, they concluded, lay in the prototype stage of a new technology – in getting a technology from the model stage onto the mass market. It is usually not a problem for an inventor to find financial backing to develop or demonstrate the viability of an idea for a new environmental technology. It is getting the capital to manufacture the model on the large scale that is the trouble. This is, first, because of the natural risk and uncertainty that is inherent in marketing a new product, and second, because of the numerous regulatory jurisdictions, each of which issues its own permit for the same technology (CARB, 1997), and in a typically slow and bureaucratic manner (Cal/EPA, 1996b). According to the participants in the partnership, that so-called 'Valley of Death' often stops good technology from getting onto the market (CARB, 1997).

The idea behind the conception of the CalCert program was to help get the best environmental technologies available for commercial use. The state would do that by working with industry to help overcome these impediments. It would evaluate the effectiveness of the new technology and, assuming it was acceptable, verify and certify it. This performance certification would make the product more credible and thus more acceptable not only commercially, but also among the regulatory agencies and jurisdictions, which would not need to retest the technology (CARB, 1997). It would thus give investors the needed confidence to finance the product onto the mass market.

This tactic by the state (as well as that by Bavaria, in its promotion of the environmental technology industry) is in accordance with Jänicke and Jacob's (2004) characterizations of lead markets for environmental innovations. According to their findings, it is the high-income countries (states in this case) that are able to bring new environmental technology successfully onto the market and reap the economic benefits from then serving as the lead market. High-income countries are characterized by high pressures for environmental protection, which is caused by high income and educational levels, and high capacities for response. Moreover, this tactic in California corresponds to the two-phase process that these authors outline in becoming a lead market in environmental technology; the first of which is the technological struggle to successfully develop a domestic market, which includes tools such as certain governmental standards and subsidies, and the second of which is the governmental promotion of the transfer of the technology through, among other means, bilateral actions with strategic countries.

Indeed, California's efforts to secure that first-mover advantage for its state-based environmental technology industry, which is an important industry in California – generating $20 billion in revenue, providing more than 180 000 jobs (CARB, 1997), and accounting for 8 percent of the global trade at the time (State of California, 1993) – did not stop at the creation of its CalCert program.[2] The state was also simultaneously working politically to help diffuse its CalCert program internationally, which would also help to open up markets for the industry. California planned to try to spread the program to other regions and nations and ultimately to the International Organization for Standardization (ISO) as part of its international environmental management standards (CARB, 1997).

By working with other important states and countries, California could exchange information and ideas to converge environmental technology certification policies enough to ensure that its policy would be acceptable elsewhere. Having these reciprocal plans would help environmental technology from abroad come into California and, conversely, it would assist California-based businesses, boasting a newly certified technology, to expand elsewhere (Cal/EPA, 1996c) – the second phase in developing a lead market. These international business implications are recognizable in a statement by BP Solar after the state certified a product manufactured by the company: 'The unmatched recognition accorded Cal/EPA certification will give us a powerful assist as we market these exciting technologies in California, across the United States and abroad' (Cal/EPA, 1998). Furthermore, having compatible plans with other regions or countries would help make the program look more enticing to an international body such as the ISO. California was interested in pushing its policy. After it was clear that the ISO was considering the CalCert program as a possible model as part of its ISO 14000 series, a state official said: 'the goal now is to develop consensus with the private sector, trading partners and other governments so that a voluntary worldwide standard for testing and verification will be set into place' (Cal/EPA, 1996a). In essence, the use of California's policy as a model for an international standard, which would then diffuse globally, would give the California environmental technology industry a competitive advantage in the global market.

Cal/EPA's modus operandi in expanding its policy worldwide can be seen through a progression of efforts. For starters, it worked with five other US states and the United States Environmental Protection Agency (EPA) to further disseminate the program across the country (Cal/EPA, 1996c). Beyond the US's borders, related efforts were made at the subnational level with Jalisco, Mexico and Guangdong Province of China, and at the national level with Canada, Russia, Indonesia and Brazil (Cal/EPA, 1996c; CARB, 1997). Included in this list is California's 1995 agreement with Bavaria, which was among its initial outreach efforts in this regard. As stated in the MoU, the partners agreed to 'work to mutually accept the environmental technology evaluations and certifications of . . . [the] respective agencies'.

Strock specifically became interested in Germany because, he said, like California they were in many ways working hard to 'reconcile an environmental economy', and so they could use each other for mutual perspective (pers. comm., 14 November 2005). As stated in Chapter 3, Germany began deliberating the then new concept of sustainable development in the late 1980s and carried out dialogs and studies on the matter over the years. It was the *Länder*, however, that began to take the consequential steps to implement the UNCED's ideals. The *Länder* minister-presidents declared their support for the development and implementation of the conference principles in 1994 (UN, n.d.). Regarding this approach, as shown above, Bavaria led the way.

THE KEY COMPONENTS FROM IDEA TO MOU

With the understanding that California could learn from Germany in sustainable development (and eventually help in what became its push in furthering its environmental policy/technology agenda), Strock contacted the German Consulate in San Francisco, and worked with Vice Consul Michael Zickerick, followed by the Consul General, Elmar Weindel. In 1994, a new Consul General was appointed, Ruprecht Henatsch, with whom Strock ended up establishing a close personal relationship. It was this connection that ultimately facilitated the states in forming a union.

But the chance to form the partnership also came to pass because of another set of burgeoning economic circumstances: the rise of the information technology (IT) economy in California in the mid-1990s, which led the German *Länder* to California, and correspondingly to the Consulate (R. Henatsch, pers. comm., 25 November 2005). As Henatsch explained, California at that time was becoming a very prominent region in economic development. Everybody was interested in learning about the new IT economy, to find out what was happening in Silicon Valley and to understand how California was achieving such 'enormous', 'exploding' growth rates. 'Everybody thought we live in a new world. It was so exciting' that all of the German states visited California to learn about it (R. Henatsch, pers. comm., 25 November 2005).

Of those many *Länder* delegations, one was led by Goppel, Strock's Bavarian counterpart. As state Minister for Regional Development and Environmental Affairs, Goppel was also exploring areas of environmental interest and ways to export the *Land*'s ideas and promote its environmental technology industry (M. Weigand, pers. comm., 6 April 2005), including sun and wind energy ('Umweltminister', 1995). The *Länder*, like the states, are competing in the United States and in Germany for foreign investment, and are therefore very active in the United States; 'all of them are trying to position themselves positively in the eyes of American investors' (R. Henatsch, pers. comm., 25 November 2005).

One of the naturally compelling features that drew Bavaria to the partnership was California's 1990 Low Emission Vehicles (LEV) program (R. Henatsch, pers. comm., 25 November 2005). 'California was leading at that time when it came to emission controls, worldwide, because they had legislation on reducing emissions even down to zero' (R. Henatsch, pers. comm., 25 November 2005). The LEV program required far more stringent vehicle emission standards, including the requirement that a small percentage of the vehicles be of zero emissions (Zero Emissions Vehicle Program, ZEV), while also allowing for more flexibility within the program (Salon et al., 1999).

Bavaria, which is home to the major auto company BMW, understood the implications of California's LEV rules. As mentioned, California had already acquired an influential role in the auto industry worldwide for its 1966 tailpipe emission standards, which spurred the diffusion of the catalytic converter. And, since the diffusion of regulations are more probable if the country (state) already has a pioneering image (Jänicke and Jacob, 2004), it is not surprising that the same was expected for the LEV program. According to the California Air Resources Board:

> All of the technology that reduces emissions from cars all over the world – from catalytic converters to computerized anti-smog systems – was developed because of the ARB's emission standards. If these [LEV] proposals are adopted, they could pave the way for a whole new generation of cars and technology [that] will redefine what we consider an environmentally acceptable car for the next two decades. (CARB, 1990, p. 11)

Plus, as demonstrated in the case of California's 1966 standards, pioneering markets with their demanding regulations 'can also send signals to the supply side outside the domestic market' (Jänicke and Jacob, 2004, p. 38). A company such as BMW can spot these indicators and work to gain some of the benefits of the lead market. '[C]ompetitive companies can advertise their ability to supply such demanding market areas as a sign of their technological competence. It can be cost efficient to orient the production to the highest standards, if there are scale effects' (Jänicke and Jacob, 2004, pp. 38–39).

Indeed, the ZEV program has helped to spur on the development of fuel cell technology (UC Davis, 2000), which was another issue that was of great interest to Bavaria and can be considered part of Bavaria's motivations for the partnership (R. Henatsch, pers. comm., 25 November 2005). There was a center for fuel-cell powered cars in Sacramento and the big

German auto companies were 'very active' and took a 'great interest' in being present, in having their cars there 'to show that they are also having a leading position in that technology' (R. Henatsch, pers. comm., 25 November 2005). This interest corresponds to the MoU in its reference to clean vehicles: 'Establish joint projects to promote the commercial viability of technologies such as renewable energy, efficient energy and clean vehicles.' Moreover, the Bavarian-based auto industry's interest in developing fuel cells corresponds to the state's overall reform goals.

With Henatsch's knowledge of the interests and goals of both Strock and Goppel, he was able to utilize the opportunity and bring the two parties together, making him crucial as the binding factor. As Strock recalled:

> Unless you have someone like that available, you're not going to have agreements or efforts that are serious with countries that are outside of the immediate sphere of the state. If Ruprecht [Henatsch] weren't there, my inquiries about Germany wouldn't have meant much. I'm sure we would have ended up focusing on the ones [countries] we were already focused on. (pers. comm., 14 November 2005)

Henatsch's facilitating role was not enough to create a transatlantic partnership; Strock and Goppel recognized the unique common interests and goals of the two states regarding sustainable development and the environmental technology industry, which convinced them to seize the opportunity to capitalize on what a partnership could provide. It was simply considered a 'natural thing to do' (J. Strock, pers. comm., 14 November 2005). It reflected the aforementioned goals that both states had, respectively, regarding their reforms. The content of the agreement, for instance, was visibly inspired by California's CalCert program. Conversely, it reflected Bavaria's goals of exporting its ideas and promoting its environmental technology industry to other countries.

But the 'naturalness' of the partnership not only stemmed from similar goals; it was based on the similar, unique backgrounds, which added to the general attraction between the two. Both states have leading economies on a global scale and were pursuing leadership in the business of environmental technology (California already claimed 8 percent of the global trade). They are both long-time leaders in their respective countries in environmental protection, having served many times as a model for other states/ *Länder* and their federal governments.

Economically, Bavaria is not only a strong state within Germany, but it also surpasses 19 out of the 25 European Union (EU) member states in gross national product (Bavarian MEAITT, 2009); it represents 17 percent of Germany's gross domestic product (Kern, 2008). Because of its policies, the state, as claimed in 2009, transformed itself into a national and international leader in almost all new technologies, including environmental and energy technologies. It consequently became a central point of the 'New Economy' and a globally significant economic partner (Bavarian MEAITT, 2009). California, for its part, would be ranked anywhere between the sixth and the tenth economy in the world if it were a sovereign country, depending on the source. The US state claimed in 2006 to be home to more environmental technology companies than any other state in the United States (Cal/EPA, 2006a).

Bavaria and California are long-standing leaders in environmental protection. Bavaria became home to the world's first 'ring sewerage system' to keep Lake Tegern clean in 1957 (Bavarian State Government, n.d.). The state also claims that it was taking sustainable development-like measures as early as 1970, two decades before the UNCED called for it, when it established the State Ministry of Regional Development and Environmental Affairs, which became responsible for both territorial development and environmental protection (Bavarian State Government, n.d.). This made Bavaria the first German state to institutionalize environmental protection into its government (Kern, 2008). In 1972, Bavaria established the first environmental protection agency in the country (including before the federal government) and by the following year it had enacted the 'most advanced environmental legislation in Europe' (Bavarian State Government, n.d.). In 1974, Bavaria set up the first automated air pollution control network in Europe; the network consists of measurement stations that monitor air quality 24 hours a day throughout the state (Bavarian State Government, n.d.).

Bavaria also became the first state in Germany to chart natural habitats in the flatlands in 1974 and 1975 and in the Alps from 1976–1979. In 1976, it created the first Academy for Environmental Conservation in the country. In addition to those efforts, the Bavarian Environmental Protection Act has produced some pioneering legislation in preservation of natural habitats including in wetlands protection in 1982 and barren and arid lands protection in 1986. Moreover, Bavaria was the first state in Germany to add environmental protection to its constitution in 1984 (Bavarian State Government, n.d.); this did not occur federally until 1994 (Kern, 2008). The state also was the first to make three-way catalysers mandatory for all vehicles containing four-stroke internal combustion engines (the federal government required more than 60 percent to be fitted with a catalyser) (Bavarian State Government, n.d.).

Bavaria considers itself, in general, the reform state in Germany; it also recognizes its role as a major player on some national-level reforms. Bavaria served as a chief force behind getting the federal government to agree to include in its Maastricht treaty, negotiating package the creation of a subsidiarity and what became the Committee of the Regions; these were written into the treaty in a way that was acceptable to the *Länder* (Jeffery, 1996; Kaiser, 1999; Stoiber, 1994a). It has also been the motor for bureaucratic cutbacks and simplifications, also regarding the federal level (Stoiber, 1994a).

California, similarly, had early noteworthy accomplishments. In 1947, the state enacted the Air Pollution Control Act, which authorized the establishment of an Air Pollution Control District in every county (CARB, 2008a). That same year, the Los Angeles County Air Pollution Control District was set up, making it the first of its kind in the nation (CARB, 2008a). In 1959, California enacted a law requiring the Department of Public Health to set air quality standards and restrictions for vehicle emissions (CARB, 2008a), marking the first air quality program in the country (Cal/EPA, 2006b).

In 1966, California adopted another innovative policy, as stated above, setting auto tailpipe emission standards for hydrocarbons and carbon dioxide, which forced technology and diffused internationally (CARB, 2008a). It also helped California become grandfathered from federal mobile emission regulations, which were established after California's in 1967. Moreover, the Porter–Cologne Act of 1970, the foundation of the state's water quality program, served as a model for the federal government's Clean Water Act. In 1988, an amended California Clean Air Act (CAA) was signed into law; this act served as a model for Congress' 1990 CAA Amendments (Cal/EPA, 2006b). Also, 1990 is the year California approved standards for Cleaner Burning Fuels, and LEV and ZEV, also as mentioned.

Even though these similar, unique background characteristics cannot be considered as the primary reasons for the partnership, they provided the foundation upon which the present-day outlooks and goals were built. Moreover, they contributed to the overall feeling of 'naturalness' of the partnership. They can thus be seen as a secondary motivation. As a result, for all of those reasons, Strock and Goppel signed an agreement to cooperate on environmental technologies.

IMPLEMENTATION AND GENERAL RESULTS

Subsequent to the MoU signing, the two states engaged in some implementation activities. They traded information on technology certification; looked at ways to get new environmental technologies commercialized faster, for example through the central government; and compared information on how each realized commercialization, since it is a different process and history in both states. There were also some technical interchanges, for example all the details and specific permitting and regulation issues that occurred governmentally (J. Strock, pers. comm., 14 November 2005).

Goppel and Strock also used each other to gain support in their states for policy advancement. Goppel spoke in California several times, raising issues of global perspective. Likewise, Strock spoke in Bavaria, describing situations in California to help give the Bavarians perspective on how they should think about what Goppel was proposing there, to help give a context for their reforms (J. Strock, pers. comm., 14 November 2005).

> I can recall . . . where I spoke with . . . Goppel at his request to various groups about how we were doing new environmental technologies in California because he was reforming his process there. And he wanted them to hear, directly, from somebody in a situation similar, but far enough away that defensiveness would be limited. And he did similar things here. (J. Strock, pers. comm., 14 November 2005)

In this regard, the agreement with Bavaria (and that with Canada) served to help push California's program along (CARB, 1997). These agreements functioned not only as an idea exchange (J. Strock, pers. comm., 14 November 2005) and an information exchange on certifying procedures to reach program reciprocity (Cal/EPA, 1997), but also as a type of informal validation of the program (or reform) from within the state through the demonstration that important foreign regions/countries agreed with it (J. Strock, pers. comm., 14 November 2005); they provided assurance for California that it was on the right track – that its international goals, the program and its mechanics, procedures and technologies would receive broad acceptance (CARB, 1997).[3]

Scholars recognize this approach as a political tactic. Policymakers who refer to viable technologies and policies in other countries help to 'legitimize' their own initiatives compared to those who do not (Jänicke and Jacob, 2004, p. 41). Advocates of a policy will often portray lessons from abroad as 'politically neutral truths', while opponents will utilize them as 'political weapons' (Robertson, 1991, p. 55). This use of lessons selectively 'to gain advantage in the struggle to get . . . ideas accepted' is one way to utilize lessons in policy transfer (Dolowitz and Marsh, 1996, p. 346).

But despite these exchanges and activities, most of the officials with knowledge or experience with this partnership do not consider it to be very successful. Among the reflections were: 'Not much came out of it'; 'nothing much happened from it, it was just kind of a piece of paper'; 'it was one of these Memoranda which are not so well founded . . . it was not so serious as other Memoranda of Understanding'. Moreover, most sources of information did not mention any related activities or developments after the MoU signing. In subsequent speeches and documents out of Bavaria referring to international environmental partnerships, the 1995 partnership is never mentioned. Bavaria's partnership with Wisconsin, however, is frequently referred to, and sometimes its 2000 partnership with California.

While there is no question that the partnership was short-lived, lasting only as long as Strock headed Cal/EPA, which was only two years after its formation, the general disappointment and negative responses as to the outcome of the partnership indicate that much more was expected of it, for instance that it serve as a foundation upon which to build, that it develop into something long-lasting or permanent, that it become institutionalized. The partnership was not institutionalized because it was formed on a personal basis – the personal venture of a couple of actors, Strock and Goppel. If a partnership does not get institutionalized, then when the personal figures are gone it collapses, which is what happened (R. Henatsch, pers. comm., 25 November 2005). Furthermore, even with interested actors, without institutionalization, the agent must keep the agreement as a priority. 'Somebody at the top has to be focused for whatever reason otherwise it's going to get lost' (J. Strock, pers. comm., 14 November 2005). In this case, one can safely say that the partnership was over when Strock retired.

Moreover, a lack of institutionalization means that financing the partnership is going to be an issue, which was the case (R. Henatsch, pers. comm., 25 November 2005). There was very little money available on either side, which meant simply an exchange of information, of visitors and the like, a bit of traveling and diplomacy on both sides, with good intentions, but no establishment of a kind of lasting infrastructure, which is what was needed for substantive developments. But to set something like that up, money would be needed. And the question of how to fund the written goals was not covered, 'not even touched upon' (R. Henatsch, pers. comm., 25 November 2005). 'If you really want to establish some kind of institutionalized relationship in terms of a working group, regular meetings, exchange of information, then . . . you need money in the budget for that. And there was . . . really not much available on either side' (R. Henatsch, pers. comm., 25 November 2005).

The German Consulate, under Henatsch, made some efforts to keep it going after Strock left, but that was the extent of it since it was a state matter, not a federal one. Although there was still some interest in it, it was not enough to keep the partnership alive (R. Henatsch, pers. comm., 25 November 2005). Moreover, Strock's counterpart, Goppel, also left his position about a year later. Without the personal push, financing or an institutional framework, the partnership just faded away.

This discrepancy points to the complex relationship between governance and the institutional workings of government. Possibly the most important point about Type II governance is that it is usually embedded in Type I; it has been observed within and therefore is bound by the legal structures of Type I (Hooghe and Marks, 2003). Since the partnership was created out of personal efforts there was no money set up for it in California, which would have had to come out of the legislature or from discretionary funds, with staff resources dedicated to it. Nor did it fit the criteria of an informal institution (with patterned interactions, the existence of some stability over time and the like) (Peters, 2005). Thus, this is an example of the snag that Type II governance runs into through its entrenchment in Type I structures.

In Bavaria this situation is slightly different. Keeping up with international activities is the task and duty of the ministers; it is not necessary to have a law from parliament. The Environmental Ministry, thus, has a budget for international affairs and it is essentially left to the discretion of the minister what affairs they will tend to, with the consent of the cabinet (M. Weigand, pers. comm., 5 August 2008). But as Henatsch stated, there was very little money available, which still implies that this type of governance was not taken seriously enough within the traditional *Land*-level structure in Germany either. Thus, the analysis is the same.

But despite having been ephemeral and with just a couple of achievements (any additional benefits or effects stemming from the mutual political backing that Strock and Goppel provided each other by traveling and holding talks are intangible), there were some concrete developments, particularly in California, to which the partnership may have indirectly contributed. A little over a year after the MoU signing, Cal/EPA announced that the ISO was considering its CalCert program as a 'leading model for determining baseline standards for verifying performance claims made by environmental technology manufacturers' for inclusion in its ISO 14000 series on environmental management systems. More relevant, however, is that a Cal/EPA official attributed the state's agreement with Germany and its discussions with Mexico and Canada regarding its certification program as the 'foundation' for its 'work with the ISO' (Cal/EPA, 1996a).

Another development that occurred later that year, in December 1996, was that the CalCert program won the 1996 Innovations in American Government Award of the Ford Foundation and the John F. Kennedy School of Government at Harvard University. The award is given to 'creative solutions to pressing social and economic problems' (Cal/EPA,

1996d). The primary function of the award is to help spread the program nationally and internationally (Cal/EPA, 1996d).

In sum, the CalCert program, which moved forward partly due to the partnership with Bavaria, received worldwide interest and served as a model at both the federal and state levels, and internationally (CARB, 1997).[4] Regarding the goals of policy convergence, transfer and diffusion on environmental technology certification policy, whether based on a direct outcome of the partnership or not, it can be said that this aspect was rather successful.[5] Likewise, over the next several years, Bavaria's reform policies, particularly its Environmental Pact, attracted attention both nationally and internationally, on the subnational, national and supranational levels, and has served as a model for similar programs elsewhere (Schnappauf, 1999). Furthermore, the state has gained a global reputation for its environmental technologies. In this regard, based on the advancement of these respective goals, it can also be concluded that both sides succeeded to a certain degree in the furthering of both their economic and their environmental protection goals.

There were also some indirect results of the partnership. Strock continued even outside of government to connect Germany and California. He has been particularly active with the German-based non-governmental organization (NGO) Deutsche Umwelthilfe on the issue of climate change. In 2005, Strock even had a meeting with the Cal/EPA secretary and the head of the Deutsche Umwelthilfe to discuss climate change issues. Strock and the head of the German NGO were able to get approval to get supportive quotes from the governor and the secretary on some environmental questions that are occurring in Germany. These quotes were publicized in about 40 or 50 newspapers (J. Strock, pers. comm., 14 November 2005). Furthermore, Strock expected that interaction to result in a series of informal contacts (J. Strock, pers. comm., 14 November 2005). Finally, the partnership can be considered partly responsible for acting as a springboard for the 2000 California–Bavaria partnership (R. Stephens, pers. comm., 14 February 2006). The 2000 partnership was a renewal of the 1995 partnership in addition to a cooperative effort on regulatory innovation, modeled on the 1998 Bavaria–Wisconsin agreement (M. Weigand, pers. comm., 6 April 2005).

ANALYSIS

The driving forces leading to the idea for the 1995 California–Bavaria partnership began in the early 1990s, with the end of the Cold War and the rapid rise of globalization, the complexities of which included: (1)

globalization of the economy, information and the environment; (2) international-level calls for reform to address changes; and (3) the emergence
of global governance. These factors, the structural changes in the international system and the international-level pressure, not only provided
a role for non-nation-state and/or non-traditional actors and institutions
in global governance, but they also served as indirect coercive forces, as
per Dolowitz and Marsh's continuum, for reform in both California and
Bavaria, compelling policymakers to act (one can also see these as situative factors that spurred the pursuance of innovative ecological modernization policies and attempts for lead markets), as the status quo became
no longer acceptable.

As explained in the innovative environmental diffusion literature, the
characteristics of the policy innovations can reveal the diffusion mechanism that is at work. The partnership demonstrated both regulatory and
ideational competition. Concerning the former (the political), California
was trying to diffuse its CalCert program both horizontally and vertically,
pushing it all the way to the ISO, which was in the process of developing
a series of EMS standards. This policy was also linked by global trade
and thus economic competition. To this end, California and Bavaria
had ecological modernization plans for their environmental technology
industries. In their MoU, the two parties stated their desire to 'promote
environmental technologies', and were consequently attempting to use the
partnership partly as a stepping stone for their diffusion ends, which is a
strategy of trying to become a lead market. Both states tie their ecological
modernization goals to globalization, causing economic challenges in both
states and their consequential aims to pair environmental protection with
economic growth and thus a promotion of the environmental technology
industry. Bavaria, home to BMW, was particularly interested in learning
more about California's LEV program and its fuel cell developments.
With its reputation of sparking the worldwide diffusion of technology in
the past, it seemed this might also happen with the LEV program as the
policy had already forced fuel cell technology in California. In terms of
ideas, California wanted to learn from Germany on reconciling an environmental economy, which it believed it was working hard to do. In the
1990s the *Länder*, in particular, took the lead in Germany in implementing
the Rio principles.

This partnership largely fit the characterization of Type II multi-level
governance (MLG). In terms of structure, while the partnership on the
surface was made possible by two subnational governments from two
countries, with the help of the federal government of Germany, the
greater dynamics included the international level (the influences and
goals in many ways transcended traditional governmental hierarchy)

and the private sector – that is, the environmental technology industry. Furthermore, it was based on a common function and a common need to work together, it was voluntary and easy to enter and exit, and it was intersecting as opposed to nested, operating (at least regarding the larger dynamics) on many scales.

Whereas the key components in the first stage of the process leading to the idea to form the partnership were structural, the main factors in the process leading to the official agreement were primarily agency driven, but also with structural components. There were three key players, without whom the partnership would not have been possible: Strock, Henatsch and Goppel. Within this tripartite group, the chief importance lay in Strock's networking, in the personal relationship that developed between Strock and Henatsch, in Henatsch's networking and, finally, in Strock and Goppel's policy entrepreneurialism. The key institutions were thus the states of California, Bavaria and the federal government of Germany. The exogenous components were the timely circumstances of Goppel's visit to California and the German Consulate, and the fact that the states seemed evenly matched because of their similar policy goals, and similar background characteristics regarding their respective strengths economically and in environmental protection.

There were several layers of objectives on both sides of this partnership. These included: (1) to learn from one another, both in a general and a specific context; (2) to gain support for policies and reforms for political purposes; (3) to benefit economically (including becoming a lead market) in their respective ecological modernization objectives; (4) to contribute to environmental protection goals; and (5) to transfer, converge and diffuse policy. In many instances these motivations intertwined. Thus, these findings demonstrate that the policy entrepreneurs were not only interested in policy learning and diffusion, but that they were also acting out of bounded rationality, as per Dolowitz and Marsh's continuum.

The general ('natural') interests in learning from one another stemmed in large part from their many exclusive leadership and pioneering similarities, that is, their economic standing, long-standing leadership roles in environmental protection, and their propensity for pushing the envelope within (and sometimes beyond) their countries. California's specific interests included learning about sustainable development policies. Bavaria's interests included California's cutting-edge vehicle emissions control policies and its developments on fuel cells.

The second tier was political; the partnership was used (whether intended or not) as a tool for the environmental leaders, Strock and Goppel, to acquire support from within their respective states for their reforms, which according to Kingdon is a tactic of policy entrepreneurs.

This aspect only becomes clear, however, in the implementation phase. The third level was economic (in conjunction with ecological modernization); it is apparent that both sides believed that they could directly profit economically from the partnership. The environmental technology industry was considered a very important industry for both states' economies. Moreover, they were both striving to become a lead market, because being a frontrunner on an innovative policy is economically advantageous. The fourth level was environmental protection: the industry they intentionally chose to support was environmentally friendly (contributing to the sustainable development goals of the two states); and using the partnership for help with reforms also had major environmental implications. Both of these points were the result of concerted policy efforts to combine environmental protection with economic growth.

The fifth layer involves the primary way they planned to realize the environmental policy and/or the promotion of the environmental technology industry, which is more abstract but nonetheless still a reason for the partnership; it involved the goals of policy transfer, convergence and diffusion. In other words, the two states wanted to converge on a policy, which means learning from one another and then transferring aspects of a certain innovative policy to make sure it was mutually acceptable to jointly and thus in a more powerful way – as two powerful, front-running, transatlantic states would be – diffuse it elsewhere. Intended to promote the environmental technology industry, the diffusion of the policy would thus open up markets in both states for their state-based companies with certifications in environment technology and attract others to their respective states to create more jobs.

In looking at the implementation and results, most people with any knowledge, direct or indirect, of the partnership consider it a failure. But in looking at the aforementioned laid-out objectives, even though most of them are not quantifiable, it cannot be totally seen in this light. The first objective, learning from one another, cannot be an assumed failure since the two main agents, Goppel and Stock, facilitated policy and idea exchanges. But in terms of the understanding that the partnership could turn into something solid and be built up into something significantly concrete, the partnership failed; ironically, it fell short for the same reason that it succeeded in coming together: because it stemmed from the personal efforts of the heads of the respective environmental agencies. The innovative agents were ultimately bound to the traditional state structure if they wanted to carry the partnership beyond personal efforts into something institutional, with staff, program dedication and thus funding – something beyond the MoU.

Secondly, the partnership can be said to have been at least somewhat successful as having been used as a political tool by both Strock and Goppel to gain support from within their respective states for their policies. And was shown, the CalCert program did diffuse to other subnations and nations. It can thus be concluded that they succeeded, based on the spread of the CalCert program; that they advanced both their economic and environmental protection goals. Furthermore, it indirectly served as a springboard and as a tool for other developments and contacts between the two states. Thus, the presence of these policy entrepreneurs did make a difference in the implementation of the partnership. This was proven when the partnership came to a halt after the policy entrepreneur in California left office.

This partnership demonstrated that certain subnational-level governments are aiming to become and have become relevant players in a sort of Type II international multi-level governance regarding sustainable development (at least the lead up to and the dynamic of it), both in implementing the international agenda in this broad area and in influencing certain, more specific policies and technologies therein. Within this multi-level structure was a two-way vertical and horizontal diffusion process (starting at the international level) in which these two respective subnational governments were seeking a frontrunner role, specifically in policies supporting environmental technology and the innovative technologies themselves. In terms of its success, the partnership demonstrated that there is a necessity for the traditional legal structures in governance, as it could not sustain itself on agents, circumstances and external factors, which in the multi-level governance literature supports the idea that Type II multi-level governance is embedded in Type I; in other words, it needs to function within the parameters of Type I if it is to function effectively.

In conclusion, this 1995 partnership was the outgrowth of several factors: the causal factors of the dynamics of the international system (globalization), coupled with the right set of unique structural commonalities between the two states, the drive of specific political actors and chance circumstances. While there were several dimensions to the partnership, the primary objective of the partnership was that it would serve as a means for both Bavaria and California to progress their ecological modernization plans. Among other revelations, the partnership illustrates that certain subnational-level governments are aiming to become, and have become, relevant players in a type of international multi-level governance regarding sustainable development, in both implementing the international agenda in this broad area and in influencing certain, more specific policies and technologies therein. The lack of a more lasting success between the two leading states, however, shows the necessity of the state structure in such governance; that is, that the legal structures and institutions of government are necessary in governance, as the partnership's lack of institutionalization led to its demise.

NOTES

1. Later, as outlined in the Environmental Initiative and in accordance with the new environmental concept regarding the need to communicate and cooperate across sectors, Goppel established the Environmental Forum of Bavaria in early 1996 to bring different societal groups together to solve current environmental problems (Stoiber, 1995; STMUGV, n.d.-a). Out of this forum, the Bavarian Agenda 21 was developed at the end of 1997 (Schnappauf, 1999).
2. A later 1997 program included the Environmental Technology Export Program, to help promote the development, manufacture, utilization and export of environmental technologies, products and services (US EPA, 2000).
3. No data were obtainable on how these exchanges impacted Bavaria; it can be assumed that at the very least they also provided assurance and validation.
4. No data were obtainable as to whether and to what degree the ISO adopted the California program.
5. But despite all the fanfare and the diffusion, the CalCert program ultimately failed, in 2002. The first problem was that the program was supposed to be self-supporting – in other words, the companies would pay for the costs – but it was actually quite expensive given the time and effort required to do a full-blown review and authentication of technology. It deterred a lot of people from coming to request a certification. The second problem was that there was some political opposition to it in terms of 'government choosing winners in technologies', in which 'some felt that that was an inappropriate thing for government to do' (R. Stephens, pers. comm., 14 February 2006).

5. Wisconsin and Bavaria (1998)

THE MEMORANDUM

On 1 December 1998, in Munich, Wisconsin Governor Tommy Thompson, on behalf of the Wisconsin Department of Natural Resources (DNR), and Dr Werner Schnappauf, State Minister of the Ministry for Regional Development and Environmental Affairs,[1] signed a Memorandum of Understanding (MoU) to create a Regulatory Reform Working Partnership. This official document, which is reasonably straightforward about its intentions and justifications, listed three overarching objectives and ten specific goals and methods for the partnership. The primary objectives were: first, to achieve a sustainable economic and environmental system both in and beyond the two states; second, to attain more cooperation between government and business than is attainable under the command-and-control method; and third, to explore voluntary agreements and environmental management systems (EMSs) as the facilitating instrument (Wisconsin DNR and Bavaria MRDEA, 1998).

The crux of the ten specific goals and methods was to establish 'joint projects' to encourage private sector participation in 'EMSs verified/certified to EMAS/IS0 14000 et seq. standards according to the principles of performance audits and legal compliance' (Wisconsin DNR and Bavaria MRDEA, 1998). In addition, the partners aimed to support an academic partnership between experts in environmental management and new regulatory systems as well as in engineering and technology, and to promote research into the development of environmental technology. Moreover, the two states agreed to work together on a 'common international environmental law project' (Wisconsin DNR and Bavaria MRDEA, 1998).

The other stated methods for attaining the objectives involved both independent and bilateral efforts. Mutual efforts included exchanges from all societal sectors to share and learn 'best practices' and 'publish[ing] annual statements' of ongoing results (Wisconsin DNR and Bavaria MRDEA, 1998). Individually, both governments agreed to cooperate with the private sector and NGOs on the new systems approaches and to conduct public awareness campaigns on the need for such approaches 'in the new era of environmental law' (Wisconsin DNR and Bavaria MRDEA, 1998).

The document outlined the reasoning behind the promotion of EMSs. Many of these arguments pointed to the many economic and environmental advantages compared to the prescribed regulatory approach. It stated that these systems fulfill the wants of both the private and public sectors that more efficient systems be competitive; yet they also provide the ability to produce the environmental results beyond the already established standards. Other arguments pointed to some external factors, for example as a way of complying with the United Nations Conference on Environment and Development's (UNCED) Agenda 21 and sustainable development goals (Wisconsin DNR and Bavaria MRDEA, 1998), and as a way of complying with the 1995 US–EU New Trans-Atlantic Agenda that calls for closer collaboration in areas including trade, environmental issues and technologies.

As presented, the document largely speaks directly about the partners' intentions and justifications. The goals of combining the Eco-Management and Audit Scheme (EMAS) and the ISO 14000 systems and the desire to diffuse such a system 'beyond' the borders of the two states indicates their drive to work toward and contribute to global environmental policy convergence on EMSs and compliance. The details of the MoU do not entirely outline the goals of the partnership, nor the extensive reasons behind it, as other documents and interviews revealed. The rest of the chapter aims to fill in these blanks.

THE DRIVING FORCES

Reform in Bavaria – Environmental Pact

As shown in Chapter 4, Bavaria began pushing through major reforms in reaction to changing world dynamics, increasing economic competition and pressures from international governing bodies in the early 1990s. The most relevant reform to this study is the Environmental Pact of Bavaria, created in October 1995. Based on the argument that 'the overall goal of sustainable development as promoted by Agenda 21 was not being met' and that 'a limit of acceptance' was being reached on the number of laws and regulations – at more than 4000 (Weissbach, 2000)[2] – Bavaria wanted new approaches to developing environmental law; the belief was that it is possible to deregulate while maintaining environmental standards (M. Weigand, pers. comm., 6 April 2005).

The Environmental Pact represented that new approach to protecting the environment, moving from the 'command-and-control' method to governmental collaboration with industry and environmentalists (Torinus,

2004). It exemplified the first agreement of its kind in Germany in which the public and private sectors formed a partnership to work together to establish an 'environmental policy based on consensus' (STMUGV, 2000, p. 3). The Business and Environment's Global Analysis even went as far as to say that 'Bavaria has done the most work in Europe on alternative regulatory programs' (Wisconsin DNR, n.d.-e).

The agreement, initially to last for five years, was voluntary, yet the goal was to achieve a greater level of environmental protection (STMUGV, 2000). The European Union's (EU) EMAS was set up as an environmental management instrument to meet the desired environmental ends (Stoiber, 1995). By the time of the partnership, Bavaria boasted that one in six companies using EMASs in Europe was located in Bavaria, making it a leader in its implementation in Europe (Schnappauf, 1998; Wisconsin DNR, n.d.-d). EMAS is a tactic in the creation of lead markets (Jänicke and Jacob, 2006).

This type of innovative method was within Bavarian's autonomous rights as a state in the German federal system. In environmental law, while legislation is mixed between the federal and state levels, its implementation and enforcement primarily occurs at the *Länder* level. This is what the Environmental Pact was, as it did not contain new legislation but was rather the state's unique way of implementing and enforcing environmental legislation, of actually exceeding legislative standards. It is not necessary to follow the command-and-control way (M. Weigand, pers. comm., 5 August 2008).

Another major goal of the partnership, which corresponds to the state's efforts to promote the environmental technology industry, is Bavaria's goals for diffusion and lead market creation (see Chapter 4 in this volume). While the Pact serves to help meet global responsibilities, its objective is 'to spread worldwide the idea of environmental protection and the high standard of environmental protection achieved in Bavaria, and to further increase exports of environmental technology and services by Bavarian entrepreneurs' (E. Müller, 2005, p. 21), to become an export leader in this market (Schnappauf, 2004).

Further International and Supranational Developments

The growing importance of ISO standards
Since the 1995 partnership and the commencement of Bavaria's Environmental Pact, and especially after the International Organization for Standardization (ISO) published its 14001 standards in September 1996, the importance of international EMSs grew for Bavaria and Wisconsin. Although the standards have been somewhat controversial

because of the organization's make-up and the value of the standards themselves (Clapp, 2005), once they were published, a widespread interest in the business community arose. In the United States, it was expected that certification might eventually be required in some international markets to do business and that it might also be required or encouraged domestically for many suppliers by their customers. It was also thought that businesses and other organizations might see such an international certification as a chance to improve their image to both regulators and the public as being more environmentally friendly (Andrews et al., 1999).

An added level of importance was given to the ISO standards by the WTO's acceptance and promotion of them as a way to reduce 'technical barriers to trade' (Clapp, 2005, p. 236). This acceptance had the weight of globally legitimizing them even though the WTO was operating from its own market-based principles. The WTO has demonstrated a preference for the ISO and its activities over the actions of other international bodies. Although the ISO's EMS standards are voluntary, the WTO considers them 'standards', and thus a way to reduce barriers to trade (p. 236); conversely, the WTO does not accept similar actions set by governments or intergovernmental organizations, such as the United Nations, as 'standards', but instead calls them 'technical regulations' and thus 'potential trade barriers' (p. 236).

One of the partnership's key figures on Wisconsin's side, Jim Klauser, emphasized the relevancy of the growing importance of international EMS standards as one of the major stimuli of the state's interest in and development of EMSs and the partnership (pers. comm., 21 March 2005). Correspondingly, Schnappauf acknowledged and promoted the international developments as necessary in a world where industry is globalized (Schnappauf, 1998). The ISO standards were also of special importance to Bavaria because of the discrepancy they posed with Europe's EMAS. Bavaria had been priding itself on being the leader of EMAS implementation in Europe and had been pressing hard to promote it as a key instrument in its 1995 pact. But this regional-based policy posed the exact predicament the ISO was attempting to eliminate through the creation of its international-level standards: the loss of competitiveness or the detrimental trade effects for companies if they have to contend with different sets of standards, particularly at a time when competition is at its toughest. This point was not only significant for transnational companies; it also applied to businesses exporting to EU countries. About 80 percent of the environmental legislation in Germany comes from the European level; these rules cover not only products that are manufactured within the EU but also imports, making this a matter of 'international significance' (E. Müller, 2005).

Schnappauf (1998) indicated that in the longer term an improvement of the basic legal framework would be necessary. This foresight was referring to the EU's revision process of EMAS (since 1997), in part to reconcile the differences and comply with the international standards (EC, 2009b; Schnappauf, 1998; Wisconsin DNR, n.d.-c). But for Bavaria, the considerations of combining systems needed to be tested and exchange of experience needed to take place; and since Wisconsin was developing and testing its own EMS program and was eager to learn from Bavaria in this regard, this proved to be a compelling partnership motive (Schnappauf, 1998; Thompson, 1998a). A statement describing the newly created partnership explained:

> The dual certification process allows the EMAS approach to 'compensate for [ISO] EMS' shortcomings.' . . . [T]he European EMAS approach does an 'excellent' job of predicting performance down the road through a company's requirement to publicly report its performance – which the EMS approach does not require. This also indicates to regulators which facilities they have to pay more attention to, while those who institute these systems will move to the 'head of the line' for regulatory relief. (Wisconsin DNR, 1999)

EU's 'mistrust' of Bavaria's pact

Despite the international and supranational developments of EMSs and approaches, Bavaria also found itself involved in a struggle with the EU about autonomy concerning its innovative pact. 'The bureaucracy of the EU . . . is to a certain extent mistrustful of models such as the Environmental Pact . . . and [is] trying to delay them or to put up resistance to them' (Schnappauf, 1999).[3] Schnappauf pointed out that this conflict was not unique to Bavaria, and that lower-level governments trying to take action based on the accepted approach from the UNCED were running into the same 'fundamental disputes . . . about the nature and function of government activity' whether with the national or supranational levels, which has made it all the more important to 'exchange experiences' (Schnappauf, 1999).

Lack of Significant National-Level Action

Even with the international calls for a paradigm shift in approaches to environmental protection, Bavarian and Wisconsin leaders point out that not much was being done nationally in their countries. Wisconsin officials indicate that the environmental debate at the federal level has not progressed since the early 1990s (Hassett et al., 2004). They argue that the fragmented approaches can no longer produce the environmental, economic and community results required of these times. Wisconsin's environmental reform policy, Green Tier, which is a system that rewards companies that achieve excellent environmental performance with regulatory incentives and breaks, is a step toward a new, needed phase in environmental law (Hassett et al., 2004). Bavaria State Secretary Emilia Müller (2005) also said that the 'limited scope of national legislation' contributed to the prompting of calls for new forms of international cooperation.

Reform in Wisconsin – The Road to 'Green Tier'

Like Bavaria, Wisconsin was hit by the same transformational forces of the 1990s. The state was particularly impacted by economic globalization, which caused an intense competition among the states to attract businesses to create jobs and made some regions, particularly manufacturing, especially vulnerable. Manufacturing has been a significant part of Wisconsin's economy, accounting for about 22 percent of employment, compared to 14 percent nationwide (Daykin, 2002). Because of this, both public and private representatives believe that reform is essential if such industries are to remain economically competitive in a global marketplace (Hassett et al., 2004).

The state paired these economic pressures to the environmental protection regulatory system that they believe does not adequately address the environmental, economic or community conditions and sustainability goals of the twenty-first century. This thinking was in accord with the global view. 'Unless we create this "Green Tier" system that removes unproductive regulatory constraints and allows companies to achieve their full environmental and economic potential, we will never be fully able to achieve ecological sustainability in this world' (Meyer, 1999a).

Wisconsin also had technical reasons for reform, such as that there was not enough immunity for self-auditing compared to other states, and that there was a general dissatisfaction with the status quo. 'Regulators, activists, lawyers and businesses were frustrated with what laws failed to do or how much they cost' (Hassett et al., 2004, pp. 11–12). According to the DNR:

> Current law does not allow us to differentiate between good environmental performers and those performing at or near the regulatory minimum. Current law may, at times, prevent or discourage performance beyond the minimum or diminish the importance of unregulated practices. The consumption of staff resources to regulate good environmental performers does not yield environmental results proportional to the investment. Failure to tap the capacity of good companies to produce substantive environmental results leaves pressing environmental problems unsolved. (Wisconsin DNR, 2005a)

Another internal driver was that there was an acceptance by environmentalists of innovative ideas. Moreover, there was the sense that innovation was occurring elsewhere and awareness that new tools were needed. For instance, the ISO's standards and the round-tables and institutions they prompted, which included the DNR (for example the Multi-State Working Group on Environmental Performance (MSWG), see below), provided learning and network opportunities and fueled the desire for change (Hassett et al., 2004).

In 1996, the DNR proposed a pilot project, the Environmental Cooperation Pilot Program (ECPP), which was, albeit on a much smaller scale, very similar to the Bavarian pact (Meyer, 1999a; Weissbach, 2000; Wisconsin DNR, 2005b). The crux of the program, which became the Cooperative Environmental Agreement Program, was to evaluate EMS methods by allowing the DNR to enter into up to ten agreements over five years with facilities that legally require licenses or permits (Meyer, 1999a; Wisconsin DNR, 1998). The idea behind the agreements was to provide the freedom needed to achieve greater environmental and eco-nomic performance through the use of an EMS – one which abides by the ISO 14001 standard and: (1) 'is clear and firm on legal compliance'; (2) 'produces measurable results'; (3) 'has a two way communication with the public'; and (4) 'addresses both regulated and unregulated environmental problems' (Meyer, 1999a). This approach is along the lines of what the partners strove for in their agreement, with the dual certification process, which they later referred to as 'ISO Plus'. Another important aspect of the new law was that it encouraged reports of early and minor violations, thereby eliminating what had become the 'don't ask, don't tell' custom (Meyer, 1999a).

The agreement program was considered the 'most comprehensive regulatory innovation law in the United States' (Meyer, 1999a). It was an even more extensive experiment on the matter than those that were underway federally, such as through the EPA's Project X-L, the Common Sense Initiative and the Environmental Leadership program (Meyer, 1999a). It ultimately served as the foundation for regulatory innovation in Wisconsin, which became known as the Green Tier concept in 1999 and later became law (see below).

The state also took non-traditional avenues in its search for reform. In the fall of 1996, Wisconsin became one of the MSWG's founding members (see Chapter 3 in this volume). As DNR Secretary Meyer (1999a) pointed out: 'The regulatory innovation being pursued by the states in the US are signs that we are not satisfied with the status quo.'

The question as to how two seemingly unequal states could come to have an innovative policy in common is especially interesting since one of the main factors that brought Bavaria and California together in 1995 was their many exclusive leadership and pioneering similarities, for example their economic standing, long-standing leadership roles in environmental protection and their propensity for pushing the envelope within (and sometimes beyond) their countries (see Chapter 4).[4] First, Wisconsin has a stable economy compared to most other states (US DOC, 2000). Second, it has a history of occasionally putting forth innovative programs, for example its sulphur dioxide (SO_2) emissions trading program of the 1980s to curb acid rain, which was adopted federally and later served as a model for the EU's carbon dioxide (CO_2) emissions trading system (J. Smoller, pers. comm., 3 March 2005; Sereno, 2002; Shoup, 2009), and its pioneering welfare reform, which also diffused nationally and internationally. Third, the state had innovative policy entrepreneurs at the helm, which is discussed below.

Idea to Form the Partnership

The idea to form the partnership began on a personal level, through an interaction between Jeff Smoller, a special assistant to the DNR secretary, and Dr Matthias Weigand, Head of Division, Cross-Sectoral Law, of the Ministry for Regional Development and Environmental Affairs (a legal advisor), at a US–European EMS round table event in California in February 1998 (M. Weigand, pers. comm., 6 April 2005; Smoller, 2006). The meeting was one of a series that took place on both continents, a 'transatlantic US, EU partnership network', organized by lawyers in the United States (M. Weigand, pers. comm., 6 April 2005), in particular by Edward Quevedo, who was an environmental lawyer and consultant and connected to BMW (J. Smoller, pers. comm., 31 December 2008). One of the topics was the development of EU environmental laws; Weigand presented the Bavarian incentives for regulatory innovation (M. Weigand, pers. comm., 6 April 2005). Smoller and Meyer found Bavaria's approach the most attractive in their search for examples of performances approaches because of its Bavarian pact, as a structured program, and because of the executive leadership led by Minister President Stoiber, whom they characterized as both 'stable and aggressive' (J. Smoller, pers. comm., 3 March 2005). Based on these mutual interests and projects, Smoller proposed the idea of working together to Weigand (M. Weigand, pers. comm., 6 April 2005).

THE KEY COMPONENTS FROM IDEA TO MOU

Formation of the Partnership

The two civil servants, Smoller and Weigand, then presented the idea to their higher-ups, Meyer and Schnappauf, both of whom readily welcomed it. In the fall of 1998, Meyer approved Smoller's trip to Germany, whereby he and Weigand drafted the first MoU (J. Smoller, pers. comm., 3 March 2005). Then, while on a trade mission in December of that year, Gov. Thompson, who was also very supportive of the agreement, signed the MoU.

Motivations and Objectives

Expanding upon what was stated in the MoU, it can be seen that there were several motivations and objectives for the partnership, including policy learning, transfer, testing, convergence, and international diffusion and convergence of an environmental policy approach that centered on EMSs and compliance. The most direct aim was that Wisconsin learn from Bavaria's environmental policy reform. Bavaria's aim was to transfer its policy and also the corresponding innovative technology that its pact impelled. Regarding convergence, anything learned and transferred would lead to a certain degree of convergence between the two programs. That said, there was a specific convergence goal, to assure that both states base their policies on a combined EMAS and ISO 14001 approach.

Beyond the development of a dual approach, the transatlantic cooperation would serve as a way to test and thus verify and validate these management systems as a substitution of regulatory approaches as part of an effort to get a successful policy diffused domestically and internationally, which would mean some degree of global convergence. As Gov. Thompson (1998b) said at the time of the signing: 'Bavaria and Wisconsin can share innovations, success stories and advice. With a stronger European Union and emergence of states in the US, we can influence greater Europe and the entire US, sometimes acting alone and sometimes together'. Weigand discussed the partnership in context with the drive to try to influence the development of the international standardization. '[I]f we want to confirm our ideas in the background of driving the regulatory innovation all over the world and with international management systems like ISO 14001 and not only EMAS in Europe then we need many partners and we need very strong partners' (pers. comm., 6 April 2005). This attempt to take the lead in this policy area, especially when considering the new arena for pioneers in global environmental policy, indicates that the two transatlantic states were acting as pushers in trying to transfer their policy innovation to the higher level.

One of the motivations for these objectives was economic gain. The combining of systems, in which companies in both states would be certified and verified to both EMAS and ISO standards, would facilitate transatlantic trade, especially since Bavaria and Wisconsin have significant industrial ties. As a matter of fact, transatlantic trade was one of the agreement's 'key elements' (Wisconsin DNR, 1999). It is not coincidental that Gov. Thompson signed the MoU as part of a trade mission that included visiting a BMW research center and speaking at a Quandt gathering on transatlantic cooperation (Wisconsin DNR, n.d.-d). 'The world wants better ways to protect the environment at a time when government resources are increasingly limited but trade's potential is not' (Wisconsin DNR, 1999).

On the larger scale, being a frontrunner in driving policy in global environmental governance (influencing the international standards, which would at some point internationally diffuse) is also economically advantageous. That said, on a basic level alone, as stated, policies such as the pact or Green Tier (the nature of EMSs) are said to be beneficial both environmentally and economically. In diffusing its pact, for instance, Bavaria is also positioning itself, as a frontrunner, to advance the resultant technology. This point has been confirmed in speeches by top officials.

Another reason for the partnership was to garner political support. Wisconsin needed to win support within the state for its reform. Bavaria, as just stated (and also Wisconsin secondarily), wanted to acquire interest and diffusion in the policy and resultant technology. It also needed support as it was up against scrutiny from the European level. As Schnappauf pointed out, subnational-level governments face an uphill battle in engaging in global environmental governance, in the non-hierarchical approach.

Primary Supporting Factors

Behind the scenes of the partnership's formation there were some additional supporting factors that contributed to the success of reaching an agreement. The main factor was leadership. Another component was the key support and connections from certain governmental and nongovernmental institutions and officials. Additionally, there were: the natural connections between the two states; the unique similarity of the policy reform; the agreement's scope and potential; and good timing. These points are examined below.

Agents – innovative leaders at the helm
The process leading to the bilateral agreement was predominantly driven by the agents themselves. Many of these actors, however, were not new when it comes to innovative policies. Some of them were even leaders in the promotion of state autonomy in the face of globalization, particularly in relation to the ever increasing supranational and international organizations and governing bodies. Gov. Thompson was a proponent of

state autonomy, as evident from his service and leading roles in organizations such as the Council of State Governments, and support for the international agreement with Bavaria (Meyer, 1999a; Thompson, 1991). Thompson's legacy also included steering through the above-mentioned welfare reform. What may have been just as important was the innovative and autonomous atmosphere he fostered in his administration. Thompson believed in supporting innovative thinking in lower-level public officials (Thompson, 1998b). Thompson's counterpart, Minister-President Stoiber, was also a big proponent of subnational autonomy, as discussed in Chapter 4 in this volume, and was also highly essential regarding the state's environmental reforms of the early 1990s, which promoted environmental technologies and created the Environmental Pact.

Likewise, Sec. Meyer advocated state roles in environmental protection, has a reputation for being a 'national leader in regulatory reform thinking', and was 'a strong supporter of a systems approach to management' (Wisconsin DNR, n.d.-d). Meyer helped found the Environmental Council of the States (ECOS) and MSWG (ECOS, n.d.-a; Meyer, 1999b), forces in regulatory reform efforts. Meyer's counterpart, Schnappauf, had only become minister in October 1998, but was nonetheless a great proponent of the discussed innovation and reform policies and a great supporter of the partnership with Wisconsin (BDI, 2007; Meyer, 1999a; Smoller, 2006; Wisconsin DNR, n.d.-d). What is most important regarding Schnappauf, and also Meyer for that matter, was their allowing Weigand and Smoller, respectively, to pursue innovative ideas. Weigand recognized how unusual it was that two civil servants were allowed to begin cooperation on a broad basis (pers. comm., 6 April 2005). The partnership would not have been possible without the support of Meyer and Schnappauf.

Smoller and Weigand, for their part, have shown themselves to be policy entrepreneurs. The instigation of the partnership, which was among the first of its kind, demonstrated their innovative tendencies. As a matter of fact, it was these regulatory reform inclinations, not merely chance, that led them to the same forums and to subsequent discussions. Both Smoller and Weigand referred to each other as strong drivers. 'The bottom line is . . . [Weigand] wanted it to happen. He's a player throughout Europe. He's a very well respected attorney within the EU and among the various regulatory organizations. He's trusted by his boss. It's as simple as that' (J. Smoller, pers. comm., 3 March 2005). Smoller played an important role in advancing innovative EMS policy for the DNR. Moreover, he represented the state in becoming one of the original MSWG members and leaders and was behind the initial push for the partnership with Bavaria. He was also able to push the partnership through different administrations, leaving Weigand to classify him as one of the 'special persons' who works behind the scenes making the partnership work and who provides the 'guarantee for cooperation' for Bavaria (pers. comm., 6 April 2005).

The federal level, non-governmental organizations and key individuals
In Wisconsin, there were some preconditions that had to be met before the partnership could even be conceptualized. This required not only the development of environmental regulatory reform policy but also the ability to establish the policy within the federal system, which entailed collaboration with the federal government (see Chapter 3 in this volume).[5] To begin with, the United States Environmental Protection Agency (EPA) and Environmental Council of the States (ECOS) signed an innovations agreement in April 1998 entitled the Joint EPA/State Agreement to Pursue Regulatory Innovation. The agreement was part of ongoing state and federal efforts in which the two governing levels would work as partners to give states more flexibility to pursue regulatory innovations that result in better environmental protection ('Joint EPA/State', 1998). The primary building block for this was the National Environmental Performance Partnership System ('Joint EPA/State', 1998) (see Chapter 3 in this volume).

Because of the belief that it needed to take its cooperation with the federal level further to convince businesses of the potential regulatory flexibility (businesses were uncertain about the role of federal oversight), Wisconsin and the EPA finalized a Memorandum of Agreement (MoA) (Wisconsin DNR and US EPA, 1999) in March, 1999, outlining guidelines for both in their execution of the 1998 agreement and the objectives of the pilot agreement program (Meyer, 1999a; Wisconsin DNR and US EPA, 1999).[6] This agreement also marked the first between a state and the EPA to correspond to the April 1998 agreement and outline reinvention of government (US EPA, 1999; Wisconsin DNR, n.d.-d). It has since become a model used by other states and the EPA (Hassett et al., 2004; Meyer, 1999b). The March 1999 MoA also stated its unity with a May 1998 agreement between the MSWG and the EPA, which was an accord to coordinate efforts to evaluate the efficacy of EMSs as a way of achieving environmental protection results (US EPA et al., 1998; Wisconsin DNR and US EPA, 1999). This shows both the crucial role of organizations such as ECOS and the MSWG, and the federal government's willingness to assist in the experimentation with federal and state innovation. These joint efforts are highly representative of the decentralization and New Environmentalism movements in the United States as discussed in Chapter 3.

Another significant force in Wisconsin came from Klauser, both in his capacity as a public official and later as a major player in the energy sector. Klauser served in the Thompson administration, as secretary of the Department of Administration and continued as an honorary advisor after leaving public office (J. Klauser, pers. comm., 21 March 2005). In 1998, Klauser became Senior Vice President for Wisconsin Energy Corp. A 'strong force in the partnership' (J. Smoller, pers. comm., 3 March 2005), Klauser even attended the MoU signing event in Munich with Thompson (J. Klauser, pers. comm., 21 March 2005).

> The interest of business in Wisconsin was a very important factor . . . [F]or instance, Mr. Klauser, a very important man in Wisconsin for the government in the past and now for energy companies . . . stood behind the project and said, yes, we go to Bavaria; we want to learn from Bavaria . . . I think it was not a problem for him to organize also the financial background for such delegations. It is the interest of business which made such delegation events possible. (M. Weigand, pers. comm., 6 April 2005) (also see below, 'Funding and Other Support')

Klauser's interest stemmed both from his concurrence with the policy and from his and Wisconsin's connections to Germany. As senior cabinet secretary, Klauser and his colleagues were looking at various innovative ways government could operate, particularly in education, finance and the regulatory area, while Smoller at the DNR was trying to 'modernize' the regulatory approach in the environmental department (J. Klauser, pers. comm., 21 March 2005). Klauser linked these efforts to the larger reinventing government movement in the United States. So, their reform ideas were not happening in a vacuum. In the mid-1990s, the last state budget Klauser put together included the program for cooperative agreements with businesses (J. Klauser, pers. comm., 21 March 2005). Klauser also had significant experience with Germany on policy transfer as he was an active participant in the sister-state partnership between Wisconsin and Hesse, which began in 1976 (see below). He received awards from Germany for his efforts in the relations between the two countries (WEC, n.d.).

Natural connection
The drive to the collaboration in Wisconsin was made easier due to the natural inclination that Wisconsin has for Germany. Wisconsin shares a similar cultural heritage with Germany, which provides a sense of connection. According to the US Census, 47 percent of Wisconsin residents claimed German ancestry. For perspective, the next highest percentage was 16.3 declaring 'other' (US Census Bureau, 2002). This fact was pointed out by different partnership affiliates. Klauser emphasized this connection at the onset of the interview. '[T]o put this in perspective:

Wisconsin is ethnically by percentage of population the most German state in the United States. So having relations with Germany is not unusual' (pers. comm., 21 March 2005). Smoller, likewise, said that there is 'clearly a comfortableness between Wisconsin and Germany, in general, and Bavaria and Wisconsin, in particular' (pers. comm., 3 March 2005).

That Wisconsin had other ties to Germany enhanced the familiarity that helped make the partnership possible. Klauser stressed how the arrangement was not an isolated exchange and how he saw it as one component of the state's overall relations with Germany (pers. comm., 21 March 2005). For starters, Bavaria, in the American mind, is the prototypical German state because it was part of the United States occupied area after World War II. Moreover, Wisconsin has had an ongoing sister-state relationship with Hesse that is now 30 years old, to which Klauser significantly contributed. Beyond that, Wisconsin had studied Bavaria's educational system. It had also worked with Berlin's business centers to see how they provide information to the workforce. Finally, since 1984 Wisconsin has had a trade office in Frankfurt, Hesse, which has helped to facilitate relations (J. Klauser, pers. comm., 21 March 2005).

Secondary support from non-governmental institutions
Other useful support, although not crucial to the partnership's formation, came from a couple of Bavarian-based non-governmental entities: the Quandt Foundation and BMW. It is not a coincidence that the MoU signing took place at a Quandt Foundation event. Quandt, the foundation behind BMW, is very active in transatlantic cooperation and likes to cooperate with governments (M. Weigand, pers. comm., 6 April 2005). Quandt's cooperation with the Bavarian government is somewhat exceptional; the special ties have to do with the foundation's large coffers and huge marketing system, which is linked to its connection to BMW, the firm that Bavaria considers one of its most 'impressive'. Hence, there is mutual support between Quandt, BMW and the state government (M. Weigand, pers. comm., 6 April 2005).

But more importantly for this case, Bavaria was working with Quandt because one of its divisions was deliberating international conditions and environmental law. BMW had become one of the most important (international) businesses in Germany working with EMAS and is probably Bavaria's top example for best practices in management systems and EMSs. Due to Weigand's good contacts at Quandt, the Foundation funded the conference, bringing the two parties together for the Memorandum signing event. While Quandt was not critical to the partnership's formation, it did contribute to its momentum and was a help (M. Weigand, pers. comm., 6 April 2005). Quandt played even more of a supportive role in the first couple of years of the partnership's implementation phase.

Unique connection through similar policy reform

Even though the historical, cultural and personal ties, and the other support, added to the greater momentum of the partnership's formation, one of the biggest conditions necessary was also the most obvious: the unique similarity of their policy reforms – that the two states were a natural fit in what they were seeking. These two subnational governments were leading the efforts in their respective countries and there were hardly any other partners to be had, if any at all. The key factor was that the two states were interested in new approaches to developing environmental law, emphasizing EMSs and compliance.

Scope and potential of agreement

The degree to which the players found that their approach was important and influential regarding its impact on future policy both domestically and beyond indicates that the scope and potential of the agreement was another factor for the partnership's successful formation. This perception is ubiquitous in remarks by state officials and other affiliates with the partnership from early on and over the years. Leaders have said that the partnership serves as a good example for transatlantic relations (E. Müller, 2005; Meyer, 1999a); that it is historical and will be influential on subnational, national and supranational levels (Thompson, 1998a, 1998b); that it will 'inform and encourage' new leaders in government, non-governmental organizations (NGOs) and in business (Meyer, 1999a); and that it will serve as an example for sustainable development (Hassett, 2004). Both Gov. Thompson and Sec. Meyer discussed the agreement in terms of leading the world in creating the next generation in environmental policy for the next century (Meyer, 1999a; Thompson, 1998a).

Timing

Timing was also a significant factor for the partnership's formation. The idea to cooperate began with a chance encounter with Weigand at a US–European EMSs round table event in California (J. Smoller, pers. Comm., 3 March 2005; Smoller, 2006). But there was another type of timing that was also relevant: the timing of the issue. Meyer said the agreement was well timed because 'the worlds of regulation are changing simultaneously. States can seize the moment or fall behind in promoting commerce and environmental quality together' (Wisconsin DNR, 'Wisc.'). Thompson (1998b) also emphasized the influence of timing:

Timing is everything! Successful innovation happens with good timing. An appreciation for timing and its consequence applies to all sectors and society, all of which are changing . . . The timing of these changes, along with government reinventing, presents an opportunity for innovation because the 'tipping point' of change is occurring simultaneously in business and government.

IMPLEMENTATION AND GENERAL RESULTS

Bavaria and Wisconsin did not waste any time in beginning the implementation of their agreement and remained strikingly active through 2008. It is beyond the scope of this study to cover every incident and lesson learned by the partners, which were numerous. The highlights, however, include having created two implementation plans (1999 and 2004), carried out numerous transatlantic exchanges and delegations, attended conferences and moved forward on their respective reform efforts.

The first implementation plan addressed reform, governance and leadership. It called for the convening of leading state, federal and European Commission officials to address the incorporation of environmental regulatory reform into existing and new laws and to create an information exchange for businesses to address how these matters and new approaches affect them. The plan also targeted specific industries and companies to learn about and/or collaborate on EMSs and regulatory reform. Furthermore, it included: developing communications with the municipal level to promote sustainable and livable communities and local responsibility; establishing activities in academia to exchange information and research between universities on environmental problem-solving between the EU and the United States; and learning about Bavarian policies on river restoration (Meyer, 1999a; Wisconsin DNR, 2008a; Wisconsin DNR, n.d.-e).

In 2004, after assessing the first phase, the partners established a phase two implementation plan and new partnership commitment (Wisconsin DNR, 2004). The partners planned to complete a report revealing the policy innovation achievements that resulted from their reform policies. They also listed specific areas and industries to exchange best practices including small and medium-sized businesses, the manufacturing sector and land development. Additionally, the document stated the objective of exchanging information on all aspects of the co-location of energy, road, rail, water, communications and recreation functions. The partners also put forth plans to create a network of cross-sectoral 'environmental performance managers', improve cooperation with NGOs and support universities on the new policies (Wisconsin DNR, 2004).

To these ends, the partners had numerous transatlantic exchanges. The exchanges ranged from the traveling of a couple of officials, to entire delegations. Generally, there was some kind of exchange every year. On the small scale in the first year alone, Weigand went to Wisconsin to brief state officials on innovative policies (J. Smoller, pers. comm., 3 March 2005; Wisconsin DNR, 2005b). BMW officials also briefed DNR leaders on environmental performance systems and business needs (Wisconsin DNR, 2005b). Furthermore, the partners made a joint presentation on regulatory substitution at an MSWG workshop (Wisconsin DNR, 2005b; Wisconsin DNR, n.d.-c). The two parties also met with EPA enforcement officials to discuss regulatory substitution (Wisconsin DNR, n.d.-c). In addition to these types of exchanges, the partners attended three Quandt Foundation conferences, which were organized over the course of the first three years (J. Smoller, pers. comm., 3 March 2005).

The major delegations consisted of Wisconsinites traveling to Bavaria. These started immediately in 1999 and the last major one was in 2004. Each delegation grew in size, reaching 31 members. They also increased in delegate diversity, consisting of state, municipal, utility, regulator, university, environmental group and media representatives.

The goal of the first trip was for Wisconsin to see how Bavaria's policies consistently resulted in a higher level of environmental protection than was legally required (Hassett et al., 2004; Smoller, n.d.). Other activities included visiting BMW to learn about its use of EMSs, and touring Bayernwerk's coal combustion and nuclear facilities (Wisconsin DNR, n.d.-c). For the second delegation in 2002, most of the time was dedicated to visiting power plants and utilities since the state was up against impending decisions on energy generation (Smoller, n.d.). The facilities showcased cleaner and more efficient technology (Kassulke, 2002), waste resourcefulness (Sereno, 2002), community efforts or 'good neighbor' policies, which included considerations such as noise and aesthetics (Kassulke, 2002; Smoller, n.d.), public outreach efforts (Kassulke, 2002) and the cooperative approach. The delegates also learned about insurance and banking related to climate change; renewable energy including wind energy and hydrogen and fuel cells; and how energy is used in a typical household (Kassulke, 2003). The delegation in 2004 traveled to Bavaria after the Green Tier was enacted into law ('Kedzie', 2004) to find ideas for policy options under the new law (UW, n.d.; Williamson, 2004). While legislators were interested in the legal policy components, the other delegates also had their own industry-specific goals during the trip.

These efforts helped produce all types of lessons, ideas and policy (and technical) advancements as well as contacts and alliances in both states among all sectors, levels of government and on an individual level

(Wisconsin DNR, n.d.-c). Many of the delegates, for example, returned to Wisconsin with different ideas and applied them in the state. A particular impact was made on the printing, building and transmission industries. The printing industry 'went green' as a direct result of the visit. There is now a printing institute in Waukesha and it is going to try to brand the industry as 'green'. The building industry also 'went sustainable'; they became convinced of the Green Tier concept. The energy transmission industry got ideas about the co-siting of energy, transportation and communication services, a concept that has been applied to an energy distribution decision made by the Public Service (utility) Commission, which also was in the delegation (J. Smoller, pers. comm., 31 December 2008).

While the delegates were compelled by the public–private collaborative arrangements that were based on incentives versus prescription and litigation, and the industry public outreach on energy issues (Kassulke, 2002; Sereno, 2002; Still, 2002), an equally valuable lesson was the consensus among the delegates about these. This common ground was, consequently, built upon and helped to push the reform along. This harmony demonstrated that the inclusion of a large and diverse delegation was a shrewd foresight as many of the individuals who made the enactment of the Green Tier law possible also participated in the delegations (Hassett, 2004).

Each year of the partnership saw advancements (sometimes setbacks) in Wisconsin's regulatory reform, ranging from the signing of the regulatory agreement with the EPA to the enactment of the Green Tier law in 2004 (Hassett et al., 2004; Wisconsin DNR, 2005b). In addition to providing a specific policy model, the agreement also functioned as a political tool for officials in Wisconsin to push their reform agenda through (Hassett, 2004; Hassett et al., 2004). Using lessons from abroad is a tactic for advocates of a policy 'to gain advantage in the struggle to get . . . ideas accepted' (Dolowitz and Marsh, 1996, p. 346). The proponents of the reform policies used the lessons to convey that the state did not want to miss out on the regulatory ways of the future, but also to ease fears about being the very first in such a reform policy (Hassett et al., 2004).

The Green Tier program was established as a two-tiered system beyond the normal regulatory system, in which a company that demonstrates superior environmental performance would receive regulatory incentives and breaks. While both tiers require companies to achieve above minimum compliance, Tier I is entry level and Tier II a more superior level (Wisconsin DNR, 2008b). A company has to 'earn' its way into Tier II. This means that Tier I remains comparatively inflexible, severe and costly in its transaction and administrative costs, while Tier II is more flexible on how environmental standards may be reached (Meyer, 1999b). The company itself decides how it will achieve superior environmental performance, but the results must be measurable. EMSs are required to assure predictable performance. Incentives range from the use of the Green Tier logo to fewer inspections. Overall, the DNR states that the system saves time, lowers costs, promotes innovation, limits liability and adjusts to market demands (Wisconsin DNR, 2008b).

The Green Tier system (which utilizes what the partners dubbed 'ISO Plus', as discussed below), helps the state overcome its inability to differentiate between companies that reach superior levels of environmental compliance and those that barely reach the minimum standards, which is an ineffective use of taxpayer money since it has to use the same amount of resources in overseeing both of types of companies (Wisconsin DNR, 2008b). It also adds a 'competitive edge' to the state (Wisconsin Office of the Governor, 2004). On the basic level, the state essentially offsets (indirectly) the costs for a company to become more efficient economically and environmentally (Wisconsin DNR, 2008b). Moreover, in the global economy, it tells both businesses thinking of expanding in Wisconsin and those already there that the state is serious about its economy and environment (Wisconsin Office of the Governor, 2004). The long-term contracts communicate regulatory confidence and thus provide greater certainty for investors (Hassett et al., 2004). In 2006, Green Tier was chosen as one of 18 finalists for Harvard University and the Ash Institute's Innovations in American Government Award.

As for Bavaria, based on its experiences with Wisconsin's Green Tier legislation and its contacts with the EPA, the German state gained some 'important insights' which it planned to use for reforming environmental laws both subnationally and federally (Wisconsin DNR, n.d.-c). Over the years, it assessed and renewed its pact twice, in 2000 and 2005, furthering its goals of reducing the state's CO_2 emissions by increasing the number of companies with EMSs. Also, because of its success, it began suggesting that a national pact be developed along the same lines, making it an 'Environmental Pact of Germany' (E. Müller, 2005).

Bavaria also saw significant further developments of the idea of EMSs and compliance by the MSWG, in which Wisconsin played a major role (Wisconsin DNR, n.d.-c). One of Bavaria's first actions after the MoU signing was that it got involved with the MSWG (M. Weigand, pers. comm., 6 April 2005, 5 August 2008). The German state was trying to address what it could see as a future policy conflict caused by the non-related approaches regarding EMS and compliance of the different governing bodies. As Weigand (pers. comm., 6 April 2005) explained:

[The MSWG] couldn't talk about EMAS . . . but they could only talk about ISO 14001, the international standard, and this was a very, very important question for us if we work in Germany and in Bavaria and in the EU on the EMAS basis [because] we cannot only work within Europe, we have to work on an international basis and the international basis is influenced by ISO 14001. And the MSWG is working on the basis of ISO 14001 and tries to influence [the] federal EPA with ideas of regulatory innovation and so our approach must be international and cannot only be European related.

That said, both states (Wisconsin through the MSWG initially) were outright trying to influence the ISO standards, which was part of the reason for collaboration (M. Weigand, pers. comm., 6 April 2005). The partners expressed their goal in their 2004 assessment report that the ISO standard should be reformed into an ISO 14001 'Plus' based on the EU's EMAS II, which was a combination of EMAS and the ISO's EMS standard (Wisconsin DNR, n.d.-c).

Early on, Bavaria learned that EMAS was better than ISO 14001. The difference between EMAS and ISO 14000 is the following: ISO 14000 is only a management system, which means it advises a company on how to best organize itself, and its sites, to have the best management system for environmental issues. There is no guarantee for compliance. In contrast, EMAS, which also contains a management system (EMAS II adopted the ISO 14001 standard for management systems in 2001), also promises compliance. This assurance means that the administration or government can rely on the compliance of this company, knowing that it has been checked by licensed experts, by verifiers, who in turn are monitored and supervised by the administration or government, and that it would not have to force it to follow any command-and-control legislation. In sum, ISO is only an agreement, a standard among business people, while EMAS is a regulation, which enforces (M. Weigand, pers. comm., 5 August 2008).

To bridge the differences between the international and EU systems, the Bavarian ministry came up with the 'ISO Plus' concept, which as stated above is really EMAS II; it contains the ISO standard for the management systems but also contains what became known as the three added values of EMAS: (1) the compliance approach; (2) continuous improvement; and (3) reporting to the public. ISO Plus was for companies based in Bavaria that needed the ISO standards for their international contacts, yet that wanted the same benefits as provided to those who use EMAS under the Environmental Pact (that is, the same substitution and privileges in enforcement). It was also a way of trying to globalize EMAS (M. Weigand, pers. comm., 5 August 2008). For the Bavarians this is essential since German efforts to try to convince the ISO to incorporate EMAS or the three added values into its standards have been so far unsuccessful.

That is not to say that ISO officials have not or are not discussing the idea of an enforcement standard; they are just negating it at the moment (M. Weigand, pers. comm., 5 August 2008).

Bavaria also made significant progress in spreading its ideas and policies to other governing bodies, for example to the US federal government (Wisconsin DNR, n.d.-b). Bavaria was also a part of MSWG's international outreach efforts, which together with the European Environmental Agency and the United Nations Environment Programme (UNEP) created the UN Best Practices Network (EEA, n.d.; Wisconsin DNR, n.d.-c). It also further pursued partnerships over the years in climate protection, for example, in Austria, Quebec, Shandong and West Cape (E. Müller, 2005). By the mid-2000s, the pact had diffused to a great extent including to ten other *Länder*, not to mention Wisconsin (and as a model for other states), setting it well on its way to becoming an 'export hit' (Bavarian MEPH, 2004; E. Müller, 2005; Wisconsin DNR, n.d.-d). As Weigand stated:

> This idea of deregulation and substitution of supporting industry with new self-responsible instruments was born in Germany, in Bavaria, and so we try to go on with these ideas worldwide and we try to export these ideas and we think since 1995 as we began to work with these ideas we got a lot of support, a lot of positive comments and there is a development worldwide in this direction. (pers. comm., 5 August 2008)

Diffusion of the policy also helps promote trade with those states and countries that implement such management systems and compliance standards. In addition, the pact's 'Climate Dialogue' aspect, which is a dialog with industry to establish pilot projects and incentives that will result in emissions reductions, had produced a CO_2 monitoring system for Europe (Schnappauf, 2003).

Difficult Transitions – Implementation and Results 2007–2011

In 2007, the partnership's activities and advancements (and some MSWG activities) began slowing down. While speculations for this included the 2008 presidential elections, funding issues, Quandt's availability, EPA personnel changes, setbacks with the Green Tier and political changes in Bavaria, there were significant political changes in Wisconsin that were the real clincher. Firstly, Secretary Hassett resigned and was replaced by Matt Frank. Secondly, Smoller received new duties at the DNR (M. Weigand, pers. comm., 5 August 2008). His previous position was eliminated. Thirdly, in July 2008, because of his change in position at the DNR, Smoller resigned as President and had nothing more to do with the MSWG. While Frank did end up strongly supporting Green

Tier, it became clear that there was no more potential for the partnership (J. Smoller, pers. comm., 31 December 2008; M. Weigand, pers. comm., 5 August 2008).

But Bavaria planned to carry on with its work on regulatory innovation. While Bavaria did have an influence on Wisconsin's Green Tier policy, Weigand said there is still much work to do on regulatory innovation both in Europe and the United States. There have been many interesting developments in this field, yet there are still many difficulties to contend with (M. Weigand, pers. comm., 5 August 2008).

For starters, Bavaria was working on an 'environmental code'; it was comprehensively collecting all of the environmental regulations in Germany into an environmental law book to examine if it would be possible to simplify and streamline the country's environmental provisions.[7] Supranationally, EMAS III was in process. The draft was completed by the European Commission (on 16 July 2008) and Bavaria planned to work with it in the ensuing months to see what its parliament and the Bundesrat would do with the draft with the hopes that the European Commission would also be ready to make some changes on it (M. Weigand, pers. comm., 5 August 2008). As stated earlier, the Bavarians were hoping that EMAS III could become the globalized standard regarding EMSs. And as also mentioned, Germany has tried to get the ISO to adopt the compliance approach of EMAS. Even though that has not been successful, Weigand believes that it is just a matter of a few years until the EMAS and ISO standards are essentially the same, and that both systems will follow the compliance approach 'because the future of environmental legislation will be a voluntary basis of compliance and not command and control'. It helps that some of Germany's experts on EMAS at the federal level are also a part of ISO associations, which means that the transmission of ideas is guaranteed (M. Weigand, pers. comm., 5 August 2008).

As for Wisconsin, Smoller planned to work on his own time and outside of the DNR through WisPolitics and WisBusiness.com to try to keep it going (J. Smoller, pers. comm., 31 December 2008). But as of 2011, with new leadership in DNR, an interest in supply chain management, and because of the interest of the American Council on Germany, the partnership was underway to being reignited again (J. Smoller, pers. comm., 29 June 2011). How the partnership has since played and continues into the future remains to be seen.

Changes in Administration/Government and 'Special Driving Persons'

While the aforementioned delineation portrays the types of efforts necessary for the agreement's implementation, it does not cover them all.

One issue that had to be reckoned with over the years was the changes of administration and government. In fact, this was really only an issue in Wisconsin as both Minister-President Stoiber and Schnappauf were in office until 2007. In Wisconsin, from the time of negotiations on the agreement until the present day, there have been four governors of different political parties and five different environmental secretaries.

From the time of the partnership signing until the first change in administration, only a little over two years had passed, which was not much time to guarantee the agreement would carry over. It is crucial to have what Weigand referred to as 'special driving persons' – in this case Smoller – who are behind the scenes making the partnership work (pers. comm., 6 April 2005). Smoller made the case to each new secretary linking the importance of the partnership with the Green Tier reform. That is how Weigand explained the partnership's survival through such changes. This was the case until Sec. Frank came into office. While it is unknown what Frank's reasons were, it is also clear that Smoller no longer had his selling point that he gave to new DNR secretaries of needing to learn from Bavaria to help get its Green Tier law completed.

This is to say that while a policy-entrepreneurial bureaucrat has to have the ability to drive the partnership, it is nonetheless of primary importance that the top leadership at least agrees to the arrangement. Smoller makes it clear that the secretaries also deserve credit since they allowed the partnership's continuation (pers. comm., 3 March 2005). But regarding the development of additional contacts, such as important departmental colleagues, business contacts and contacts in the law department, Smoller was always the key (M. Weigand, pers. comm., 6 April 2005).

Funding and Other Support

The financial component of the partnership was less of an issue during its creation because this stage was limited to a couple of players. After the signing, however, this type of support needed to be addressed. While there was no mention of funding in the MoU, it was referenced in a statement: 'Funding is being sought but costs generally are with the parties' (Wisconsin DNR, n.d.-e). There was also mention of and hopes for support from the Quandt Foundation and the Council of State Governments, in that they would sponsor conferences at which the partners could provide one another with updates (Thompson, 1998b; Wisconsin DNR, n.d.-e). Ultimately the Quandt Foundation did host several events including the MoU signing ceremony, which 'added to the momentum' and provided some initial structure at the beginning of the implementation process helping the two parties 'connect' (J. Smoller, pers. comm., 3 March 2005), but it did not provide any kind of substantial funding.

Outside of such minor assistance, there was a lack of institutional funding in Wisconsin. Wisconsin's delegations to Bavaria were generally not state funded, even though their reasons for traveling there were in reference to state policy. The only governmental representative who the state paid for was Smoller, and that was not in full. As Smoller explained:

> The state government funded me, but I paid part of my cost on some of the trips just because it's under scrutiny every time you leave the state. Some legislator or a member of the press might think it's a junket and think that you were out there having a good time when you're really working some long and exhausting days. (pers. comm., 3 March 2005)

Businesses paid for their representatives, while businesses, one of the utility foundations, one of the utilities and a trade association paid for the NGO representatives (J. Smoller, pers. comm., 3 March 2005). The German Marshall Fund of the United States provided some funding for delegates (Still, 2002; Sereno, 2002). Aside from that, everybody else paid out of their own pockets (J. Smoller, pers. comm., 3 March 2005). On a more conceptual level, this is to say that these aforementioned entities and willing agents made the implementation of the partnership possible.

The reason for the funding difficulties is that outside of the opinion of policy entrepreneurs, the perception reigns that there is nothing to gain beyond state borders (J. Smoller, pers. comm., March 3, 2005). But, to push through innovative ideas, this is exactly what the state needs to do, coordinate and cooperate. At the 1999 US–German State Leadership Conference in Washington, DC, at which the two states met, Sec. Meyer (1999a) explained why it is difficult for innovative ideas to triumph over the status quo:

> We can't do it alone. As one might imagine, the path of regulatory innovation for states can be difficult [for] staff resources to test these ideas, implement what works and learn from what does not. The reason is that the status quo controls the fiscal resources and the owners of the status quo control the communications infrastructure. Finding the resources needed to form innovation partnerships – especially partnerships across the Atlantic – is a daunting challenge, indeed. That is why the support of the Quandt Foundation and the German Marshall Fund is so critical to creating the structure and process of sharing what we do, so that we can learn and develop together – as new leaders with new ideas.

Bavaria had some institutionalized funding, albeit not limitless. The full Bavarian cabinet supported the partnership in 1999 (Wisconsin DNR, n.d.-e), which ensured its institutionalization in the Bavarian government and access to the budget allotted to international affairs (M. Weigand, pers. comm., 5 August 2008). That said, the state had fewer expenses since it was not the one sending the major delegations.

Conditions for Successful Partnership Implementation

The Wisconsin–Bavaria partnership is a success story, not least because of its duration. The partnership largely achieved its original objectives and accomplished the goals that were subsequently added onto the agenda. As planned, Wisconsin incorporated ideas of Bavaria's Environmental Pact agreements into its Green Tier program, and thus Bavaria transferred components of its policy based on the ISO Plus concept. Furthermore, this convergence 'brought about an amendment of the European EMAS Regulation (EMAS II) to include parts of the management descriptions contained in ISO 14001' (Wisconsin DNR, n.d.-c). In addition to the original objectives, Wisconsin learned from Bavaria regarding some of its pressing issues that emerged during the implementation process, such as energy generation. The highlights of these activities and achievements were discussed above. The better and more revealing angle to sum up the achievements is that one is hard-pressed to point to anything significant that the partners did not accomplish, especially considering the institutional and financial limitations. And considering these confines, there are those who imagine what the partnership could have been if it had been considered as core DNR work.

Key factors behind accomplishment of goals

There are several reasons behind the agreement's successful implementation. One of the most important factors was the will of the primary players. While the support of respective secretaries and ministers was crucial, the role of Smoller and Weigand also cannot be underrated; this was due to their willingness, abilities, personal rapport and job positions. The first two points were demonstrated above. Also significant was that there was a good working rapport between them, even a kind of friendship that developed over the years. Furthermore, both were non-politically appointed bureaucrats, which allowed them to remain in place through changes in administrations and governments.

Other critical factors were the types of action taken, such as the drafting of a detailed implementation plan which, designed to include different societal sectors and levels of government, provided concrete goals and guidance. Also important was the setting up and participating in numerous exchanges, large and small, which contributed to the inspiring of the delegates, the garnering of cross-sectoral support, the building up of trust and rapport among the partners and a sense of validation of the partnership. Such exchanges also contributed to the transferring of ideas and learning (goal fulfillment). In accordance with the value of these activities, yet no less crucial in its import, was the swiftness with which the first major dealings took place (the first year of the partnership alone consisted of Bavaria joining the MSWG, the creation of the implementation plan, a Quandt conference and several transatlantic exchanges, including one major delegation). Furthermore, the regularity and continuity in which these activities occurred over the years contributed to keeping the partnership central. Up until the slowdown of activities, there was at least one exchange per year and that was in addition to other types of important partnership and reform advancements. Finally, the perceived potential of the partnership in terms of the two states' respective goals was a key factor. For Wisconsin, the arrangement was intrinsically linked to the completion of its reform policy; and for Bavaria it was connected to the multi-level diffusion goals of its ISO Plus concept.

The non-traditional institutionalization of the partnership in Wisconsin

Additional factors in Wisconsin contributed to the successful implementation of the partnership, which was not formally institutionalized. Even though it was formally created through an MoU, it was not established or funded through the state legislature or a DNR discretionary program. These components are important to ascertain since Wisconsin was more in the active, learning position.

One of the decisive factors was the actors' networking and inclusion of all segments of government and society in the implementation process, which was a successful tactic for garnering extensive and in some instances crucial support (not to mention pooled resources) for both the partnership and the reform policy. That said, Wisconsin was fortunate to have had from the outset some specific backing in its favor including, from the federal level, which was vital to this process. In addition, the partnership gained authority by having been played off of the Green Tier reform (they were played off one another). Moreover, its association with the reform policy helped it to gain legitimacy due to its more traditional institutional legitimacy. Also, the partnership was able to acquire weight through its staying power and successes, which required the special driving person and his ability to make the case (which was compelling) to the powers that be (and their acceptance) to guarantee its survival over the years. Finally, the consequential informal institutionalization of the partnership contributed to its momentum. Each of these points will be looked at more closely.

One of the most decisive tactics was the agents' purposeful networking and inclusion of all segments of government and society in the implementation process of the partnership to gain widespread support for both the partnership and the reform policy. Gov. Thompson explained the importance of such an approach: 'Organizational and social culture must support innovation and see change as a friend. Leaders must credibly and effectively communicate about change. This is difficult in risk-adverse cultures like government. Reaching out opens a dialogue that builds trust and allows individuals to adapt to change and commit to innovation' (Thompson, 1998b).

Within the executive branch alone, the Wisconsin state agencies that were involved in the implementation included the departments of Natural Resources, Commerce, Administration and the Public Service Commission (Wisconsin DNR, n.d.-e). Even more key, however, was the comprehensive inclusion of all societal sectors. Looking at the delegations to Bavaria alone shows this range of representatives. There were government officials, including from the legislative branch, representatives from the Green Tier's advisory committee, the manufacturing and commerce lobby, academia, business, utilities, local government, environmental groups and the media. This inclusion won over these various groups both on the partnership and the reforms, not only because they were more directly included in the policy process, but also because they were exposed to seeing the issues from other perspectives and saw such cross-sectoral cooperation transpiring successfully in Germany. Moreover, upon their return, delegates who were members of the media, and others, wrote positive articles about the trip and on what was learned, which also contributed to the education of the public. Thus, it became not only a cooperative effort that other sectors supported, but also one that had pooled resources from them. This proved to be a highly successful approach.

A similar course was taken with the Green Tier program; naturally, the partnership itself was part of the agents' outreach efforts for this policy. In their hard work to bring about reform, to get the regulatory policy signed into law, which took years, public officials in Wisconsin continually promoted its concept in different settings, even beyond state borders (Wisconsin DNR, 2005b). And, as with the partnership with Bavaria, support and recognition of the concept grew throughout the years from different societal sectors, including from the federal level, and not least from Bavaria (Wisconsin DNR, 2005b).

A couple of these supportive non-governmental entities also served to provide some early structure that contributed to some of the initial momentum. The partners, for instance, had the whole apparatus of the MSWG on their side, which provided a kind of surrogate institutional backing before the partnership stabilized. Another example, albeit less critical, was the usefulness of the Quandt Foundation's conferences.

Wisconsin was also fortunate to have had vital support from the outset. The role of Klauser was critical, especially when he was later serving as a high-ranking energy representative as he enabled some delegation funding, which helped to gain backing not only from the business community but also from NGOs. Federal support was crucial for the formal institutionalization of Wisconsin's reform law, and thus indirectly for the partnership. Without the agreements with the EPA, Wisconsin could not have passed its Green Tier law, which would have adversely affected the partnership since it was based on this regulatory reform.

In addition to (and also further contributing to) the garnering of support over the years, both the Green Tier concept and the partnership gained further authority by having been played off of each other – one was used to justify the other; one may not have succeeded without the justification of the other. When the delegates traveled to Bavaria, they came back supporting regulatory reform. Likewise, the reform was used as a reason to continue the partnership. For instance, as explained above, each time a change of administration occurred, Smoller convinced each new secretary of the importance of continuing the partnership by connecting it to the ultimate success of the Green Tier reform (since each new secretary wished to complete the Act) and thus guarantee its future.

Moreover, the fact that the Green Tier program was also on the path toward formal institutionalization added more of a feel of legitimization to the partnership. The reform was slowly making its way through the state legislature. According to state officials, this type of institutionalization was necessary, as they believed that innovation would only be possible within the safety of law (Smoller, 2006). Basing his argumentation on some of the problems that the EPA had with its Project X-L program and the perception of its regulatory legitimacy, Smoller (2006) said: 'Without that safe place in law, we believed there were too many reasons why businesses, government employees and citizens would not take the risk to be an environmental innovator.' Moreover, Wisconsin's reform had the seal of approval from the federal government, a legitimizing force in itself. And since the partnership was associated with this program, such formalities were also helpful to this end.

Another key condition for the successful implementation of the partnership in Wisconsin was that it acquired staying power; the partnership secured institutional footing through its ability to survive and succeed over the years. Staying power required a bureaucratic driver, in this case Smoller. Also important was that Smoller had a compelling case to present: that is, the importance and timing of the policy that was connected to the partnership. And the acceptance by the successive secretaries as a condition for its continuance was necessary.

Many of these components contributed to what can be considered the informal institutionalization of the partnership, based on the definition of Peters (in other words, a network of interacting organizations). The interactions developed something of a predictable pattern, especially in reference to exchanges. The partnership gained stability over time as it proved its survivability over the years. It was able to affect the behavior of its members and was deemed important; there were shared values, which is why the partnership began in the first place. This type of institutionalization contributed to the status and momentum of the partnership and its successful implementation. Had it been formally institutionalized, however, it could have had more longevity, as others may have been able to step forward and carry it on (J. Smoller pers. comm., 31 December 2008) after Smoller changed positions.

ANALYSIS

The partnership between Wisconsin and Bavaria showed deep multi-level coercive elements in its structural influences. This included ISO's EMS and the EU's EMAS standards as well as the epistemic community MSWG; Wisconsin wanted to learn from Bavaria (ideational competition) but it also wanted to be a frontrunner with its innovative Green Tier policy (regulatory and political competition), which employed a policy featuring EMSs plus compliance. Bavaria was an even bigger competitor. Already a frontrunner, Bavaria tried to policy push both the EU and the ISO as well as to internationally diffuse its reform policy, the Environmental Pact, which utilizes the EU's EMAS. Wisconsin was involved in this competition, also a frontrunner, but more so through the MSWG (and with regard to influencing the ISO, through MSWG, this was only early on). These aims were also prompted by global trade (economic competition) as both states were driven to pursue some type of EMS approach in order to help their businesses be as competitive as possible because of tough global competition (together with the need for worldwide sustainable development). Finally, Bavaria's policies were linked to its ecological modernization aims, as it also planned to diffuse its technologies along with its environmental policies. Bavaria (and to a much smaller degree Wisconsin) was aiming to create a lead market for itself.

In addition to this international influence, these subnational governments were also acting because they found a lack of adequate federal-level polices; this criticism seemed to be stronger in the United States. And for

Bavaria, there was a discrepancy between EU and ISO standards as well as the EU's mistrust of its pact. But in Wisconsin, the EPA played an enabling role in other ways, having signed agreements with it so that it could enact its innovative reforms. All three were involved in the MSWG, a state-dominated epistemic community.

This partnership provides more of a comprehensive perspective of the role that subnational governments, via such partnerships, have in global governance for sustainable development. It reveals a multi-level dimension from the international to the subnational level, in which Bavaria and Wisconsin were significant actors in a two-way vertical and horizontal diffusion process regarding certain policies within this global governance.

There were smaller reasons why Bavaria and Wisconsin came together, including the similarity of their pioneering reforms themselves. Both states had introduced or were trying to introduce a like-minded innovative regulatory reform based on a state–business type of cooperative governance that utilized EMSs and compliance. This common interest, combined with a sense of its global importance, led representatives of these subnational governments to the same transatlantic event in this subject area. There they gained knowledge about the other's activities. Personal exchanges and a connection between the would-be primary partnership agents subsequently developed, leading finally to the idea to form a partnership in this area.

This pioneering impulse, and consequently the idea to create a transatlantic subnational collaboration, would not have transpired without the leadership of agents and policy entrepreneurs. The states had leaders that were both prominent and active in innovating on the state level and determined in endorsing state autonomy. The key players, without whom the partnership would not have been possible, were Smoller, Weigand, Meyer and Schnappauf. The secondary key players, those not directly involved but nonetheless in some way important to its creation, were Thompson, Klauser and Stoiber.

Another building block, without which there would not have been reform in Wisconsin and, consequently, a transatlantic collaboration, was the support from and connections to certain state-supporting entities and the federal EPA, which laid some foundational groundwork on regulatory reform. This included agreements worked on and signed by the EPA with ECOS, the MSWG and Wisconsin. This clearly needed support was only specific to Wisconsin because of the make-up of the US federal system. Thus, altogether, the key institutions necessary for the partnership were the states of Wisconsin and Bavaria, the US federal government and two state-driven NGOs – the MSWG and ECOS.

These crucial support agents and institutions point to another important feature: the right combination of personal connections and networking that served to help the partnership form and get off the ground. First, there was the connection made between Smoller and Weigand. Second, there was the link between Smoller, Weigand and the MSWG, and Meyer's tie to ECOS (these organizations helped Wisconsin in its reform). Third, there was the collaboration between these organizations and the state of Wisconsin with the US federal government. Fourth, there were Weigand's ties to BMW and Quandt. Fifth, there was Klauser's linkage to the top tier of the Wisconsin government, his association to the reform proposals, his relationship to the business and energy world, and his connections to Germany. Sixth, there were Wisconsin's previous political connections to Germany, through its sister-state agreement with Hesse and others. Finally, there was the natural-historical connection between the two that added a special affinity between them.

Timing was also a significant component leading to the formation and thus success of the partnership. There was good timing in the two states coming together and in the innovation itself. It was a seizing of the moment of changing regulations.

But it was that the two states were a natural fit in the potential that the partnership could provide them regarding their like-minded, frontrunner reforms, on both the small and large scales, that was one of the most significant factors. The scope of objectives of the partnership can be organized into four categories: (1) the larger, overarching aims; (2) the many smaller, specific goals and mechanisms; (3) the secondary aims; and (4) the numerous objectives that arose throughout the course of the partnership. The overarching and primary goals included to achieve policy learning, transfer, convergence (between the policies of the partners), testing, and diffusion and convergence (beyond partners) of a policy approach that centered on EMSs and compliance. The most direct and initial aim was that Wisconsin learn from Bavaria's policy reform, particularly its Environmental Pact, while Bavaria's goal was to transfer its policy and corresponding innovative technologies that its pact impelled. In reference to motivations, here we see the bounded rationality of the agents. In terms of convergence, anything learned and transferred would lead to a degree of convergence between the two. That said, there was a specific convergence goal, to ensure that both based their policies on a combined EMAS–ISO 14001 approach. Beyond that, the objective was to test these approaches and to influence the upcoming EMAS revisions (Bavaria's aim) and the ISO standards, which would ultimately mean diffusion, as an international standard would diffuse globally.

The partners also laid out numerous smaller and specific goals and mechanisms in both the MoU and in the first implementation plan. The gist of these aims included exchanges between representatives of different sectors regarding the overarching goals. There were also targets to foster the communications between the respective states and the cities within them. Many industries and some individual companies were named specifically, together with concrete objectives. Brownfield redevelopment and river restoration were also targeted as concentration areas.

The partnership contained some secondary objectives. One was to gain political support for reforms in both states; this is also an example of bounded rationality. Cooperation is needed any time a state is trying to push through an innovative reform. For subnational-level governments facing an uphill battle in engaging in global environmental governance, cooperation was seen as a plus. It was also to quell any mistrust of the reform: in Wisconsin's case within the state (and at the federal level), and in Bavaria's case at the EU level. Winning political support also helps with the objective of garnering interest in the policy both domestically and internationally, to help it (both the policy and the resultant innovative technology) diffuse.

There were also objectives that arose over the course of the partnership. One of these many aims, caused by impending decisions on energy generation in Wisconsin, was that Wisconsin would learn from Bavaria on energy matters. Also, after the Green Tier legislation became law, another goal became to find ideas in Bavaria for all sectors that Wisconsin could implement under its new law. Phase two also put forth a new list of partnership goals mostly to exchange best practices in several areas including in several business sectors, the manufacturing sector, and regarding small and medium-sized businesses, and rivers protection.

There are several reasons behind the successful implementation of the partnership. One of the most important variables was the will of the primary players. While the support of both respective secretaries and ministers was crucial to the partnership, the role of the key bureaucrats also cannot be underrated; this was due to their willingness, abilities, personal rapport and non-politically appointed job positions. This suggests that the presence of policy entrepreneurs post-MoU signing is an important factor for its implementation. Other critical factors were the types of action taken, such as the drafting of a detailed implementation plan, the setting up and participating in numerous exchanges and delegations, large and small, and both the swiftness with which the first major activities took place as well as the regularity and continuity with which these actions occurred throughout the years. The perceived potential of the partnership in terms of the two states' respective goals was also a crucial factor.

Since the partnership was not formally institutionalized in Wisconsin and since Wisconsin was more in the active, learning position, there were several additional conditions in Wisconsin alone that made a successful implementation possible. First, Wisconsin's agents achieved a successful cross-sectoral outreach, which not only resulted in widespread, aggregate support for the partnership (and the reform) but also served as a source of funding. Second, there was some crucial support and foundational pillars at the outset from which this networking grew, from the EPA, the MSWG and ECOS, which allowed regulatory reform in the state. Third, the agents were able to play the partnership and the reform policy off of each other, gaining more authority. Fourth, the partnership acquired legitimacy from the fact that the Green Tier reform policy was moving through formal institutionalization (in other words, legislative) channels. Fifth, it secured institutional footing through its staying power and successes. Its durability was largely because there was a 'special person', namely Smoller, who was the key player not only in the formation of the partnership but also during the implementation process, and who had the ability to make the case to each successive secretary; seventh, the case was compelling – the reform, and thus the partnership, was seen as important and the timing was right. Eighth, each new secretary, until Frank, supported it. Finally, what became the informal institutionalization of the partnership also contributed to its momentum. These findings support the notion that institutionalization requires more than an MoU. And while it supports the idea that a policy entrepreneur can initiate a partnership but will have difficulty sustaining it without formal institutionalization, it suggests that informal institutionalization may function as compensation.

The partnership between Bavaria and Wisconsin is an example of a successful transnational, subnational environmental partnership. It illustrates what the necessary conditions for successfully forming this type of partnership may be and what the essential requirements for ensuring a positive outcome are. It also provides further knowledge of the process of policy transfer and of the origins of policy diffusion, especially as it emanates from the subnational level regarding who initiated it and why, how learning occurred, how and why the states conspired to prompt diffusion, and what the dynamics involved in these processes were.

This partnership largely fits the characterization of such Type II multi-level governance (MLG) in that it is voluntary, task-specific and based on a common need to work together; it also has a flexible design and is intersecting as opposed to nested. Moreover, the dynamics of the partnership contain many influential jurisdictions, like a 'marble cake'. In accord with the notion of two types of MLG existing side by side, however, this partnership is a window into how these two forms of governance – the first of which is very much based in the traditional legal system and nested institutions – can operate in a parallel fashion. It also shows how they may interact and, consequently, the necessity of this. The success of the Type II partnership was very much linked to its informal institutionalization in Wisconsin, thus in its quasi-incorporation to the Type I system. Its ultimate hindrances however, as alluded to, were because it was not formally institutionalized, or fully brought into the Type I legal system.

NOTES

1. As of 13 October 2003, the ministry became the Bavarian Ministry of the Environment, Public Health and Consumer Protection.
2. Stiober's (1995) tally of administrative regulations, orders and laws was at more than 8000.
3. EMAS was intended to be an additional system, rather than one of substitution. European officials first wanted to implement good command-and-control systems in all member states. Most younger member states did not have good enforcement systems, unlike the United Kingdom, France and Germany, which had been enforcing with command-and-control since the 1960s and 1970s. And even though the European Commission accepted the efforts of states with long-standing enforcement systems to find new instruments for improvement, it was nonetheless careful to keep up traditional systems and not allow substitution too early (M. Weigand, pers. comm., 5 August 2008).
4. In addition to the examples of Bavaria's leadership in Chapter 4 in this volume is Bavaria's 'frontrunner' status in renewable energy use in Germany at approximately 11 percent, which is three times more than the national average. Likewise, its CO_2 emissions per capita are the lowest of all the states at 7 tonnes (Stoiber, 2003).
5. A framework for coordination was formalized in 1986, within which the regional offices and most of the states enter into annual agreements establishing roles, responsibilities and commitments for enforcement and compliance. Standards are set so the EPA can measure whether national enforcement is necessary; but generally, the idea is that the federal level and states cooperate to realize goals (UNEP, n.d.-a).
6. This was a way of proving that the EPA approved of Wisconsin's regulatory efforts (Meyer, 1999b).
7. For potential future partnership efforts, Bavaria would be interested in seeing whether Wisconsin would do something similar in its own state to innovate its environmental laws (M. Weigand, pers. comm., 5 August 2008).

6. California and Bavaria (2000)

THE MEMORANDUM

On 15 September 2000, in Dresden, Dr Robert Stephens, Assistant Secretary for Environmental Management and Sustainability at the California Environmental Protection Agency (Cal/EPA), on behalf Sec. Winston Hickox, and Dr Werner Schnappauf, Bavarian State Minister for State Development and Environmental Affairs, signed an agreement entitled 'Memorandum of Understanding to Create the Bavaria–California Regulatory Innovations Partnership' (Bavaria MSDEA and Cal/EPA, 2000). The agreement renewed the 1995 environmental technology partnership and added an innovative regulatory approach, similar to the one in the 1998 partnership between Bavaria and Wisconsin (M. Weigand, pers. comm., 6 April 2005). Objectives were to learn from one another and achieve some level of convergence among the two states' policies: that is, to promote dialog, create an international learning network and encourage interstate benchmarking regarding 'EMSs [environmental management systems] which incorporate provision[s] for compliance with statutory performance standards' (Bavaria MSDEA and Cal/EPA, 2000).

To make the learning possible, the partners agreed to share information and to have an exchange of experts, primarily through a partnership website. Through this medium, both sides would report their 'experiences, successes, opportunities, risks and challenges of new legal instruments' (Bavaria MSDEA and Cal/EPA, 2000). The two parties also agreed to confer periodically to develop further cooperation and to produce annual progress reports.

One of the reasons mentioned for the union of the states was their unique policy similarities. Both states were developing new methods to protect the environment – working more in collaboration with industry and public interest groups, instead of commanding and controlling them – and focusing more on the overall environmental performance of industry, which entailed allowing for more flexible regulations, instead of prescribing the 'end-of-pipe' technologies. Moreover, both parties placed a high priority on their efforts to create such innovative solutions to environmental protection and had been experimenting in this area. They saw it as important to demonstrate the 'effectiveness and utility' of EMSs that incorporate a compliance component with legal standards. Finally, regarding the renewal of the previous partnership (1995), the two states concurred that their new collaboration on regulatory innovation would be an important tool in the promotion of environmental technologies (Bavaria MSDEA and Cal/EPA, 2000).

The Memorandum of Understanding (MoU) appears clear on its objectives of developing (including learning more about) and advancing regulatory innovations, namely, EMSs together with legal standards and a compliance component. The background behind the promotion of this approach is the search for more effective ways to both improve environmental protection and promote economic growth. But the fact that these two leading states had wished to converge on their innovative policies implies that there are some larger objectives involved. The weight of their consensus on an innovative policy suggests it would be intended to serve as a model for others. This point was only hinted at in the MoU through the declaration of importance given to and the need for 'demonstrating' the 'effectiveness and utility' of environmental management systems together with legal standards and a compliance component (Bavaria MSDEA and Cal/EPA, 2000). Other public statements further divulge this greater objective.

THE DRIVING FORCES

Further Development of the Global Events and International Pressures that Influenced both California and Bavaria

Both California and Bavaria, as explained in Chapters 4 and 5 in this volume, started feeling the pressure in the early 1990s (end of the Cold War, globalization, international environmental agenda, increased multi-level competition) to reform their environmental protection policies. The one issue that really grew in importance to both states since the 1995 partnership was environmental management systems. Both California and Bavaria were determined not only to be among the first that acted on these environmental management system standards, but also to assure that they were appropriate and acceptable. Bavaria's additional objective was to examine and reconcile the discrepancies of the European Union (EU) and International Organization for Standardization (ISO) standards. The two states sought to influence the international standards. To achieve this, innovative ideas were being pursued. The key player on California's side, Stephens, said that the reason many subnational-level governments are seeing a different role for themselves in today's world is because many of the innovations in areas such as economic or environmental politics are happening at the regional or local levels, not at the national level. Because of this, they are reaching out to other regional and local governments to form these kinds of partnerships so they can help one another. 'It's as simple as that' (R. Stephens, pers. comm., 14 February 2006). Within their modern-day position regarding global governance for sustainable development, subnational governments are also in many ways compelled to work with one another.

California's Reform Efforts and Search for Innovative Policies

California's search for innovative environmental policies to deal with the pressures of globalization, which were causing economic difficulties in the state, stems back to the early 1990s (see Chapter 4 in this volume). The then Cal/EPA secretary, Strock, decided to pursue sustainable development ideas, one of which resulted in the 1995 partnership with Bavaria. These endeavors toward sustainable development, however, were not enough. According to Stephens, California's system of managing the environment – whether part of the regulatory system, the various policy structures or the legal structures – needed to be reformed (R. Stephens, pers. comm., 14 February 2006). The system had many 'problems', it was 'disjointed' in many ways, 'it was not outcome focused' and it was 'very inefficient' (R. Stephens, pers. comm., 14 February 2006). The state's objective had become to retool the government's environmental policy system and the legal system that underpinned it, to create a more 'rational', 'integrated' system, and EMSs were a part of the reconstruction (R. Stephens, pers. comm., 14 February 2006).

Meanwhile, the ISO standards were 'slow to take off' in the United States (NRCA, n.d., p. 21). This was because of 'mixed regulatory signals' from the EPA and states, in addition to minimal outreach efforts by the specific US bodies that took part in the development of the ISO standards (NRCA, n.d., p. 21). The standards were also somewhat controversial. Critics question the legitimacy of the ISO to establish an environmental standard, especially since it is industry dominated; they question the transparency and democratic value of the organization and they question whether the standards themselves would lead to environmental improvements (Clapp, 2005). Yet the standards have become publicly accepted, which in turn, pressures states (see Chapter 5 in this volume). The World Trade Organization recognizes them 'as legitimate public standards and guidelines' (Clapp, 2005, p. 224). The standards have, consequently, essentially become embedded in the existing global trade rules. Moreover, they are simply increasingly accepted and widely seen as the standards of the future: '[S]tates and other international bodies are increasingly recognizing these standards and incorporating them into national standards, governmental regulations and intergovernmental policies. In this way they are becoming embedded in broader international structures of governance, which in turn increases their legitimacy among states' (Clapp, 2005, p. 235).

As a result of this state of affairs, in 1996, as a representative of Cal/EPA, Stephens founded the Multi-State Working Group on Environmental Performance (MSWG),[1] to 'determine the effectiveness' of EMSs (particularly ISO 14001 systems) as a policy tool to improve both the environment and the economy (see Chapters 3 and 5 in this volume) (Cal/EPA, 2005a; PDEP, 1999).[2] Over the years, the MSWG has refined its objectives and has grown exponentially and into a multi-level, multi-sectoral network (see Chapter 5 in this volume). It has been described as 'a forum for determined change agents from all sectors who respect each other's views and want to go environmentally further than we are today. . . . [It] also helps change agents leverage their combined knowledge and experiences to strengthen communities and build economies while improving the environment' (MDEQ and MSWG, 2005, p. 10). The organization has received recognition for its innovative thinking and it has been dubbed a '21st century organization' (MDEQ and MSWG, 2005, p. 2). In essence, the MSWG can be defined as an epistemic community, or an agent for policy convergence, according to the following definition:

> An epistemic community is defined as a network of policy experts who share common principled beliefs over ends, causal beliefs over means and common standards of accruing and testing new knowledge. These actors play an important role in issue areas where state leaders are uncertain about the consequences of different policy options and where interdependence demands coordination. Under those circumstances, transnational epistemic communities can mold state preferences over various regulatory options, making negotiations easier and more likely to lead to a harmonization of policies. (Drezner, 2001, p. 63)

Not surprisingly, included in the MSWG's broadened objectives is international outreach: 'as we share information and learn from each other and through international outreach that we feel that the international community will learn from the innovation and the creative thinking, which is in the US' (R. Stephens, pers. comm., 14 February 2006). The MSWG has also since teamed up with the European Environmental Agency (EEA) and the United Nations Environment Programme (UNEP) to initiate the UN Best Practices Network (see Chapter 5 in this volume).

Scholars point out that such efforts are also tactics for policy diffusion. The pressure not to have to later adjust to the 'global convergence of environmental governance patterns' leads international entities to 'increasingly seek to foster the diffusion of innovative approaches in environmental policy through the documentation and broad publication of national best practices' (Kern et al., 2001, pp. 5–6). According to Jänicke and Jacob (2004):

> There is a political competition between countries that requires an arena. International agencies like OECD [Organisation for Economic Co-operation and Development] or UNEP and global networks of all kind [*sic*] provide a basis for benchmarking and competition in global environmental policy. The competition is motivated by the willingness to support domestic innovative industries or to protect the national regulatory culture against pressures to adapt to policy innovation from abroad. (pp. 36–37)

A few years after the founding of the MSWG, and a couple months prior to the signing of the partnership, California state officials announced a program that furthered their EMS efforts at home. On 6 June 2000, Cal/EPA Secretary Hickox declared the commencement of the Cal/EPA EMS Project (signed into law by Governor Davis in 1999) by approving seven pilot projects. The aim of the project, which marked the first phase out of several in which the ultimate goal was to develop a plan to achieve a sustainable state, was to see if collaboration between government, business and public interest groups could produce higher levels of environmental protection and better public information on protection programs as opposed to the traditional regulatory approach (Cal/EPA, 2000).

Bavaria's Continued Frontrunner Efforts

As has been well established, Bavaria's reforms began in the early 1990s due to the global structural changes as well as international and supranational (EU) developments, which contributed to the Bundesland's sense that the growing number of environmental laws, rules and regulations, caused by the additional levels of authority, was making its system to protect the environment confusing, costly and ineffective (M. Weigand, pers. comm., 6 April 2005). By the end of 1994, the state government began formulating some of its objectives in terms of new environmental initiatives and approaches, but with the goal of being on top, being a pioneer in this area and realizing innovative environmental policies. One of Bavaria's major attempts to materialize its goals and reforms was through the 1995 Environmental Pact of Bavaria, which was assessed and continued for another five years, around the time of the formation of the partnership, containing a renewed emphasis on the state's diffusion and convergence efforts:

> The parties to the pact will step up their efforts to influence legislation at federal, European and international level[s] with the aim of contributing to genuine harmonization and systematization of environmental laws and environmental standards in Europe, while reducing the administrative costs for companies and authorities to the greatest possible extent. To this end, they will enhance reciprocal information and coordination. (STMUGV, 2000, p. 20)

Adding to the importance of influencing legislation internationally was the fact that the EU became skeptical of Bavaria's pact. At a conference in Washington, DC, on German *Länder* and US states, Schnappauf (1999) discussed the implementation of Agenda 21 at the subnational level in both countries, pointing to the tie between the goals of the Rio conference, the battles of autonomy between different levels of government, and the subsequent need to cooperate internationally with other subnational governments:

> [There are] problems of political power, such as those encountered, for instance, in battles between bureaucracy and politics, or between the different political levels. The bureaucracy of the European Union, for example, is to a certain extent mistrustful of models such as the Environmental Pact of Bavaria, and trying to delay them or to put up resistance to them. All those present will know from their own experience those fundamental disputes, painful as they are, about the nature and function of government activity in the wake of the Rio conference. The discussions our American interlocutors have with their federal bureaucracy will essentially not be different from those we have with bureaucracies in Bonn or Brussels. This exchange of experiences is therefore all the more important. (Schnappauf, 1999)

The pact also prompted international action due to the fact that one of the key instruments chosen to achieve the desired environmental ends was the use of the Eco-Management and Audit Scheme (EMAS). And since EMAS only pertained to Europe, and Bavaria not only works within the realm of Europe but also within the international realm, and since one of Bavaria's goals was to internationally diffuse its program, the ISO standards were also 'very important' for the German state (M. Weigand, pers. comm., 6 April 2005) (see Chapter 5 in this volume). This is not even including the fact that EMAS was under revision considerations. This is why Bavaria not only teamed up with Wisconsin in 1998 to examine, test and transfer a combination of the standards, but also why it joined the MSWG. It was this organization that ultimately served as a forum for the key players in the partnership to get to know each other, compare notes and come up with the idea to form a partnership.

THE KEY COMPONENTS FROM IDEA TO MOU

In the late 1990s, the MSWG began building relationships with people outside the United States. While most of these connections were in Europe and Canada, there was also some outreach to some extent in the Far East. Through these efforts the MSWG became aware of the reforms that were going on in Bavaria (R. Stephens, pers. comm., 14 February 2006). As discussed in Chapter 5, Bavaria became involved with the MSWG in early 1999, shortly after the formation of the partnership with Wisconsin, which was also part of the MSWG (M. Weigand, pers. comm., 6 April 2005, 5 August 2008). In this context, Stephens got to know Weigand, whom he characterized as essentially his counterpart in the Bavarian ministry with respect to innovation programs, the development of the Bavarian compact initiative and the use of environmental management systems and regulatory policy (R. Stephens, pers. comm., 14 February 2006).

During the course of their discussions, and as they compared notes on what they were doing in their respective states, Stephens and Weigand not only realized that they had common objectives (R. Stephens, pers. comm., 14 February 2006) – that is, similar innovative regulatory reform goals coupled with the high priority they attached to this area (Bavaria MSDEA and Cal/EPA, 2000) – but they also recognized that both were leading their reform efforts in their respective countries (and Bavaria possibly also within Europe; M. Weigand, pers. comm., 6 April 2005). With these commonalities, the two states believed that they could learn from one another. As Stephens (pers. comm., 14 February 2006) said: 'We think the Bavarians are doing some really interesting things, we in California; the Bavarians thought the Californians were doing some interesting things . . . Let's try to learn from one another'.

One of the major reasons it was believed that learning from one another would be advantageous was because it would assist in achieving 'interstate benchmarking' (Bavaria MSDEA and Cal/EPA, 2000), for starters, and hence in convergence between the two states on these policy matters. This benchmarking would, in turn, help in international diffusion – in both 'influencing the development of ISO 14001 in the international standardization' (M. Weigand, pers. comm., 6 April 2005) and thus 'achiev[ing] regulatory innovation at an international level' (STMUGV, 2000). According to Weigand (pers. comm., 6 April 2005):

> If we want to confirm our ideas in the background of driving the regulatory innovation all over the world and with international management systems like ISO 14001 and not only EMAS in Europe, then we need many partners and we need very strong partners . . . California . . . for us, was always a leading state in the US.

For the MSWG, influencing the ISO was more of an initial issue (R. Stephens, pers. comm., 14 February 2006). That said, its international outreach concerning EMSs, and influence in that respect, was and remains the emphasis.

The literature on the diffusion of innovative environmental policy suggests that pioneers or 'first-movers' in regulatory innovation frequently establish the international standard, which pressures other countries to act and thus leads to an increase in 'regulatory competition' (Kern et al., 2001, p. 4). It also potentially lessens the cost of having to later adjust politically or economically to the rule or to try to block it. The larger pay-off is that it is economically advantageous, particularly in light of the 'growing globalization of environmental policy' (Kern et al., 2001, p. 15). When regulatory innovation is quickly diffused internationally, it is 'usually accompanied by an expansion of markets for environmental protection technologies developed in the frontrunner countries' (Kern et al., 2001, p. 4). '[I]t is no accident that the biggest exporters of environmental technologies in the world – the United States, Germany and Japan – have at least at times introduced the most progressive environmental policies' (Kern et al., 2001, p. 4). And taking this point a step further, both California and Bavaria are leaders (or budding leaders) within their respective countries in environmental technologies (and highly prioritize them). With the knowledge of both states' promotions of environmental technologies (as shown in their 1995 partnership and the extension of it in 2000), and with the understanding of the economic benefits that come with being a first-mover, it can be concluded that another motivation for the partnership was as a means to achieve economic benefits.

All of these motivations, however, are based on some deeper similarities, which led them, in part, to such like-minded goals and to the belief in the mutual value of the collaboration. While it has been stated that global and international factors influenced both Bavaria and California to embark upon similar reforms, it should be noted that their mirror reactions also stem from other unique commonalities. California and Bavaria were not just any states working toward these goals. Both states, as shown in the 1995 partnership, were and are considered as being on the leading edge in environmental policy and thinking, in general, not to mention economically; and both believed that about themselves and about each other (R. Stephens, pers. comm., 14 February 2006). As shown, they were also both ahead in environmental technologies. Furthermore, California and Bavaria matched in the roles that they play within their respective countries (R. Stephens, pers. comm., 14 February 2006). They are both geographically larger, relative to other states, and both are considered leaders or frontrunners, to which other states, the federal governments and other foreign entities (as shown, not least, in the example of this partnership) turn for ideas. In essence, as Stephens summed it up, there was a 'real interest in getting together, and so it happened'.

Also helpful in the creation of the partnership was the interest of other players and their connections to each other and the would-be partners. As Stephens and his colleagues were spanning the globe looking for progressive corporations that were trying to redo the way they managed their businesses, as part of their outreach initiatives, Stephens had gotten to know some people at BMW because of what they were doing in that regard (R. Stephens, pers. comm., 14 February 2006). Through this connection, Stephens and his colleagues became connected to Quandt, the foundation behind BMW. Stephens said that Quandt was well informed about what they were doing in the state, and both Quandt and BMW knew that California was having productive discussions with Bavaria (R. Stephens, pers. comm., 14 February 2006). Moreover, the people at BMW had been to MSWG meetings and were knowledgeable about the organization's work. Correspondingly, these two entities – BWM and Quandt – as shown in the Bavaria–Wisconsin partnership, have a special relationship to Bavaria and Weigand.

Stephens and Weigand also became connected with Edward Quevedo, who around that time was an environmental lawyer and then the Director of the Environmental Management and Sustainability Programs of the business consulting firm WSP Environmental. Quevedo was also a member of the MSWG. Consequentially, Quevedo was also working with BMW. Moreover, through him, Stephens, his colleagues and Weigand became even more connected with Quandt.

For these reasons, also that both Stephens and Weigand were well informed of the 1995 agreement between their two states and that by then Bavaria's 1998 partnership with Wisconsin (driven by MSWG members, Vice-President Smoller and Weigand) on EMSs, was off to a good and promising start, the two policy entrepreneurs were compelled to form a partnership. Stephens and Weigand decided to try to build on the initial 1995 MoU, but also to 'put some more substance into it and try to move forward on broader initiatives, in which technology was one part' of the many 'dimensions' (R. Stephens, pers. comm., 14 February 2006). Stephens and Weigand then put together an MoU. Quevedo helped with some of the drafting of the actual language and also served as a link to BMW and Quandt (R. Stephens, pers. comm., 14 February 2006).

In the policy transfer literature, the involvement of a player such as Quevedo in the making of the partnership would not be surprising. 'Consultants' are listed as one of the nine 'main categories of political actors engaged in the policy transfer process' (Dolowitz and Marsh, 2000, p. 10):

> It is becoming increasingly clear that policymakers, at both the national and international levels, are relying on the advice of consultants whether individuals or firms, who act as policy experts in the development of new programs, policies and institutional structures. Their role is particularly important because they tend to offer advice based upon what they regard as the 'best practice' elsewhere. (Dolowitz and Marsh, 2000, p. 10)

After the document was drafted, Stephens and Weigand ran it up their respective political chains, to Secretary Hickox and Minister Schnappauf, respectively, where it was positively received (R. Stephens, pers. comm., 14 February 2006). Then, since Hickox and Stephens were invited to a Quandt Foundation conference in Dresden that fall (the same one that Wisconsin and Bavarian officials attended), on public–private partnerships and new generation policies on the environment – innovations in approaches to sustainable development – they used the opportunity to sign the MoU. Hickox was not able to attend, so Stephens signed in his place (R. Stephens, pers. comm., 14 February 2006).

Here, the roles of Hickox and Schnappauf become clear. Environmental secretaries and ministers play a crucial role in the formation of an international state-to-state partnership. They are the governmental representatives who officially agree or disagree to it. What is special in this case, however, is how they allowed lower-level officials to pursue the international agreement. According to Stephens it is 'pretty rare' for someone in his position, an employee of an agency of a US state, to have been given 'broad authority to pursue an international issue like this' (pers. comm., 14 February 2006). Stephens attributed this confidence to the type of person that Hickox was: 'He was strongly supportive of this sort of outward looking policy' (pers. comm., 14 February 2006). Stephens drew the same parallel for Weigand and his relationship to Schnappauf even though he found such dynamics generally more common in regional governments in Europe than in the United States.

IMPLEMENTATION AND GENERAL RESULTS

This partnership, for all intents and purposes, never got off the ground. According to Stephens (pers. comm., 14 February 2006), after the agreement was signed some first steps were taken: a work plan was developed and some initial issues to work on were chosen, which included moving in the direction of setting up expert committees, or 'working groups' as they were referred to, to deal with these specific issues. Stephens and Weigand had discussion meetings to decide exactly what they were going to work and cooperate on to determine how they were going to take the 'very general' agreement and 'turn it into something specific' (R. Stephens, pers. comm., 14 February 2006). But despite all of the preparation that went into it, the MoU 'really never got fully implemented' (R. Stephens, pers. comm., 14 February 2006).

According to Weigand (pers. comm., 6 April 2005), the cooperation on the basis of the 2000 Memorandum was stopped because of the difficulties in California regarding the energy crisis (May 2000 until September 2001), followed by the recall change of government in 2003. Stephens went even further back with the election problems. The elections in 2002 were also detrimental to the partnership, Stephens said, because the 'budgets got a little dicey and we were fighting with legislators and things' (pers. comm., 14 February 2006).[3] At this crucial time in the beginning, according to Stephens (pers. comm., 14 February 2006), it may have been helpful if Governor Davis had taken an active role in it, or at least encouraged it within the agency, to help get it off the ground. This corresponds to Knigge's (2005) findings that revealed that the inclusion of high-level politicians increases the impact of transatlantic partnerships. But the recall elections in 2003, Stephens concurred, were the clincher, having 'turned everything upside down' and making it 'impossible' (R. Stephens, pers. comm., 14 February 2006).

When the Schwarzenegger administration came into office, everybody just 'scattered' (R. Stephens, pers. comm., 14 February 2006). Hickox left immediately, and Stephens three or four months later. In addition to the loss of the key players, information on the partnership did not get passed along to anybody and was therefore never institutionalized into the state government apparatus, which was actually part of the plan in California:

> If I recall correctly, one of the specific objectives in the work plan was to institutionalize it – put structures in place that would go beyond political changes and to actually produce valuable specific products that could be pointed to and say we're doing this because this is what it produces and it's well worth the money. (R. Stephens, pers. comm., 14 February 2006)

With institutionalization would also be funding, which is a necessity for such an activity, according to Stephens. As Stephens pointed out, even though he was able to spend time on the partnership, with respect to traveling and giving his support to it, a state-to-state partnership cannot exist with the sole efforts of one person, so there has to be money to support it (pers. comm., 14 February 2006). The budget problems in the early 2000s were one of the reasons the partnership ran into trouble on the Californian side. The agency had discretionary funds, but those were limited – enough for Stephens and sometimes a second or third person (R. Stephens, pers.

comm., 14 February 2006). But for an actual program where you would have several people focusing on it and spending most of their time on it, it would have to be a real program that would have to be in the budget, which is approved by the legislature. There is always the possibility of getting funding from outside sources, such as businesses, as occurred in Wisconsin, but there are problems with that avenue too: ethical barriers (R. Stephens, pers. comm., 14 February 2006).

The lack of institutionalization and (hence) funding indicates that the partnership was very much a personal endeavor of Stephens and Hickox: it was not linked to the state government as a whole beyond that, not even to Governor Davis, as Weigand suggested (pers. comm., 6 April 2005). This seems to be very much in line with Stephen's other endeavors and innovative thinking. As Weigand pointed out, Stephens is 'a very active person', who works 'internationally with UNEP and with the EU and his Multi-State Working Group' (pers. comm., 6 April 2005). During his tenure at Cal/EPA, he was essentially in charge of innovation change at the agency (R. Stephens, pers. comm., 14 February 2006), which means that he is very accustomed to thinking outside of the box.[4] Moreover, the fact that Weigand and Stephens continued to remain in 'close contact' outside the realm of the state or the partnership, working through the MSWG (M. Weigand, pers. comm., 6 April 2005), also demonstrates that the failure of the partnership was because it was not institutionalized rather than because there was a lack of personal effort or contact between the key players.

The issue of institutionalization, however, was part of a deeper problem in state government, according to Stephens. Partnerships such as the Bavaria–California partnership of 2000, in addition to innovative programs in general, were constantly running up against resistance: financial resistance through the legislature, or conceptual resistance, in the sense of trying to change the existing system (R. Stephens, pers. comm., 14 February 2006).

> The California/Bavaria partnership was focused as a change in innovation and learning from the Bavarians in what they were doing in terms of their initiatives, the compact initiatives, partnerships in the business community initiatives ... [Y]ou can imagine, that the idea of government entering into partnerships with the business community on innovation of policy, not everybody looks at in a positive light. (R. Stephens, pers. comm., 14 February 2006)

Institutional resistance, however, seems to be a common issue when it comes to policy transfer. In their work, Dolowitz and Marsh (1996) have found the constraints of institutions and structures on agents transferring policies as 'crucial' (p. 354).

Stephens said addressing this issue is exactly what he would have done differently if he could have started all over again (not just regarding the Bavaria–California MoU, but the entire resistance against innovative programs). Stephens would have spent more time making the case to the governor, the legislature, the non-governmental organizations (NGOs) and the business community, as to why the current environmental policy, legal structure and regulatory system needed changing. Stephens maintained that once it was analysed where California would be 30 to 50 years later, if it were to maintain its trajectory, it would have been clear that it was not heading in a good direction; and that analysis and case would never be made (R. Stephens, pers. comm., 14 February 2006):

> If you make that case that in fact, yes, we're not heading in a good direction, and we need to therefore modify our direction, then you figure out what it is, then you start asking the question what it is you need to do to get where you need to be in twenty or thirty or forty years. And one of the things you do is you look and see what others are doing throughout this country and around the world to try to correct their course so that they're not involved in a train wreck. And in the US, the California–Bavaria partnership . . . is a piece of that whole. (R. Stephens, pers. comm., 14 February 2006)

Studies show that policymakers may have an easier time legitimizing their case concerning innovative lead markets when they refer to other countries that have proven the feasibility of their initiatives, both technologically and politically (Jänicke and Jacob, 2004).

Stephens specified that the next major crisis or 'train wreck' in California will probably be in resource depletion (land and water). The cost of the regulatory system is 'escalating dramatically' and is an 'unnecessary burden' on the regulatory community since adequate environmental performance can be achieved in 'a much more efficient way' (pers. comm., 14 February 2006). Stephens said that the last thing the state needs is a needless financial burden on its economic system because it is having a hard enough time competing as it is.

The argument or case that needed to be made, as stated earlier, is that the current environmental system in the state of California is 'disjointed'; not only are the different environmental mediums – air, water, land and waste – fragmented from one another, but they also are not integrated to the economic and social systems in the country, while it is clear that they should be (R. Stephens, pers. comm., 14 February 2006). The state cannot continue in this way, considering its population growth and economic growth. Regarding the partnership, the argument would have been that 'you're not creating a California–Bavarian partnership just because you want that partnership, it's because you're trying to achieve a goal of a better system' (R. Stephens, pers. comm., 14 February 2006).

ANALYSIS

The driving forces that prompted the idea to form the California–Bavaria partnership are primarily the same as those that led them to create the partnership in 1995, with a few differences. The issue of EMS standards from both the EU and the ISO took on greater importance because of the ISO's publication of its 14001 standards in 1996 and the pending EU revisions of its EMAS standards. Just as in the other partnerships, the initial motivating components of the process leading to the partnership were structural, containing coercive elements.

The situations in both states were also slightly different five years after the original partnership: California was still in great need of major reforms in sustainable development, while Bavaria was well along its implementation path and in the process of promoting its policies internationally. In the effort to fulfill these goals the role of agency and the actors' subjective perceptions (bounded rationality) became prominent. The key policy entrepreneur and player in California founded what became an epistemic community on environmental performance with the emphasis on EMSs, the MSWG, of which the key agent in Bavaria also became a member.

The MSWG served as a forum where personal connections and networking among the players and institutions transpired and ultimately was the way in which the partnership came together. The primary players were the policy entrepreneurs Stephens, Weigand, Quevedo, Sec. Hickox and Minister Schnappauf. The key institutions were the MSWG, the states of California and Bavaria, and WSP Environmental. Also important were BMW and the Quandt Foundation. In essence, the partnership was one endeavor among others for both states in achieving their environmental policy reforms. And since both sides were engaged in cutting-edge thinking in this regard, the purpose of the partnership was to learn from one another and to help capture some of the economic leverage that comes when one is a first-mover in a new policy. It was very much a continuation of the 1995 and 1998 partnerships. Thus, their knowledge (and in one instance participation) in the 1995 California–Bavaria partnership and the successfully operating 1998 Bavaria–Wisconsin partnership also served as a building block and added momentum. Thus, the formation of the partnership required not only policy entrepreneurs, but specifically those interested in policy learning or diffusion.

The outstanding points about this partnership are the different levels and sectors involved in global (environmental) governance that occurred throughout the process of the partnership, namely:

1. The driving forces that led to the reform – that is, the international-level pressure for new environmental approaches to environmental protection and the larger role that subnational governments (as well as other non-state and/or non-traditional actors and institutions) have in the new international structure as shown by California and Bavaria's (not their respective federal governments) response to this pressure.
2. The types of reforms themselves – that is, the reforms in Bavaria involved government cooperation with business and the use of an EU-level tool, EMAS and the aim to influence policy globally; while the reform efforts in California involved the creation of an NGO network organization – the MSWG, a multi-level, public–private–NGO cooperation, established with the full intention to create and influence policy on all levels.
3. How the partnership was created – that is, not only was there influence by other non-state actors such as a consultant from WSP Environmental and representatives from BMW and Quandt, but it also stemmed from the MSWG and was very much the product of policy entrepreneurs.
4. Why it was not successfully implemented – that is, because it was very much centered in the MSWG and agency driven in California's case.

At all stages of the process leading to the formation of the partnership, the dynamics were multi-level and sectoral, while actions occurred in a non-hierarchical fashion; the partnership represents Type II multi-level governance (MLG). And within this type of governance partnership, there was a two-way vertical and horizontal diffusion process regarding EMS policies. The diffusion (coercive) mechanisms that were at work (which is comparable to the 1998 Wisconsin–Bavaria partnership), were ideational competition, as stemming from the ISO's EMSs standards and the EU's EMAS standards as well as the epistemic community MSWG (and ultimately the UNCED regime), regulatory (both political and economic) competition as triggered by the ISO, as seen through attempts of California and Bavaria to be influential (at all levels of government) regarding EMSs/EMAS and through their ecological modernization goals.

The implementation of the partnership was another story as it was hindered by the state of California itself. It was really the product of agents, run out of the MSWG and thus a problem of Type II multi-level governance failing to function within the traditional structures of Type I.

California's key player, Stephens, even believed in hindsight that he needed to win over those in the state government in order for the partnership to have been successfully implemented. This stresses the idea that while a policy entrepreneur can initiate a partnership they will have difficulty sustaining it without formal institutionalization, which requires more than an MoU. In this case, however, the presence of policy entrepreneurs subsequent to the formation of the partnership, into its implementation stage, did not make much difference. That said, the initial activities that transpired between the two transatlantic actors would not have occurred in their absence. Moreover, as recognized by Stephens, it would have been up to him to make the partnership work.

In sum, this partnership is demonstrative of the role of two leading sub-national governments in global governance for sustainable development, specifically on EMSs. The process of the formation of the partnership, starting from before the concept was conceived – the forces that led to its conception – to the formal creation of the partnership, was a window into this aspect of global environmental governance. The failure of the partnership revealed both the necessity of the involvement of the traditional governmental structure and the difficulty of getting both structures to successfully function in harmony. This task, however, does not seem to be impossible, as the key player in California himself believed that had he made the case to the powers that be within the state apparatus, then the partnership could have been successfully implemented in the state.

NOTES

1. Stephens founded the MSWG and was its President until 2006.
2. The informal group of almost a dozen states and the EPA (MDEQ and MSWG, 2005) came together out of a dissatisfaction with the status quo regarding the entire management system between government (at all levels) and its relationship with the business community, and because of the developments of the ISO standards (Hassett et al., 2004; Meyer, 1999a; R. Stephens, pers. comm., 14 February 2006).
3. The primary elections were held on 5 March 2002 and the general elections took place that fall on 5 November; Gray Davis was re-elected. The recall effort began slowly in February 2003 and acquired momentum throughout the spring and summer. The elections took place on 7 October 2003, the results were officially certified on 14 November, and Schwarzenegger was sworn in on 17 November 2003.
4. As Assistant Secretary for Environmental Management and Sustainability, Stephens led the agency's program on regulatory innovation based on EMSs, public–private partnerships, and environmental and economic sustainability. Moreover, although not really a part of the 1995 partnership, Stephens knew about it and had jurisdiction over the California Environmental Technology Certification Program (CalCert) at the time – the program which was of central relevance to that partnership. Furthermore, Stephens served as chair of the ISO Task Group developing the Testing and Verification Standards for environmental claims.

7. Maryland and Schleswig–Holstein (2002)

THE MEMORANDUM

On 5 July 2002, the Acting Secretary of the Maryland Department of the Environment (MDE), Merrylin Zaw-Mon, and the Minister of the Ministry of Environment, Nature and Forestry of Schleswig–Holstein (MUNF), Klaus Müller, met in Tönning, Schleswig–Holstein to form an environmental partnership. The two signed a Memorandum of Understanding (MoU) to collaborate on sustainable development, energy conservation, renewable energy, greenhouse gas (GHG) emissions reductions, 'green' building development and land and watershed management. The primary aim of the cooperation, as alluded to throughout the MoU, was to learn from one another to advance policies in these areas.

The stated mechanisms for achieving this objective were through 'exchanges of information and technical assistance', 'study tours, workshops, work sessions, training courses, conferences and symposia'. The parties also listed some possible short- and long-term activities. The short-term activities were: (1) 'setting up links to homepages'; (2) 'collecting best practices case studies on green buildings, watershed management, wind energy, "smart growth" or coastal zone management'; (3) 'inviting individual speakers to conferences or workshops'; and (4) 'convening bilateral conference[s] including different actors of society (business, science, NGOs [non-governmental organizations] etc.).' The long-term activities were: (1) 'joint grant writing for additional peer-to-peer exchanges'; (2) 'specific technical research between universities/institutes'; (3) 'implementation of pilot projects subject to further specification'; and (4) 'business co-operation in the environment sector'. To this end, the secretary and minister were to establish a coordinator, if not themselves, to be responsible for organizing the implementation and realization of the goals (MDE and MUNF, 2002).

The MoU listed two reasons for the cooperation. First, the two parties were promoting, or had interest in promoting, similar policies in the aforementioned subject matter; in other words, they had mutual interests in advancing such policies. Second, by collaborating in these areas of joint interest, they believed that both sides could benefit – that the joining of forces could bolster their respective efforts (MDE and MUNF, 2002).

While the MoU specifically listed many areas in which the partners wished to collaborate and learn from each other, and many possible mechanisms for cooperation, and details such as who would be in charge of implementing the partnership, it was nonetheless very vague as to the specific ideas and goals, the reasons behind the motivations, the expected concrete benefits of collaboration, and how and why the partnership came about. Furthermore, the issue of funding seemed precarious, as the document hinted how the partnership depended on the availability of funds (which would apparently only be through outside grants) and personnel. The rest of the chapter focuses on filling in these blanks.

THE DRIVING FORCES

International and National Influences and Pressures

Maryland and Schleswig–Holstein's coming together was much more complex than portrayed in the MoU. The 'mutual interest' that both states had in working together was the outcome of a compilation of driving forces from all levels of government that led the two to form policies that earned them both frontrunner status. Both states were influenced by the unfolding international events of the 1990s that dealt with climate change and sustainable development, as was shown in the content of the MoU. They were also driven by a transatlantic advocacy network[1] that promoted such policies. Moreover, they were influenced by the subsequent domestic activities, or lack thereof, at the national level in both countries. These points are discussed further below. But the additional drive of both Maryland and Schleswig–Holstein to form leading policies and later the partnership was the result of problems and opportunities that were unique to both states and due to the political will of both states' leaders at the time.

Political Climate in Schleswig–Holstein

As stated in Chapter 3, throughout the 1990s and beyond some German *Länder* carved out a frontrunner niche for themselves by having enacted ambitious types of sustainable development and climate change policies. Schleswig–Holstein was one of them, having earned a leadership position in climate change and renewable energy policies. Schleswig–Holstein's policy decisions, in addition to being prompted by the region's special circumstances and its relation to the federal (and international) policy positions in these areas, can be attributed to the state's leaders at that time, which MUNF Minister Müller described as 'open-minded' and 'progressive' (K. Müller, 2005).

This issue of climate change has posed both special challenges and opportunities to Schleswig–Holstein. This *Land* is particularly vulnerable to rising sea levels since it is located between two seas and has an estuary (K. Müller, 2002b). This issue has also cost it a lot of money; since the early 1960s, €1.5 billion has been spent on coastal protection (K. Müller, 2005). Schleswig–Holstein has a high stake in the effective handling of climate change; ambitious targets to this end are in its best interest. That said, officials also saw that these challenges and regional circumstances provided new opportunities. Representatives posited that having a 'modern environmental policy' would be economically advantageous – that such a policy approach would not only be 'one of the keys to ecological innovation' but also a means to 'greater global competitiveness and more jobs' (K. Müller, 2002b).

The state leaders made use of federal policies, and combined them with state policies to gain a lucrative position in renewable energies. In 1995, Schleswig–Holstein created its own climate protection program, which was fashioned to complement federal policies (K. Müller, 2005). The state set four major goals for 2010. It called for: (1) an overall reduction of carbon dioxide (CO_2) emissions by 15 percent; (2) a 25 percent share of renewable energies at end energy consumption; (3) a 50 percent share of renewable energy at electricity consumption; and (4) a 30 percent share of electricity of CHP (combined heat and power) generation. Then, under the state's Red–Green coalition (as of 1996), the state financially supported measures to promote some individual sources of renewable energy and energy conservation (K. Müller, 2005). The four areas the state chose to emphasize were wind, biomass and solar energy, and 'green' buildings. Out of these foci, Schleswig–Holstein became a frontrunner in 'green' buildings and wind energy.

As early as the late 1980s and early 1990s, Schleswig–Holstein earned leadership status in 'green' buildings, through the implementation of new standards for energy saving in new buildings. These standards resulted in a 75 percent reduction of energy use in modernized buildings compared to other buildings (K. Müller, 2004). In this regard, and as a way to reconcile economic development and environmental protection, the state endorsed projects such as its Sustainable Building and Dwelling project (K. Müller, 2005), which was created to consider all of the environmental components in the construction and use of buildings and include the involvement of all stakeholders from the beginning (house building societies, the construction industry, investment banks, the tenants' association, environmental associations, the Chamber of Architects and Engineers of the state, and the state government) (Lotze-Campen, 2001).

Wind energy, however, got the most attention. 'Schleswig–Holstein was one of the first worldwide, if not the first, to systematically use wind energy, by promoting the adequate policy and administrative framework, by establishing financing models (for example, 'Bürgerwindpark'), by supporting centers of expertise and by actual wind installations' (Anonymous, pers. comm., 25 October 2004). One of the main reasons the *Land* chose to emphasize wind energy was because of its coastal geography, which is 'perfect' for large-scale wind energy generation (K. Müller, 2005). At the time of the partnership, wind energy contributed about 17 percent of the total power consumed in Schleswig–Holstein (K. Müller, 2002a). By 2004, it provided 30 out of 31 percent from all renewable energy resources, and was expected to reach 50 percent by 2010 (K. Müller, 2005).

The Renewable Energy Sources Act of 2000 helped transform Schleswig–Holstein into a dominant wind-energy generating state. Because of this federal law, the wind energy industry made €350 million in 2004. At the *Land* level, support activities included: (1) land-use planning; (2) local resident ability to operate and earn money from the turbines; (3) financial support in the late 1980s and early 1990s; and (4) networking and support for research and development activities (K. Müller, 2005).

Regarding other important state-level considerations, the state also made the search for 'modern approaches' a top priority (K. Müller, 2002b). In 1996, for instance, Schleswig–Holstein established its biomass initiative, a cooperative arrangement between the ministries of the environment, agriculture and energy, and the energy foundation of Schleswig–Holstein, to promote bioenergy. The state believes that this energy source, which is used in the electricity, heating and fuel markets, has the potential to contribute up to 13 percent of energy use; it currently contributes 1 percent (K. Müller, 2005).

In water management, the state primarily follows the European union (EU) Water Framework Directive to attain a certain ecological, biological and chemical level by 2015. That said, due to the wet nature of the *Land*, some significant advancements were made in this area earlier in the state's history. One of its more contemporary policies includes the promotion of organic farming to prevent eutrophication. It also began a campaign on the significance of water and how to correctly manage it (K. Müller, 2002b). Moreover, the *Land* pursued a decentralized approach, involving the participation of stakeholders (K. Müller, 2002a).

Overall, the state's push for such environmental policies and for the development of environmental and renewable energy technologies has provided significant business activity. At the time of the partnership, the state was already employing more than 32 000 people in about 700 enterprises tied to the renewable sector, bringing in €1.89 billion annually (K. Müller, 2002b). The wind energy industry alone is increasingly considered one of the state's most important exports. This industry had already created around 3500 new jobs by 2002, reaching 5000 in 2005, and expected to double by 2010 (K. Müller, 2002b, 2005).

Political Climate in Maryland

By the turn of the century, Maryland had made a national and international name for itself for its innovative urban sprawl and water quality policies. These policies and ideas were a consequence of the state's distinct environmental problems and were also evidence of certain policy entrepreneurs in state government. They were forerunning environmental policies that reflected the new generation of environmental approaches.

Maryland is a small state that has to contend not only with the impact of two major cities but also with the largest estuary in the country. Some of the major challenges within the state have to do with urban sprawl and water quality, and particularly the effects of urbanization on the bay, overnitrification and sedimentation (D. Medearis, pers. comm., 16 September 2004). Contributing to the sprawl is the steadily increasing population – which grew 25 percent from 1970 to 1995 and is expected to increase another 20 percent by 2015 – combined with the migration trend from cities and towns to newly developed suburbs. The result is new roads, which contribute to run-off into the bay, and longer commuting distances, which worsens air quality (Abbruzzese et al., 2002). Development is a top environmental concern and receives a lot of attention (Abbruzzese et al., 2002; D. Medearis, pers. comm., 16 September 2004).

Officials in Maryland, under Gov. Parris Glendening, decided to take new and creative approaches to dealing with these problems. In early 1997, the state enacted land management policies referred to as 'Smart Growth' to reduce urban sprawl and encourage growth in existing communities. The law had three major objectives and five core initiatives. The objectives were: (1) to save the remaining natural resources; (2) to support development in already existing communities; and (3) to save taxpayer money on the cost of infrastructure that supports sprawl. The five initiatives were: (1) the 1997 Smart Growth Areas Act to discourage sprawl by denying subsidies for it and supporting existing communities; (2) the 1997 Rural Legacy Act to protect natural and cultural resources that could promote resourced-based economies and provide greenbelts around developed areas; (3) the Brownfields Voluntary Cleanup and Revitalization Incentive

Programs to stimulate the reuse of brownfield sites through subsidies; (4) an updated Job Creation Tax Credit Program to encourage businesses to expand or relocate to Maryland; and (5) the Live Near Your Work Program to provide incentives for people to buy homes near their workplaces (Cohen, 2002).

The state earned immediate recognition for being bold and innovative regarding growth management, even before the programs were implemented. In October 2000, Smart Growth was one of ten winners in the annual Innovations in American Government program of the Ford Foundation and Harvard's John F. Kennedy School of Government (Cohen, 2002). In sum, in the years leading up to the partnership, Maryland had become a frontrunner and model with its Smart Growth initiatives, which began to diffuse both nationally and internationally.

Maryland was also receiving international attention in the watershed area, due to its cutting-edge work on the Chesapeake Bay. The 1983 Chesapeake Bay Program, spearheaded by a US Senator from Maryland, is a regional partnership to restore and protect the bay (Blankenship, 2003). This program became a model for its focus on public participation and cooperation among the federal government, a number of neighboring states and numerous local governments. This cross-sectoral, multi-level effort allowed for a comprehensive approach, which was the only solution for addressing the diverse pollution issues affecting the bay. This policy was almost a decade ahead of its time, as such multi-level and horizontal integration types of approaches were not on the international agenda until 1992 (through the United Nations Conference on Environment and Development (UNCED)) or the national agenda until 1995 (through the United States Environmental Protection Agency's National Environmental Performance Partnership System program).

These two Maryland initiatives were not the only ones that corresponded to the international agenda. The state administration took some initial and deliberate steps to address climate change, which in the context of the times was quite progressive and a politically autonomous statement for a state. The Glendening administration put together an inter-cabinet working group on climate change. The purpose of this group, which consisted of all the various departments relevant to climate change impact, was to discuss potential policies and programs in this area (F. Hoover, pers. comm., 9 March 2005).

Furthermore, Glendening signed an executive order in March 2001, on energy-related activities within state agencies that had some climate impact. The order contained a 'green buildings' requirement for all state-owned and -leased facilities (Glendening, 2001). It also had a 'green' power procurement requirement for state-owned facilities, that 6 percent be generated from 'green' energy, making it, at that time, the highest percentage in the country (F. Hoover, pers. comm., 9 March 2005; Glendening, 2001). Furthermore, the order contained specific energy-efficiency goals for facilities and fleets, which included decreasing energy consumption by 10 percent by 2005 and 15 percent by 2010 relative to the year 2000; increasing renewable energy use, including supporting the federal Million Solar Roofs program; buying Energy Star (energy-efficient) products; reducing agency waste; and purchasing alternative fuel vehicles (Glendening, 2001). Among other initiatives and agreements, these last goals were in accord with the Maryland Clean Energy Incentive Act of 2000, which provides tax incentives for energy-efficient and renewable energy products to the state's residents and businesses, including sales tax exemptions for Energy Star appliances; tax reductions for electric and hybrid-electric vehicles; tax credits for the installation of a solar or photovoltaic system; and tax credits for the use of biomass fuel to produce electricity (Pew Center, n.d.-a).

Maryland was also taking some major steps in renewable energy. The legislature was discussing utility deregulation that contained a renewable energy component (there was no previously renewable energy policy in the state). Moreover, through this legislation, the administration was attempting to get a Renewable Portfolio Standard (RPS) enacted into law (F. Hoover, pers. comm., 9 March 2005). By 1999, the Electric Customer Choice and Competition Act was signed into law, which restructured the electric industry, giving customers the choice to select 'green' power (SMECO). The RPS, however, did not remain a part of the legislation (until 2004) (F. Hoover, pers. comm., 9 March 2005).

In addition to those renewable energy endeavors, the Maryland Energy Administration was encouraging the deployment of renewable energy, particularly wind energy. At the time of the partnership, the state had begun the siting process for wind power generation in Western Maryland. Considerations for wind turbines off the coast were also occurring (F. Hoover, pers. comm., 9 March 2005).

Another significant non-conventional policy approach under Glendening that was no less important when it came to the partnership was the enhancement of the MDE's international activities. Gov. Glendening was a firm supporter of international partnerships, which allowed MDE Secretary Jane Nishida and then Deputy Secretary Zaw-Mon to engage actively in international work (J. Nishida, pers. comm., 24 March 2005). The governor's interest in this area was the result of a couple of experiences, from which he learned of the value of such activities.

The first experience was an outgrowth of the Smart Growth and Chesapeake Bay Program projects. Maryland received a great amount of international attention and interest for these programs. It was this interest and subsequent visits from abroad that prompted the realization that the state had valuable information to contribute. Likewise, as the state met with other governments, it became clear that there was also much that it could learn from elsewhere. Glendening became interested in finding another state government that was addressing similar issues so that the state might collaborate on effective solutions (J. Mitchell, pers. comm., 1 March 2005).

This high volume of international attention was also because of the globalization of communications and the rate in which information travels. It became possible for governments on other continents to learn about the programs and decide if they want to learn more, whereas it was not as common before (J. Mitchell, pers. comm., 1 March 2005). Former MDE Secretary Nishida elaborated on this point: '[T]hrough the use . . . of Internet, [and] international conferences . . . people are waking up to the similarities that you see from abroad . . . You can communicate more easily than in the past' (pers. comm., 24 March 2005).

Thus, the governor provided Nishida, a policy entrepreneur in her own right and also interested in pursuing international activities, room to engage in such ventures. Nishida made the most of this support from her superior compared to previous environmental secretaries. Others considered her to be very active in promoting international environmental exchanges. According to John Mitchell, who was the MDE's international activities coordinator at the time: '[I]t wasn't as if international . . . [activities were] new, but Jane [Nishida] certainly took it to a completely new level and we had many, many more projects and she really expanded the state's international environmental profile' (pers. comm., 1 March 2005).

Nishida was aware of the unusualness of this approach and felt fortunate that she worked for a governor who promoted international exchange programs and international travel. 'There is still a stigma associated with international travel, so it's harder, I think, for some states like mine to do the international exchange programs I did' (J. Nishida, pers. comm., 24 March 2005). That said, Nishida believes there is a growing acceptance of the importance of international corroboration and the benefits from it.

The second valuable experience that contributed to the governor's interest in increasing the MDE's international activities was a cooperation that the MDE had with Chiang Mai, Thailand, made possible by funding the state received 'for the first time' in 2000, from the NGO, Council of State Governments (CSG) (J. Mitchell, pers. comm., 1 March 2005). This funding, which came from the federal US Asia Environmental Partnership, allowed the state to become more proactive internationally. As Mitchell explained, the department prior to the funding 'never had any money to do any traveling'; it had been essentially reactive in international activities. Mitchell would be informed that a foreign delegation was coming to visit

– between 12 and 30 foreign delegations would visit annually – and about what they were interested in seeing and learning, so he would work out the speakers, arrangements and site visits if relevant. But the MDE was not reaching out itself and trying to set up such interactions (J. Mitchell, pers. comm., 1 March 2005).

This lack of active international endeavors had to do with the Board of Public Works (the governor, treasurer and a third party), which has to approve international travel. Often, one of the parties was a person who had been in his position for about 40 years and who essentially had a parochial view and did not see how international work was also beneficial to domestic work (J. Mitchell, pers. comm., 1 March 2005). And since states are cash-strapped, it is difficult to justify spending limited travel money for such work (M. Zaw-Mon, pers. comm., 29 October 2004). Basically, any time an MDE official, like Nishida, traveled, it was when she received an invitation and the other party was paying (J. Mitchell, pers. comm., 1 March 2005). That is why it was so essential to get funding from external sources; participation depended on it (M. Zaw-Mon, pers. comm., 29 October 2004).

The CSG funding for the program with Thailand, however, 'changed the dynamic' and the MDE really started to engage internationally (J. Mitchell, pers. comm., 1 March 2005). Through the course of this work, which expanded into other areas and included high-level delegations to meet the governor, the value of such international work became clear to both MDE representatives and the governor – that there was a great amount of best practice that Maryland had to pass on, but there was also quite a bit it could learn (J. Mitchell, pers. comm., 1 March 2005). This realization was the watershed moment for the rapid interest in international activities.

The third experience was a transatlantic exchange of three US states (Maryland, New Jersey and Minnesota) and three German states (Baden Württemburg, Saxony and Saxony-Anhalt). This exchange demonstrated, among other things, the possibilities of such international relations and the promise of something even more long term (J. Nishida, pers. comm., 24 March 2005). Moreover, this exchange sparked the idea to pursue a partnership with an individual German state. As such, the following takes a closer look at the construction of this exchange and consequently at the origin of the partnership.

The Origin of the Partnership

The transatlantic environmental exchange was the fruit of the work of three closely networked policy entrepreneurs: Dale Medearis of the United

States Environmental Protection Agency's (EPA) Office of International Affairs, Nishida and Reinhard Bütikofer, co-chairman of the Baden-Württemberg Green Party (1997) and then executive director of the Federal Party (1999) (S. Müller-Kraenner, pers. comm., 27 October 2004). They approached the Germany-based, Green Party-affiliated Heinrich Böll Foundation (S. Müller-Kraenner, pers. comm., 27 October 2004) and the US-based NGO Center for Clean Air Policy (CCAP) (S. Gander, pers. comm., May 26, 2006), to carry out and fund the program (S. Müller-Kraenner, pers. comm., 27 October 2004).[2] The idea was to bring together environmental practitioners from these six subnational governments for a series of meetings in both countries (S. Müller-Kraenner, pers. comm., 27 October 2004) between 1997 and 1999 (Scherf et al., 2000), 'to share ideas and experiences on regional responses to the issue of sustainable development' (J. Nishida, J. Sherman and B. Struever, letter to Sen. Barbara Mikulski, 29 January 1999).

The initiative provided Maryland experience in environmental exchanges with Germany, the insight into the value of it and the desire for something more 'permanent' with a German state (J. Nishida, pers. comm., 24 March 2005). Furthermore, it contained the 'right' mixture of like-minded, networked people who were also motivated to put together a partnership. This is where Medearis was instrumental (J. Nishida, pers. comm., 24 March 2005). Medearis came up with the idea of matching up Maryland and Schleswig–Holstein, due to his extensive knowledge of and connections in the two governments. Medearis recognized that there were very strong analogies not only politically and geographically, but also regarding the size of both states relative to other states in their respective countries (D. Medearis, pers. comm., 16 September 2004). This connection corresponds to other findings regarding the value of policy entrepreneurs in lesson-drawing, in that in addition to their advocacy of lessons, 'their concern with a special subject . . . leads them to build up a nationwide or international network or contacts that are a source of ideas for new programs' (Rose, 1993, p. 56).

THE KEY COMPONENTS FROM IDEA TO MOU

Formation of the Partnership

Once the idea was born to pursue a transatlantic partnership with Schleswig–Holstein, Medearis, Bütikofer, Nishida and the Böll Foundation utilized the six-state exchange to pursue this. While Nishida was on one of the trips to Germany as part of the program, the others talked to Klaus

Müller, Minister of MUNF and also a Green Party member, about the idea of a partnership, and he responded with interest; so they arranged for her to travel to Schleswig–Holstein to meet him (J. Nishida, pers. comm., 24 March 2005). One could say that these were the activities of a transnational advocacy network. During this visit, both environmental heads recognized the similarities and potential and agreed that the partnership was worth pursuing. To this end, 'leadership was key', according to Nishida (pers. comm., 24 March 2005): 'You had to have committed people on both sides willing to see the value in this.'

From that point on, the two states corresponded from opposite sides of the Atlantic. They worked out the particulars of the agreement, what their mutual interests were and in which areas they wished to cooperate, and arranged for a Maryland delegation to travel to Germany as the official beginning of the partnership. The Heinrich Böll Foundation was set to pay for the trip of two Marylanders in the delegation.[3] The key agents in this phase were Alfred Eberhardt, the deputy head of the Department of Sustainable Development at MUNF, and Mitchell; they were in charge of 'making the partnership happen' (J. Mitchell, pers. comm., 1 March 2005). As Mitchell pointed out: 'Once the decision is made to make it happen and there's the political will on both sides, it's just basically up to the staff then to make sure that it does happen' (pers. comm., 1 March 2005).

But before the delegation made it to Germany, Nishida left office (26 April 2002). Mitchell, in charge of executing it, filled in the new Acting Secretary, Zaw-Mon, on the details and she approved (J. Mitchell, pers. comm., 1 March 2005). From then on, Mitchell spent a lot of time corresponding with Eberhardt, working out the fine points of the partnership and the logistics of the upcoming meetings (J. Mitchell, pers. comm., 1 March 2005). On 4 July 2002, the approximately seven-head delegation arrived in Schleswig–Holstein. The group consisted of environmental, energy and trade officials, as well as federal representatives.

Motivations and Objectives

The partners had numerous motivations and objectives for collaborating, including learning from each other. There was also a strong economic component, especially for Schleswig–Holstein, regarding wind energy. Finally, both subnational governments were interested in using the partnership to address international objectives.

Environmental lesson-drawing
Despite the geographical distance, Maryland and Schleswig–Holstein have an extraordinary resemblance in natural physical features, which means

they face similar environmental issues. Both are small states relative to the other states in their respective countries (D. Medearis, pers. comm., 16 September 2004). Moreover, both contain major bays – the Chesapeake Bay and the Bay of Kiel, respectively; and they are coastal states, located on the Atlantic Ocean, and the Wadden (North) Sea and Baltic Sea, respectively. The two subnational land masses, therefore, have similar watershed and coastal zone management issues. In addition, both Maryland and Schleswig–Holstein have to contend with major cities – Baltimore and Washington, DC, and Hamburg, respectively – amidst their considerable rural areas. Likewise, they both have similar land management issues.

Studies show that when it comes to drawing lessons the degree of similarities is more important than the geographic proximity. Moreover, geographic distance can actually be very fruitful: 'studying familiar problems in an unfamiliar setting can expand ideas and inspire fresh thinking about what is possible at home' (Dolowitz and Marsh, 1996, p. 351). Nishida confirmed this understanding when she said that the seeking out of the partnership with Schleswig–Holstein had to do with the fact that the state was 'looking at creative ways to solve Maryland's problems' (pers. comm., 24 March 2005).

In addition to these physical analogies, both states had likeminded environmental leaders who were accordingly pursuing or interested in establishing the same types of policies to address comparable issues. This aspect was influential when the original policy entrepreneurs were considering the possibility of a partnership. Correspondingly, the innovative policies for which both states became frontrunners (Smart Growth and the Chesapeake Bay Program in Maryland, and wind and 'green' building policies in Schleswig–Holstein), also were harmonious with these leaders' interests. On the occasion of the bilateral convention, Minister Müller acknowledged this aspect:

> When I met Jane Nishida some two years ago it was not just this similarity in the countries' nature but even more the pattern and strategies of environmental policy which encouraged us to get in closer contact and to establish a more institutionalized exchange of experiences between our two states. I think that we both can claim that we developed quite progressive approaches in environmental policy at [the] state level. (K. Müller, 2002a)

The desire to learn outside of national boundaries was also the policy entrepreneurs' ability to take advantage of the zeitgeist of subnational empowerment and their environmental policy capacities. As Mitchell said: 'We shouldn't just expect everything to trickle down from EPA. There's a real need for state-to-state relationships. And we can learn a lot from each other; we can help each other, and that's a very good thing' (pers. comm.,

1 March 2005). Moreover, it indicated dissatisfaction with the status quo. According to Nishida:

> It was the leadership but also the vision of trying to think outside of the box and looking at international best practices as one way to enhance your tool box at home. We knew what was tried in the United States, because we mainly interact with other states and other regions within our sphere. But this was an opportunity to see how a country very similar in culture and conditions, unlike developing countries, . . . dealt with environmental challenges; you could see the comparative value of international best practices. (pers. comm., 24 March 2005)

There were several areas in which the two states wanted to learn from each other. The Maryland delegates were interested in 'green' roofs because the MDE was in the process of building a 'green' building for its headquarters in another part of the city (M. Zaw-Mon, pers. comm., 29 October 2004) and because of the 'green' buildings requirement as called for in the afore-mentioned 2001 executive order of the governor (Glendening, 2001). In this regard, there were 'a lot of examples of "green" buildings and "green" roofs' in Schleswig–Holstein (M. Zaw-Mon, pers. comm., 29 October 2004). State representatives were also interested in alternative energy sources, such as from biomass, particularly from animal manure, and Schleswig–Holstein had experience in this area. Schleswig–Holstein has a large dairy population, while Maryland has a large chicken population (J. Nishida, pers. comm., 24 March 2005).

Also important to Marylanders was learning about wind energy, as it was starting to deploy wind generation in Western Maryland (F. Hoover, pers. comm., 9 March 2005). In general terms, Maryland was interested in knowing how Schleswig–Holstein had achieved its 'very high percentage' of wind energy – what the policies and incentives were that helped them (M. Zaw-Mon, pers. comm., 29 October 2004). Furthermore, the state was interested in technical and logistical assistance, including siting concerns.

There were also the obvious common areas of mutual learning, such as water management and land management approaches. Schleswig–Holstein was interested in learning about Maryland's Smart Growth initiative. It was not only one of the first links between the two states, but the 2002 delegation highly focused on issues such as land use and sustainable development (Anonymous, pers. comm., 27 April 2005). '[W]e actually talked a lot about Smart Growth . . . urban development, green development and things like that, which they were sort of interested in finding out. That was the part they hadn't really focused too much on' (F. Hoover, pers. comm., 9 March 2005). Schleswig–Holstein officials were particularly interested in learning about economic development (D. Medearis, pers. comm., 5 April

2005). There was a two-way exchange potential because the Smart Growth program was an incentive-based approach while Schleswig–Holstein bases its efforts on 'quite elaborated land use planning' (K. Müller, 2002a). And as Nishida indicated, even though Schleswig–Holstein does not have the population pressures of Maryland – for example, Kiel is not a large city like Baltimore – the Marylanders were interested in knowing what motivated Schleswig–Holstein to 'grow wisely', 'to look at inner-cities as a place you want to bring your families, etc.' (pers. comm., 24 March 2005). But as to where the partnership would lead, the idea was that it eventually would branch out beyond government-to-government learning.

Economic gain
Business was one area to become part of the partnership (J. Mitchell, pers. comm., 1 March 2005; K. Müller, 2002a). In reality, this issue was already very relevant and prominent going into the partnership's formation. Nishida, for instance, informed the Maryland Department of Business and Economic Development (DBED) Secretary that there were business opportunities to be had; he sent a representative from his European office on the delegation (J. Nishida, pers. comm., 24 March 2005).

The most clear economic opportunity known to both states at the time was in wind energy, especially for Schleswig–Holstein. As discussed earlier, wind energy was becoming an important growth industry, bringing in an increasing amount of revenue, providing a growing number of jobs and becoming an increasingly important export product for the state. Thus, the Schleswig–Holstein-based companies that were making wind-power products could have sold them to Maryland-based businesses (J. Mitchell, pers. comm., 1 March 2005). And Maryland was interested in looking at the different suppliers for that type of equipment (M. Zaw-Mon, pers. comm., 29 October 2004). Another possibility under discussion was that one or more of the Schleswig–Holstein-based turbine manufacturers site one of their facilities somewhere on the East Coast if it turned out that a sufficient enough market developed in the eastern part of the United States (F. Hoover, pers. comm., 9 March 2005). If such a market developed in the East for their product, it made more sense for them, due to the size of the components, to make the investment and build a factory in the United States (Maryland in this case) as opposed to building the equipment in Germany and then shipping it over (F. Hoover, pers. comm., 9 March 2005).

The Marylanders were also exploring the economic benefits of the partnership regarding wind energy. At the time, Western Maryland had a powerful Speaker of the House of Delegates, Casper Taylor, Jr

(Democrat), who was interested in wind power. Taylor advocated setting up wind turbines in Western Maryland, for which it has the geography and from which it could economically benefit as it is economically behind the rest of the state (J. Mitchell, pers. comm., 1 March 2005). The state was keen on generating more renewable energy because it was consuming more energy every year. Wind power was seen as both a way to boost the energy generation in the state and a way to generate economic development in Western Maryland (J. Mitchell, pers. comm., 1 March 2005). Maryland also had two solar and wind energy businesses that were interested in wind and solar power, one of them in Western Maryland (J. Nishida, pers. comm., 24 March 2005). DBED, the Maryland Energy Administration and the MDE were working together to try to bring wind power to that area (J. Mitchell, pers. comm., 1 March 2005).

Addressing international issues (and lack of US federal policies)
Whereas certain international issues, such as sustainable development and climate change, certainly were indirect drivers of such policies (or policy ideas) in Maryland and Schleswig–Holstein that contributed to the motivation to collaborate, the deliberate addressing of these issues also served as a partnership objective, both officially and unofficially. The MoU states that the two states wished to promote 'sustainable development' and reduce 'greenhouse gases', in line with the international agenda. Some officials became especially moved to address the matter because of the US government's rejection of it.

Officials in Maryland believed that they might be able to indirectly influence Washington because of the proximity of the state to the US capital. Many government officials and people employed in Washington, DC, live in Maryland or Virginia; and some federal agencies and many Washington lobby organizations and NGOs are housed in these two states. As former Maryland Energy Administration Director, Fred Hoover, Jr, explained:

> If we did something in Maryland on this front and it got any kind of press coverage, then the various federal officials and congressional types actually read about it, because it was in their local newspapers. So a lot of times our thought would be, and we were encouraged to think this, that if we could . . . do some of these things, and demonstrate that they actually worked, that they might have some national import. (pers. comm., 9 March 2005)

Maryland also saw its efforts in renewable energy and sustainable development with Schleswig–Holstein as a way to address another issue where the federal government had not made adequate steps forward – rising oil dependency, despite this being a consistently voiced concern of the federal government (J. Nishida, pers. comm., 24 March 2005).

Primary Supporting Factors – the Foundational Pillars

Outside actors and institutions

The role of outside entities that created the foundational pillars upon which the partnership was built was crucial. First, those supporting the transatlantic exchange among three German and three US states, which included Medearis of the EPA, Green Party-affiliated Bütikofer and the Heinrich Böll Foundation, and the CCAP (utilizing funds from the EPA and German Marshall Fund) (in addition to Nishida), were indispensable. Second, in the MDE's cooperation with Thailand, the CSG (utilizing funds from the federal US Asia Environmental Partnership) was key. And third, in the formation of the partnership itself, the Heinrich Böll Foundation was of central importance.

In his capacity at the EPA, Medearis coordinates the agency's international urban environmental programs on how US cities and states can learn from Organisation for Economic Co-operation and Development (OECD) member countries about sustainable land use, urban watershed management, 'green' buildings, brownfield sites, transportation and smart growth policies. Medearis had first-hand experience working in Germany and in Schleswig–Holstein, and was an entrepreneur when it comes to subnational lesson-learning:

> There's this paradigm in the US that says basically that international work is conducted either in a technical assistance context – that is we export knowledge and technologies to developing countries because we have the answers, or it is national level issues, where climate change predominates all other issues. But everyone has lost sight of the fact that these very vigorous subnational partnerships that are taking place that influence mobility, 'green' housing, 'green' design, have just as much an influence on climate change, long range transboundary air pollution or other 'national' types of issues. (D. Medearis, pers. comm., 16 September 2004)

Medearis was working from within an institution of the federal government: the EPA. This means that as much as his efforts were personal and entrepreneurial, the institution of the federal government made that possible. Medearis also had a personal connection to Schleswig–Holstein, since his grandmother is from there; and with Maryland, since it is connected to greater Washington, DC, where he works.

The CSG and the CCAP are state transfer and learning institutions. The CCAP was even founded by a collection of governors who were on an exchange program in Germany to look at issues of acid rain, under the auspices of the National Governors Association. 'The motivation for CCAP was to cross-pollinate the policy ideas around sustainable development' (S. Gander, pers. comm., 25 May 2006). For its part, the Böll Foundation agreed to fund the program because it wanted to find out if the environmental approaches of the Green Party in Europe, which is based on a concept of regionalism – on the concept of the region as a political entity – also applied to the United States (S. Müller-Kraenner, pers. comm., 27 October 2004).

Entrepreneurs, networking, ideology, timing, bureaucrats and personal contact

As shown in the process leading to the partnership, these institutions contained policy entrepreneurs, who were the core behind the partnership. And as policy entrepreneurs do, they utilized their connections and networked to bring Nishida and K. Müller together knowing the political ideology of the two was a good match, making this another factor to the partnership's formation. But having similarly minded leaders at the helm with the right combination of connections also implies that timing was a factor. Nishida found this to be the case: 'Timing was definitely a factor with regards to the first component in terms of the leadership component – having the right advocates to move this forward' (pers. comm., 24 March 2005).

After Nishida and K. Müller agreed to pursue the partnership, there were bureaucrats that were key players who worked to make it happen. In this case, the importance of Mitchell and Eberhardt also should not be underestimated. As an anonymous source explained, while Nishida and Müller gave the major political impulse in initiating the partnership, the question of its concrete design was based very much on the administrative workforce (pers. comm., 27 April 2005). Mitchell and Eberhardt 'kept quite close contact and tried to elaborate an action plan and things like that. So that was not influenced too much anymore by the politicians; but they, of course, supported and approved it' (Anonymous, pers. comm., 27 April 2005). Moreover, Mitchell carried the partnership over to a new secretary after Nishida left office.

Finally, all of the personal contact and networking that occurred behind the scenes also helped to solidify the partnership (Anonymous, pers. comm., 27 April 2005). An anonymous source said that interest grew with personal contact (pers. comm., 27 April 2005). It is this type of personal contact that is arguably the most crucial for such a partnership, particularly face-to-face contact. According to Mitchell, such meetings are absolutely essential for the success of international partnerships (see below) (pers. comm., 1 March 2005).

IMPLEMENTATION AND GENERAL RESULTS

Planned and Unplanned Developments

The one and only trip that Maryland took to Schleswig–Holstein was for the MoU signing. That trip, however, served not only as a signing ceremony, but also as the first exchange between the partners. The Maryland delegation had a full agenda during their two-and-a-half-day stay. In addition to attending conferences, the partners took excursions to places such as the Wadden Sea, which included an information center, and to the town of Eckernförde, which highlighted sustainable land-use planning at the community level. They were also shown specific energy-related places of interest including a zero-energy house and a biomass incineration plant. And, not least importantly, the delegates visited many wind parks and a company that produces wind generators (Anonymous, pers. comm., 25 October 2004).

For the delegates, the trip 'confirmed, enhanced, [and] encouraged' the delegates' beliefs in terms of the policies they were pursuing (F. Hoover, pers. comm., 9 March 2005). This seemed to be particularly so regarding wind and renewable energy. On the most basic level, the Marylanders were encouraged to continue forward on their trajectory of deploying wind turbines (F. Hoover, pers. comm., 9 March 2005). Beyond that, Hoover, who engaged in the policy discussions during the delegation – including the tax incentive discussions (M. Zaw-Mon, pers. comm., 29 October 2004) – said that the trip gave him 'some ideas and concepts on how to enhance development of wind generation throughout the state' (pers. comm., 9 March 2005). Zaw-Mon added that the delegates gained a lot of information that they passed on to DBED to use in its determinations of what energy sources might be fruitful for Maryland (pers. comm., 29 October 2004).

There were also some immediate liaison activities in the business sector (wind energy), but they did not result in concrete company-to-company cooperation (Anonymous, pers. comm., 25 October 2004). These activities did not reach a stage where they were publically announced. Thus, further information was unobtainable.

Another exchange occurred immediately after the Maryland delegation: Minister Müller traveled to Maryland (among other states) to learn more about the state and its policies (MUNF, 2002). Müller opened a cabinet meeting discussing the Chesapeake Bay and gathered information from various departments, the Chesapeake Bay Foundation and the environmental police regarding their work on water protection. The minister also sought information on new energies and national park management (MUNF, 2002).

Even though the partnership started off in a successful manner – from the efforts to form the partnership, to the MoU signing, to the initial implementation – activities were stopped shortly thereafter because of external circumstances. In November 2002, just four months after the signing, Maryland's residents elected the first Republican governor, Robert Ehrlich, Jr, in 31 years. Most of the MDE's staff who had any knowledge or involvement in the partnership either had to leave because they were politically appointed, or were forced out. Mitchell, the primary non-politically appointed partnership driver, was also let go (J. Mitchell, pers. comm., 1 March 2005). The election was also momentous in that the powerful, long-term Speaker of the House, Taylor, who was engaged in utility deregulation and an ardent supporter of wind power in Western Maryland, lost his seat. Coincidentally Medearis, the driver from the federal government, also lost funding for his position at that time and was no longer available to promote the partnership. To make matters worse, there was a delay in the appointment of a new environmental secretary – it took one and a half years.

Officials in Schleswig–Holstein, and Medearis, who by then was back in his previous position at the EPA, made efforts to re-establish the partnership (Anonymous, pers. comm., 25 October 2004). The foundation and common ground that had been worked out would have to be re-established. The trust and rapport that had been built from having worked together, and met personally, would have to be redeveloped. Eberhardt's new counterpart became Tracy Gingher. But Gingher indicated that since the partnership was only a fraction of her responsibilities, she was not able to dedicate a lot of time to it; this signifies that the administration had not allotted top priority or even a significant priority to it. Nonetheless, both sides agreed to put information about the partnership on their websites, and that that would be a primary means to share information about best practices (Anonymous, pers. comm., 27 April 2005; MDE, n.d.). Within the posted information, both states referred to one another as one of the international partners they have. Moreover, they both created a link with a brief partnership description. Furthermore, Maryland posted an article about water management in Schleswig–Holstein, while Schleswig–Holstein posted two articles about Maryland: one on the Bay Restoration Fund and one on Priority Places, which is a Smart Growth initiative.

In April 2005, Schleswig–Holstein formed a new government. The Greens were out of the governing coalition. The minister assigned to replace K. Müller, Dr Christian von Boetticher, was a member of the conservative CDU party. Although this meant that Schleswig–Holstein's key player in the creation of the partnership was gone, it was thought that with ideologically similar political parties at the helm of both states again, this might strengthen the mutual interest of the partnership and maybe rekindle it.

In 2006, some life was breathed back into the partnership, as Eberhardt made some proactive efforts with some new initiatives (D. Scheelje, pers. comm., 22 September 2008). The MDE and MUNF decided to concentrate the partnership on renewable energy. Within this frame, the priority became wind energy because of Schleswig–Holstein's great capacity in this area – that is, all the segments involved in the production of wind energy: the scientists, the producers, the planners. Likewise, renewable energy in Maryland is rapidly growing (D. Scheelje, pers. comm., 22 September 2008). Representatives from various agencies and ministries such as environmental, energy, agricultural and economic, met via videoconference to discuss the opportunities including fostering research and development, economic incentives for renewable energies and siting issues (MDE, n.d.). The two parties agreed to develop a plan and to search for other areas of cooperation. They also agreed to conduct (and later conducted) a video conference to exchange information on land-use practices and Smart Growth principles (D. Scheelje, pers. comm., 22 September 2008; MDE, n.d.).

In November 2006, Martin O'Malley brought the state back into the hands of a Democratic administration. Shari Wilson, who was familiar with the partnership, quickly became the next MDE secretary. But even with the expectation that the new administration's political agenda would be a better match to Schleswig–Holstein's regarding the partnership's aims, and that it would be progressive and active on renewable energies, in reality there was precious little time for anything (D. Scheelje, pers. comm., 22 September 2008).

On the other side of the Atlantic, there was also a change of personnel concerning the partnership. In early 2008, the primary responsibility was given to Dirk Scheelje as Eberhardt began working on new tasks (D. Scheelje, pers. comm., 22 September 2008). By then, officials in Schleswig–Holstein had come to understand that a partnership only works if there are concrete and financed projects in which people can travel and meet each other. Scheelje pointed out that the videoconferences, albeit an interesting exchange of information, did not yield a concrete effect (nor was a plan thereafter created). He added that only passing information from one side to the other is not a sustainable activity for a partnership (pers. comm., 22 September 2008). Scheelje's goal became to find some real concrete projects to propose to Maryland.

One idea was to have a specific university exchange of climate change scientists. This idea came from a meeting between scientists from the two states who expressed such an interest. Scheelje also considered wind energy because of Schleswig–Holsteins' high competence and North America's growing market in this area. In this respect, some possible approaches included Schleswig–Holstein-based businesses that are interested in building up factories there, or agencies that want to plan wind parks (pers. comm., 22 September 2008).

Scheelje also planned to seek assistance on finding a solid project idea. Scheelje planned to contact Hamburg-based GADORE, the German–American Dialog on Renewable Energy, to get assistance from this organization on ideas for projects (D. Scheelje, pers. comm., 22 September 2008). According to GADORE's website, the organization is for all sectors of society and works to provide opportunities in renewable energy, help initiate US–German partnerships and assist in joint transatlantic projects on renewable energy. The organization organizes workshops, meetings and conferences to bring people together and to start projects (D. Scheelje, pers. comm., 22 September 2008). This was useful not only because GADORE has 'very good contacts in North America' (in the sense that if this organization does not know of a way to start a project between Maryland and Schleswig–Holstein in renewable energy, then no one would), but also because Scheelje himself has little time to dedicate to the partnership (D. Scheelje, pers. comm., 22 September 2008).

In the interim, Scheelje planned to attend a conference held by the German Federal Foreign Office and the Federal Ministry for the Environment entitled 'Entering a New Era of Transatlantic Climate and Energy Cooperation'. At the conference, which was created to include all societal sectors, those involved in transatlantic exchanges, such as representatives from the states of Virginia and Wisconsin, the German Marshall Fund and the Heinrich Böll Foundation, the German federal government, the German Green Party (Bütikofer), among others, were on the agenda to speak. Scheelje planned to do some networking there and speak to, among others, representatives of GADORE (D. Scheelje, pers. comm., 22 September 2008).

Scheelje planned to contact Maryland (he had already talked briefly a couple of times to Medearis) when he had a concrete project idea to propose (D. Scheelje, pers. comm., 22 September 2008). If there were a tangible plan, he said, there would be funding from the EU and the German Foreign Ministry, the German Marshall Fund and businesses that they might be able to procure. But that was only a future potential. In measuring the results of the partnership until 2008, one could not say that the partnership was really working (D. Scheelje, pers. comm., 22 September 2008). Data could not be obtained as to how these efforts unfolded.

Reasons for Lack of Success

Earlier on it was concluded that the partnership's lack of implementation success was the result of Maryland's 2002 elections. It was also inferred that the slowdown was because the political ideology of the new Maryland administration did not match up any more with that in Schleswig–Holstein. Both of these reasons (although the latter was only conjecture) are only a part of the story. Upon the passing of time and further examination, deeper problems became apparent; there were some fundamental flaws in the overall planning and structural set-up of the partnership.

The first problem was that the partnership did not have a deeper institutional foundation, beyond the formal document. Policy entrepreneurs were responsible for the creation of the partnership. In addition to the agents in the executive branch of Maryland and a governmental ministry in Schleswig–Holstein, it was created by actors from the EPA, and the Green Party of Germany. After that, in the more obvious case of Maryland, no institutionalized program was created, which left it dependent on the key players. So after all of the actors left their posts, only a remnant of the partnership remained. It is clear why Nishida did not try to get a program created through the legislature or through discretionary funding: because the state apparatus, outside of the executive branch, was not really interested in promoting these types of activities. It can be speculated that the leaders believed it would be informally institutionalized with time, or that they planned to set something up but had not had a chance to do so. But even then, the MDE still did not have a plan for funding (at least by the time the players left) except for possibly looking for grant money as indicated in the MoU.

Although it originally appeared that this lack of institutionalization had only to do with Maryland because of the dramatic consequences post-elections, the same holds true for Schleswig–Holstein. Even though MUNF has a department for international affairs (and climate change), there is really no concrete institutionalization (D. Scheelje, pers. comm., 22 September 2008). There is no person solely responsible for the partnership, nor are there specific funds for it. 'We have very, very little resources here' (D. Scheelje, pers. comm., 22 September 2008). This was one of the reasons why Scheelje, who was only able to spend a very small fraction of his time on the partnership, decided to take the small amount of resources and see if GADORE might provide the needed assistance.

According to Müller-Kraenner of the Böll Foundation, once a partnership is in force, the states have to be able to support it themselves. Seed or additional money can always be found, but whether the partners themselves pay indicates how serious they are and whether it is something they 'really want to do':

[M]y experience is that if you want to have information you can go on the Internet and get it anyway. What you need is the personal contact; the personal contact is visits and it's not only visits of minister meets minister but its practitioners meeting other practitioners, visiting projects, visiting sites, building relationships, business relationships, that kind of thing. And that costs a little bit of money and it needs someone to coordinate it. Either you commit to it or you don't. (S. Müller-Kraenner, pers. comm., October 27, 2004)

Even though some recent efforts are being made by Schleswig–Holstein, the lack of institutionalization indicates that the partnership was not given enough priority on either side beyond that of certain people. Scheelje believes it has to take some precedence or it ultimately will not work out (pers. comm., 22 September 2008). He points out that in these circumstances it is hard to make it a priority in day-to-day reality, where other issues arise and are main concerns. One will never know what would have happened had the original actors still been involved.

In addition to this structural flaw, there was also a mistake in the planning. The partners did not create a viable implementation plan to carry out the partnership. This means that the partnership remained more on the 'declaration level', and lacked 'real projects' (D. Scheelje, pers. comm., 22 September 2008). 'If you have a partnership without real projects, it's only on the level of talking' (D. Scheelje, pers. comm., 22 September 2008). Working on a common project brings 'spirit' to a partnership, according to Scheelje, as opposed to only exchanging information, in which the partnership does not grow. Moreover, when there is a concrete plan, then it is possible to get the full ministerial support and a delegation can travel to Maryland. It is not enough to ask the minister to go to Maryland and 'let's see what happens there' (D. Scheelje, pers. comm., 22 September 2008); 'But that's much work'. The bottom line is that the partnership has to move beyond personal interest into producing concrete values and results (D. Scheelje, pers. comm., 22 September 2008). And, as discussed, once there is a concrete idea, then that helps to pinpoint what type of funding is needed, and how to obtain it.

Next to having concrete funded projects so delegates can travel and meet each other is the fact that face-to-face meetings alone are invaluable for such collaboration. According to Mitchell, Müller-Kraenner, and others, as discussed above, any plan has to be coupled with face-to-face meetings (which, again, costs money). And since there were essentially no more meetings in person after the main delegation, this made the situation even worse. Mitchell, who now works in international projects at the

EPA, says that not only is it important in these international partnerships to meet face to face, but they are not possible without meeting, without traveling (pers. comm., 1 March 2005). Naturally, a great deal of work occurs in between meetings. But if an agenda is laid out and another meeting is scheduled, the work will get completed because of the pressures of having to meet again; 'face-to-face meetings drive action' (J. Mitchell, pers. comm., 1 March 2005):

> If you're going to have an international . . . or any type of partnership, you have to meet periodically. It doesn't have to be three or four times a year, but it has to be at least once a year . . . People, and again it doesn't have to be the leaders, but people have to meet, because otherwise it will fall off the radar screen. Because the things that are the most vibrant are when people are meeting. And if you're not meeting face-to-face, over time it will just lose its vibrancy. (J. Mitchell, pers. comm., 1 March 2005)

Circumstances, Timing, Political Orientation and Special Persons

If the MDE heads were banking on informal institutionalization over time, then circumstances and timing were relevant in a couple of ways. The types of leaders serving at the same time played a role. The time when Maryland elected a new governor also was instrumental in the stagnation of the partnership. Had the previous administration and all of the key players remained in place, there is a chance, based on the fact that the agency has another long-running partnership, that it would have continued in the same productive manner that it had up until that point. Sec. Nishida believed this to be true: 'Frankly, my belief is that if I had stayed on a little longer and if there weren't a change of administration this initiative would still be alive though maybe a little bit weaker but still have some format' (pers. comm., 24 March 2005).

One way in which this might have been prevented would have been if Mitchell, the non-politically appointed driver, remained in his position. The same holds true for Medearis having been transferred at that crucial time. Mitchell sums the issue of timing up well: 'It was interesting how it all came together and how it all went away so quickly' (pers. comm., 1 March 2005).

ANALYSIS

The idea for and the formation of the 2002 Maryland–Schleswig–Holstein partnership was the result of policy entrepreneurs and their networking. These were entrepreneurs who were not only on the cutting edge of thinking when it came to addressing their own regional environmental problems, but who also saw these solutions in a more multidimensional global context. Correspondingly, the creation of the partnership itself is representative of governance for sustainable development in a multi-level international system (along the lines of Type II multi-level governance). This is apparent, not least, when looking at the subnational (political and non-political), federal and non-governmental actors that were essential to the partnership's creation. Thus, factors such as the agents' networking, and consequently timing – characteristics of policy entrepreneurs – were important. Personal contact also contributed to furthering the interest. Additional or secondary actors and institutions that were not directly involved in the partnership but that provided foundational support also included state, NGO and federal entities.

There were several objectives for this partnership, some overt, while others were more concealed; and not all of the aims were from the state-based actors. The most explicit goal was mutual lesson-drawing, both in specific areas and in general ones. Thus, the partnership required policy entrepreneurs that were specifically interested in policy learning or diffusion. Another aim was to gain economically, to find areas in which to do business. Possibly the primary aim of the partners, albeit less apparent on the surface, was a combination of these two goals, specifically in wind energy. The idea was that Maryland could learn from Schleswig–Holstein in wind energy policy and deployment, while Schleswig–Holstein-based businesses could take advantage of the business opportunities (which would also help Maryland economically).

While these objectives were driven by an understanding by the partnership agents that the two states had a similar geography, like-minded leadership and goals, and complementary innovative policies, they were also influenced by a multi-level global dimension. We see that not only were the agents operating from their own subjective desires to do so (bounded rationality) but they were also responding to multi-level coercive elements. In this structural context voluntary lesson-drawing can be seen as driven by ideational competition on types of policies that are encouraged by the UNCED, the United Nations Framework Convention on Climate Change (UNFCCC) and the multi-level (and multi-sector) transnational advocacy network that was interested in promoting such policies. This was portrayed in the common motivations, such as 'conserving energy', 'reducing greenhouse gases', 'preserving ecosystems' and 'promoting sustainable economic development', and in the interests in innovative policies and technologies in biomass, 'green' buildings, wind energy and Maryland's innovative Smart Growth and Chesapeake Bay programs. There was also a drive because of lack of climate change action from the US federal government.

Furthermore, for Maryland, this ideational drive and thus urge to form the partnership also stemmed from the globalization of communications. Because of the high volume of international attention Maryland received for its Smart Growth and Chesapeake Bay Program projects, this structural factor contributed to its then budding interest in international partnerships (which led it to Schleswig–Holstein) as it clued it into the value of joint international learning and to the realization of its role as a key environmental protection policy actor in a multi-level system. For its part, Schleswig–Holstein may have been driven by ecological modernization, specifically regarding its wind energy industry, which resulted in part from state and federal climate change laws that were aiming to fulfill international obligations under the Kyoto Protocol.

Thus, there is a multi-level component from the international to the subnational level, and likewise, horizontally on a transnational level from subnation to subnation. The vertical dimension includes in part the federal level – particularly for Schleswig–Holstein, which utilized federal policies and programs to its economic advantage for wind energy. The lack of federal activity in climate change was, in part, inspiration for Schleswig–Holstein; and for Maryland, which was trying to pursue climate change policies despite the federal stance. That said, the state was utilizing federal policies to help in these aims (such as energy deregulation). In the instances of the two states' innovative programs this indicates, in any case, their going beyond the federal-level policies and programs. Moreover, there is an element of superseding the federal level in climate change, as the two respective federal governments were at odds in this area.

But while this multi-level, cross-jurisdictional diversity was a major factor for the successful formation of the partnership, it was a problem when it came to implementation. This Type II multi-level governance (MLG) made the partnership too dependent on people (including several outside actors who were not involved after the formation) and not enough on the state as an institutionalized funded program. This speaks to the notion that while a policy entrepreneur can initiate a partnership, they will have difficulty sustaining it without formal institutionalization, beyond the MoU. This means that, again, factors such as timing were crucial for the implementation; and as the key players left office, the partnership essentially ground to a halt. Hence, the absence of the policy entrepreneurs in the implementation stage negatively impacted the partnership. While it is uncertain whether it is still alive, it was by the end of the decade because one key bureaucratic player remained in place. Seen as hindering its revival to that point was that there was no personal rapport – there had not been any face-to-face meetings to build that. But this lack of contact had a lot to do with an absence of funding, and that the partnership remained too vague, instead of something with concrete projects.

NOTES

1. Defined as 'relevant actors working internationally on an issue, who are bound together by shared values, a common discourse and dense exchanges of information and services' (Betsill and Bulkeley, 2004, p. 474).
2. The funds that the CCAP provided for the program came from the EPA and the German Marshall Fund (S. Gander, pers. comm., 25 May 2006).
3. The trip probably could not have not taken place – at least not initially – without the funding from the Heinrich Böll Foundation (M. Zaw-Mon, pers. comm., 29 October 2004). Or it would have been a much smaller group (S. Müller-Kraenner, pers. comm., 27 October 2004).

8.   California and North Rhine–Westphalia (2004)

THE MEMORANDUM

On 17 November 2004, in Sacramento, the Chairman of the California Air Resources Board (CARB), Dr Alan Lloyd, and the Minister of the Ministry of Transport, Energy and Spatial Planning of North Rhine–Westphalia (NRW),[1] Dr Axel Horstmann, signed a Memorandum of Understanding (MoU) to 'help accelerate the development of hydrogen and fuel cells [technology worldwide] and foster greater links between NRW and California' (CARB and MESP, 2004). The agreement's mechanisms included: 'networking; information exchange and establishment of partnerships between the parties; research and science collaboration; consistent codes and standards; demonstration of fuel cell and hydrogen technologies; and education of . . . respective public and business on the benefits of hydrogen and fuel cells' (CARB and MESP, 2004).

The rationale for this match-up was that both states have high-level aims regarding hydrogen and fuel cells. Moreover, both are leaders in the development and advancement of this technology: California is a 'leading contributor to the international progress of hydrogen and fuel cells' and NRW 'is a well-known location' for such technologies in Europe. The drive to be such leaders was because it would result in potential environmental, economic, security and societal benefits, including 'a sustainable economic development and the creation of export markets for hydrogen and fuel cell technologies, an increasing independence of fossil fuels, cleaner air, lower health care costs, reduced GHGs [greenhouse gases] as well as a sustainable development' (CARB and MESP, 2004).

While the partners do not state how to implement and assess the partnership and their progress, they do state that it is to be financed by the two agencies within the 'available budget' (CARB and MESP, 2004). While this is vague, it clarifies that the funding would come from governmental as opposed to outside sources. The rest of the information – the objectives, mechanisms and reasons – appears straightforward.

THE DRIVING FORCES

China, India, Energy and Environmental Protection

The rise of global environmental issues and corresponding corrective approaches have become intertwined with other situative factors, such as the rapid rise of China and India as economic powers. The growth of these countries signifies their increasing need for energy and their mounting consumption of natural resources – developments that contribute to worldwide environmental degradation. According to the US Energy Information Administration (EIA), worldwide energy consumption is expected to increase 53 percent from 2008 to 2035 (US EIA, 2011). Within that projection, the energy demand of non-Organisation for Economic Co-operation and Development (OECD) countries is estimated to grow by 85 percent, mostly due to China and India, while the demand from OECD states is anticipated to increase 18 percent (US EIA, 2011).

Energy Demand, Peak Oil and National Security

The growth in energy demand implies not only further environmental degradation but also increasingly insecure energy supplies and issues of national security as many countries become more dependent on those rich in oil and natural gas. This development is compounded by fears of an upcoming peak in oil supply. Tensions are already playing out as a result of this dynamic. In a study designed to examine this issue, the authors pointed out that '[m]ajor energy suppliers – from Russia to Iran to Venezuela – have been increasingly able and willing to use their energy resources to pursue their strategic and political objectives' (Deutch et al., 2006, p. 3).

Competition for the Clean Energy Market

Consequently, the door has been opened wider for a clean energy market. And policies to promote this type of energy have also dramatically multiplied since around the turn of the century (REN21, 2005). In 2004, global investment in renewable energy set a record at $30 billion. By 2010, another record was reached at $211 billion. As of early 2011, renewables from all sources comprised about one-quarter of the global power capacity (REN21, 2011). At the time of the partnership's formation, the fastest-growing clean energy technology was grid-connected solar photovoltaic, led by Japan, Germany and then the United States, having grown 60 percent annually between 2000 and 2004; the second was wind power, led by Germany, having increased 28 percent per year. From 2005 to 2010, grid-connected solar photovoltaic continued to be the fastest-growing renewable energy technology, holding at 60 percent per year, led by Europe (Germany), followed by Japan and the United States. Biodiesel and wind followed, with wind energy growing 27 percent annually from 2005 to 2010, led by China in 2010, followed by the United States and Germany (REN21, 2011). In looking at all renewable energy capacity, excluding hydro, the United States comes first, followed by China and Germany.

Another competitor vying to meet these demands is the budding hydrogen and fuel cell industry. Tom Cackette, Chief Deputy Executive Officer at CARB, discussed the growingly problematic dependence on oil and the potential role for hydrogen and fuel cells:

> We're in a situation where we're nearly a hundred percent tied to petroleum. We know that our petroleum supply cannot keep up with the worldwide demand. And so, at some point they start diverging and the price goes way up and we have more valuable uses of petroleum than burning it at 12 miles per gallon in an SUV. So, at some point we have to start diversifying into other technologies and I think the question will be whether or not we synthesize petroleum-like fuels from our larger sources of energy like coal and tar sands and things like that or whether we try to make hydrogen from more renewable sources and make it a renewable long-term fuel solution. (pers. comm., 16 November 2005)

Cackette added that one cannot currently predict how the future of energy will unfold. If there are crises, there will most likely be a rush to figure out how to turn coal into petroleum-like products – basically coal to liquids. If there is a little more time, the goal will probably be more like biomass to liquids or to gas, which supports the hydrogen concept. And regarding the actual hydrogen concept, fuel cells are much more efficient compared to hydrogen use in an internal combustion engine or hydrogen burners. 'So, if it's planned out and logically implemented, I think there's a reasonable chance that hydrogen fuel-cell vehicles are what the future is about' (T. Cackette, pers. comm., 16 November 2005).

The European Union (EU) has cited market studies projecting growth between 40 percent and 60 percent in fuel cell-run transportation by around 2012, and that the European fuel cell vehicle market should reach €16.3 billion by 2020 and €52 billion by 2040 (EU, 2002b). The United States listed fuel cells as one of 22 essential technologies for its future economic progress, especially for exporting and national security (EESI, 2000). And, after a long history of development, hydrogen and fuel cell technology has finally become viable in the last decade (Helsinki University of Technology, n.d.; NYSERDA, n.d.).

Multi-Level Advancements of Hydrogen and Fuel Cell Technologies

National, supranational and international

As the push to make hydrogen and fuel cells a feasible commodity emerged, so did activities within the United States and Germany, in both the private and public sectors, and at the EU and international levels. Numerous measures and developments helped pave the way to achieving this end, including the formation of associations in the late 1980s such as the US-based National Hydrogen Association and the German-based World Fuel Cell Council and German Hydrogen Association ('German Hydrogen', 1998; NHA, n.d.; NYSERDA, n.d.; WFCC, n.d.). Throughout the 1990s, significant research and development funds were put forward (NYSERDA, n.d.; 'USA', 1997; US DOE, n.d.; US DOE, 1999). While this type of funding was curtailed in Germany in the mid- to late 1990s, that changed drastically after the 1998 elections as Germany wanted to maintain its strong position in this area ('Future', 1998; Geiger, 2003; 'German Ministry', 1997; 'German Parliament', 2002; US DOE, 1996). Some of this funding went to public–private initiatives in both countries (US DOE and USCAR, 2002; 'Energy Strategy', 1998; 'Germany', 1998; 'US Fuel', 1998). EU, international and transnational efforts mostly dealt with the need for policy and technological convergence (EHA, 2000; EU, 2002a; 'Fuel Cell Standardization', 1998; 'IPHE', 2003; 'Leading', 2003; NYSERDA, n.d.; UNECE, 2001).

As shown, there were multi-level activities or situative factors nationally in the public and non-public sectors on the advancement of hydrogen and fuel cell technologies in the 1990s and early 2000s, the period leading up to the partnership, that were influential on the political climate at the subnational level. There were also very concentrated activities at some subnational levels. Among them, NRW and California have made concerted efforts to be frontrunners in this domain.

Political climate in California

California, as shown in Chapters 4 and 6 in this volume, began adjusting to changes caused by globalization and to the need for a new approach to environmental protection around the early 1990s. Complementary to these efforts, the state embarked upon advancements in climate change, renewable energy and hydrogen and fuel cells (starting in the late 1980s) that have dominated the state's policies and direction ever since and for which it has earned national and/or international frontrunner recognition. While most of these activities are in response to the international and national advancements in these areas, some are also prompted by lack of action, particularly at the national level, and a drive to thrive in these areas. The following delineation of California's activities in these areas portrays what made the state appear as an attractive prospective partner to NRW.

Climate change and renewable energy initiatives
Considering the federal stance on climate change, California's activities since the late 1980s leading up to the partnership were significant. As early as 1988, the state was studying the potential impacts of climate change on the state. This spurred strategies for reducing GHGs and a climate action plan (CEC, 1998; USEPA, 2002). By the turn of the century, some significant governmental action was being undertaken, including: the California Climate Action Registry (CCAP, 2002; 'California Climate'; California Office of the Governor, 2000); the 2003 West Coast Governors' Global Warming Initiative (Pew Center, 2006); litigation against utilities to reduce their carbon dioxide (CO_2) emissions (C2ES, 2004); and arguably most significantly, the reduction of GHG emissions from cars and light trucks manufactured from 2009 onwards, which supersedes federal law, as discussed in Chapter 3 in this volume.

Changes in energy policies in California started a little bit later than those of climate change but were no less monumental. In September 1996, Governor Pete Wilson signed the first electricity industry deregulation legislation, out of which came the Renewable Energy Program (CEC, 2009b) to promote the development of a competitive renewable energy market. The Renewable Resource Trust Fund (1998) was subsequently established to finance the program, which in turn would disburse the payments through market- and performance-based mechanisms directed at both supply and demand. This program is considered to be the impetus for the state's other renewable energy resource developments (ECOS, n.d.-b).

Another milestone for renewable energy was the 2002 Renewable Portfolio Standard (RPS) Program, which required companies selling electricity in the state to increase their use of renewable energy to 20 percent of retail sales by 2017 (later changed to 2010, and 33 percent by 2020), at minimal increments of 1 percent annually, making it the most aggressive RPS in the country (CCAP, 2002; CEC, 2009a; DSIRE, n.d.). Also significant was the 2004 formation of the Clean Energy States Alliance (CESA) (by California and other states with public benefit funds) to promote renewable energy markets throughout the states.[2] A CESA delegation even attended the Renewable Energy Conference in June 2004 in Bonn (see Chapter 3 in this volume). There, a California official cited the increasing clean energy investment activities in the states and 'called upon the international community to work more closely and directly with the states' (Milford et al., 2004, p. 2). This was seen as an articulation of the states' need to 'go beyond' the federal government's concentrations on research and development to promote new means for investment and sister funds in other states and countries.

Hydrogen and fuel cell initiatives
California's advancements on hydrogen and fuel cells began around the same time as those of climate change. In 1990, CARB established the pioneering Low Emission Vehicles (LEV) program, which required far more stringent vehicle emission standards including a small percentage of zero-emission vehicles (ZEV) (Salon et al., 1999). Over the years, the program has been slightly modified mostly due to agreements reached with automobile companies (C2ES, 2003). The ZEV program is thought to have served as a catalyst helping to impel the development of fuel cell technology in the state (UC Davis, 2000).

Around the turn of the century, other major steps in the advancement of hydrogen and fuel cells occurred. CARB and the California Energy Commission teamed up with six companies[3] and formed the California Fuel Cell Partnership (CFCP) to put about 50 fuel cell cars and electric buses on the road between 2000 and 2003 and work on infrastructure issues (CFCP, n.d.; 'California Fuel Cell Partnership', 1999). Similarly, CARB adopted a regulation requiring large transit agencies (with 200 or more buses) that primarily buy diesel buses to begin using at least three zero-emission buses by 2003 (CARB, 2000). And, regarding the afore-mentioned ZEV program, a law established an incentive program for the buying or leasing of such vehicles (CARB, 2008b).

Finally, a monumental step forward in the advancement of the hydrogen economy occurred in April, 2004, through Gov. Schwarzenegger's executive order establishing the California Hydrogen Highway Network. The network would create a public–private partnership to build a Hydrogen Highway in the state by 2010. The initial network would consist of 150–200 hydrogen fueling stations, or about one station every 20 miles on major highways (California Office of the Governor, 2004a).

It can be said, coming full circle, that this Hydrogen Highway initiative emanated from the 1990 ZEV program (T. Cackette, pers. comm., 16 November 2005). Cackette discussed the link between the two programs:

> Our interest in hydrogen fuel cells initially came out of our requirement that there be zero-emission vehicles sold in California. [B]attery vehicles didn't pan out in the 1990s. Instead, fuel cells became the more likely technology because of the high investment by the auto manufacturers. Then Gov. Schwarzenegger became very interested in trying to break the barrier that's there [as to] which comes first, the stations or the cars. [H]e decided to move forward on the hydro-gen highway to put in a beginning network of stations not limited to just fleets,

so that when cars are sold they would have somewhere to fuel. (pers. comm., 16 November 2005)

Technology forcing and diffusion of policies
California's efforts in climate change, renewable energy and hydrogen and fuel cells are considerable compared to those of other states and even countries, including the federal government itself. They demonstrate the state's tendency to be progressive and a frontrunner. The state's tough environmental laws, especially the ones that have been stricter than the federal government's, have historically had great impacts beyond its borders; they have traditionally forced technology and/or diffused to other states and even countries. The classic example is the 1966 tailpipe emission standards, which spurred the diffusion of the catalytic converter. For its part, the 1990 LEV program, which includes ZEV, is also an example of a policy having advanced clean vehicle technologies. Technology forcing is one of the strategies for the establishment of lead markets (Jänicke and Jacob, 2006). And as indicated: 'The millions of hybrid and other clean vehicles on the road today exist, in part, as a result of California's ZEV regulation' (UCS, 2008). It is also an example of one of the programs that attracted NRW to California, as discussed below.

Political climate in NRW – reform

From fossil fuels to renewable energy
NRW has been hit particularly hard by economic and environmental globalization, leaving it in a 'special situation', as its economy has been historically based on heavy industries (A. Ziolek, pers. comm., 12 September 2005). NRW was formerly an industrial center of Europe with its production of coal, steel and chemicals (Höhn and Stolper, 2004; A. Ziolek, pers. comm., 12 September 2005). Particularly impacted has been the state's energy sector, which is the leader in Germany (and Europe) in both energy generation and energy consumption. NRW's long history with energy and energy technologies has been primarily based on coal (its most significant resource), mining and power plant technologies and equipment (EnergieAgentur.NRW, 2007; Höhn and Stolper, 2004; A. Ziolek, pers. comm., 12 September 2005). The breakdown of these industries, resulting in 'hundreds and thousands' of lost jobs, has prompted the state to undergo an extreme 'change in economic structure'; the state found that the solution lay in changing from fossil energies to renewable energies (A. Ziolek, pers. comm., 12 September 2005). Because of these issues (and because of some federal-level incentives and mandates, such as the Renewable Energies Act of 2000; the ecological tax reform; the

abandonment of nuclear energy; and the CO_2 emissions reduction goal), NRW redefined its objectives: (1) 'to make the region number one for future energies'; (2) 'to secure existing jobs and to create new ones'; and (3) 'to save resources and to make progress in climatic and environmental protection' (EnergieAgentur.NRW, n.d.-a). To realize these goals, the state introduced laws complementing those enacted by the federal government, outlined below.

Renewable energy initiatives   One of NRW's first major efforts to achieve these energy, economic and environmental ends was its 1987 REN program,[4] created to 'support the development, demonstration, production and application of technologies for renewable energies and more efficient energy use' (Höhn and Stolper, 2004, p. 44), providing more funds than any other German state (Immisch, 2002). But NRW did not believe that financial help alone would be enough. It held that some structural changes were also needed in which there was more of a 'consultation and networking' dynamic (Höhn and Stolper, 2004, p. 45). In 1996, it created the NRW State Initiative on Future Energies. This initiative brings together all interested experts and stakeholders of future energy technologies and has resulted in about 20 working groups and networks (Höhn and Stolper, 2004). This is a strategy to become a lead market as it provides support to the entire innovation process, from the first stages of research and development, to the promotion and demonstration of the project and the final stages of getting the product onto the mass market (*Facts*, 2005). The initiative also concentrates on: (1) increasing supply and use of renewable energy; (2) promoting energy conservation; and (3) making the primary sources of energy (such as coal) even more efficient (EnergieAgentur. NRW, n.d.-a; Höhn and Stolper, 2004; NRW-Energieministerium).

Hydrogen and fuel cell initiatives   One offspring of the NRW State Initiative on Future Energies was what is now called the Fuel Cell and Hydrogen Network NRW (FCHN) (A. Ziolek, pers. comm., 12 September 2005), established in April 2000 as a public–private partnership. In addition to the state government, more than 300 businesses and research institutes make up the FCHN. The European Union, through its European Regional Development Fund, also contributes funding. The aim of the FCHN is to:

- 'position NRW as an internationally recognized location for the fuel cell and hydrogen technology;
- [introduce] ... the fuel cell into early markets as bridges for the mass market;

- support the development of the fuel cell and of adapted system components accompanied by a targeted basic research; [and]
- support the establishment of a ready-to-market and sustainable hydrogen energy economy'. (EnergieAgentur.NRW, n.d.-b)

While the organization is linked to the state's environmental protection policies, its mandate and thus primary focus is the creation of 'new jobs' (A. Ziolek, pers. comm., 12 September 2005). The FCHN's focus is on small to medium-sized companies because they are the main drivers of the economic development in the state. And within this strategy, the *Land* also believes that it only makes sense if it works in close collaboration with the leading locations all over the world (A. Ziolek, pers. comm., 12 September 2005). This tactic of working with specified countries refers to the second phase in working toward creating a lead market (Jänicke and Jacob, 2006).

International efforts
This outward-looking component is seen as essential for NRW's survival in the globalized economy. NRW sees a new 'global socio-ecological principle': the linking of 'environmental protection and employment in the North with environmental protection and development in the South and East' (Höhn and Stolper, 2004, p. 47):

> The future ... will be characterized by international involvement and the necessity for transnational cooperation. National boundaries will continue to decrease in importance and mutual dependencies will gain in significance. NRW is not only a large industrial state in the middle of Europe, it is also a responsible and reliable international partner. Within its scope of activities, the state government will continue to advance the processes of change necessary for sustainable development. This can be the basis of partnerships for shared development – for mutual benefit and profit. (Höhn and Stolper, 2004, p. 47)

NRW touts its years of experience in partnerships, particularly development projects in countries of the south. The state also has some cooperative energy projects under way within the framework of its Agenda 21 (Höhn and Stolper, 2004). The first partner wind power plant was set up in Belarus. Likewise, a biogas facility has been constructed in a state in India.

Transformations
This once industrial center of Europe now has become defined by the service sector, which contributes two-thirds of the state's gross product. But while a great portion of German-based multinational corporations (MNCs) are located in NRW, small and medium-sized businesses, and young and innovative companies, are most characteristic of the state.

There are about 2000 environmental technology companies, making NRW one of Europe's leaders in this field (Höhn and Stolper, 2004). NRW is also the leader for renewable energy in Germany (A. Ziolek, pers. comm., 12 September 2005) and has a 'top world ranking' (NRW, 2007). In this context, NRW plans to continue to concentrate on 'pushing forward innovation processes . . . preparing the way for cooperative undertakings and strategic alliances and also accelerating the market launch of innovative products on a national and international level' (EnergieAgentur.NRW, n.d.-a).

Pioneering background
That NRW would be a leader in environmental technology and renewable energy is not surprising as it, like California, has both a high level of socio-economic standing and some historical precedent in being an environmental pioneer. Economically, the state accounts for 22 percent of Germany's gross domestic product (Kern, 2008). And in environmental leadership, in 1962, NRW enacted the first air pollution law. It also created the first renewable energy funding program in 1987 (Kern, 2008).

Idea to Form the Partnership

The partnership between California and NRW started at the FCHN within the first year or two after its establishment. Dr Andreas Ziolek, the FCHN's director and not part of the ministry, and the FCHN's ministerial liaison, Dr Achim Dahlen, were the drivers. They believed a partnership with CARB would be 'very much helpful for [the FCHN's] activities' (A. Ziolek, pers. comm., 12 September 2005).

A closer look at CARB and its leadership helps to explain the FCHN's interest in it. CARB, the part of the California Environmental Protection Agency (Cal/EPA) that addresses air pollution, was behind such pioneering efforts as the 1966 auto tailpipe emission standards that forced the catalytic converter technology and more recently the 1990 ZEV standards that played a role in prompting fuel cell technology and the Hydrogen Highway. The CARB chairman at that time, Lloyd, was a renowned figure in the world of vehicle emissions and hydrogen and fuel cells and one of the driving forces behind the zero- and near-zero-emission mandates (ICCT, 2006). In fuel cells, Lloyd had worked in public, private and academic settings to advance and commercialize this technology for which he also has received awards. The former Cal/EPA secretary also served as the first chairman of the CFCP and was a co-founder of the California Stationary Fuel Cell Collaborative. Lloyd was also connected federally as he served on the EPA's Clean Air Act Advisory Committee, the US

Department of Energy Hydrogen Technical Advisory Panel (as chairman) and the National Research Council Transportation Research Boards' Committee on Alternative Transportation (Cal/EPA, 2005b; California Office of the Governor, 2004b).

These types of vehicle emission policies and hydrogen and fuel cell activities have contributed to the worldwide attention that California has received. And California's standing in this field was what attracted NRW to it (A. Ziolek, pers. comm., 12 September 2005). To connect to California, and Lloyd, the FCHN networked through the US Fuel Cell Council and the German-based World Fuel Cell Council (Marcus Nurdin) (A. Ziolek, pers. comm., 12 September 2005).

THE KEY COMPONENTS FROM IDEA TO MOU

Formation of the Partnership

After Lloyd expressed his openness to exploring the potentials between the two states, Ziolek worked on organizing trips to California and developed ideas of how they could collaborate and what the potential topics could be (A. Ziolek, pers. comm., 12 September 2005). The first of several trips was arranged, for a small NRW delegation to go to California in 2002. During these visits NRW presented its activities to CARB and, likewise, learned about CARB. The delegation visited several places and talked to many companies and research institutes to get an overview of the activities in the United States. The two states sought out synergies and potential benefits for both sides, to determine what the basis for collaboration would be. These initial visits and meetings served as an additional motivation for the partnership for NRW, as the state came to believe that California had a 'similar way of thinking' (A. Ziolek, pers. comm., 12 September 2005).

Shortly before the November 2004 delegation, when preparations began for the MoU signing, which entailed discussions determining what both sides would allow in the agreement, Lloyd delegated the task to Cackette to 'make this happen' (T. Cackette, pers. comm., 16 November 2005). He served as a replacement for Lloyd as the point person in California from then on. For the signing in 2004, a large NRW delegation of approximately ten public and ministry-related officials and 15 representatives from companies and research institutes, accompanied Minister Horstmann to Sacramento (A. Dahlen, pers. comm., 25 May 2007; A. Ziolek, pers. comm., 12 September 2005). California also invited some representatives from a few companies and research institutions that it believed might have a future interest in the cooperation (T. Cackette, pers. comm., 16

November 2005). These participants included the National Fuel Cell Research Center of the University of California at Irvine, the CFCP, and energy, oil and automobile companies.

NRW's Objectives

The intent of the partnership portrayed in the MoU is vague. For NRW, there were some deeper and more specific objectives for wanting to collaborate, including the desire: (1) to learn from California; (2) to promote NRW-based fuel cell firms; (3) to achieve diffusion and convergence of the corresponding policies and technologies; and (4) to fight climate change. While all of these motivations are ends in and of themselves, they can also be tied to what is arguably NRW's main reason for wanting to form the partnership with California: for economic gain (as it corresponds to its ecological modernization goals).

Regarding learning, NRW wanted to learn about California's ZEV program: 'The Californian directive to force major companies to develop clean vehicles for hydrogen and fuel cells vehicles is a very good guideline and an excellent example for other regions in the world' (A. Ziolek, pers. comm., 12 September 2005). The FCHN is not interested in directly copying from California per se, but rather in learning from the state, in understanding where the difficulties in daily practice lie. This is not a 'discussion between partners on the same level'; NRW is in a good position to learn from California (A. Ziolek, pers. comm., 12 September 2005).

On the promotion of state-based businesses in the field, several indicators reveal this objective. This was shown by the number of industry and research institution representatives, approximately 15, that accompanied the ministerial officials on the 2004 delegation to California. This point is also made clear through NRW's larger role (as with other subnational governments around the world), particularly economically, in the international arena. Ziolek points this out:

> If you look to the overall activities of the [Economic Affairs and Energy] ministry . . . they have really a huge department for foreign activities. They had several trips all over the world and different technical issues. And the idea behind this is really a commercial approach to show products from NRW to find partners all over the world. (pers. comm., 12 September 2005)

These two goals can be linked back to the purpose of the FCHN, the real driver behind the partnership, to create jobs. And, as one way of doing this is by trying to bring new hydrogen and fuel cell technology onto mass markets, the FCHN attempts to identify early markets with very particular products (A. Ziolek, pers. comm., 12 September 2005). But partners who are interested in the state's products are needed to reach economies of scale. This is why the state is trying to combine markets, trying to create a small mass production, to decrease the cost of the products. It is part of the strategy to have 'close collaboration with the leading locations all over the world' (A. Ziolek, pers. comm., 12 September 2005).

The realization of diffusion and convergence of the corresponding policies and technologies is also linked to the economic goals. With these overarching ecological modernization aims in mind, it is clear why NRW, or the FCHN, also believes that it is important to integrate its activities and strategies into a global approach. This motivation is touched upon in the MoU with regard to the consistent codes and standards. The state acknowledges that it is 'too small to do big things on its own', and that it needs support and collaboration with other like-minded regions (A. Ziolek, pers. comm., 12 September 2005). Ziolek expounded on this point by referring to international regulations:

> If [you] try to have a fuel cell or a hydrogen storage system within an aircraft, an international certification is needed. This cannot be done . . . by simply following an NRW standard. An international approach is needed. . . . [I]f you try to get an international approval, you need a strong alliance to do so, because you have to do lobbying for a longer time. And . . . we are too small. [F]rom my perspective that is one of the most important reasons why we try to find partners on this issue. (pers. comm., 12 September 2005)

Being the frontrunner on an international standard is economically advantageous. That said, this quote implies more than being a frontrunner; it is demonstrative of a policy pusher.

Finally, from the ministerial point of view, the partnership was viewed in larger environmental terms. NRW's press release about the agreement was couched in terms of fighting climate change (EnergieAgentur.NRW, 2004). While the FCHN was working on the technical aspect of the partnership in terms of hydrogen and fuel cells, the ministry itself was advocating both the political angle and, correspondingly, the larger environmental angle.

California's Objectives

If the partnership was not between equals, what were California's motivations for it? Cackette believed that both parties had something to offer (pers. comm., 16 November 2005). The mutual benefits were essentially economic; they were their complementary hydrogen and fuel cell development efforts.

Cackette characterized NRW as much more focused on helping build a strong hydrogen fuel cell-related business environment where companies, particularly small and medium-sized, are able to thrive (pers. comm., 16 November 2005). California was impressed with the number of companies that were active in this area and with the strong government support that is given to help them move forward as a business development and energy issue. The state support of businesses in this field is much less prevalent in California (T. Cackette, pers. comm., 16 November 2005). In contrast, California is focusing on the infrastructure components (which, inadvertently, provides a major source of business). So California may be ahead (or appear so) in organizations such as the CFCP and the Hydrogen Highway and in actually putting vehicles and infrastructure on the road, but NRW has a stronger focus on individual technology companies, which California does not normally see (T. Cackette, pers. comm., 16 November 2005). There were, thus, a couple of possibilities for mutual benefit: (1) that NRW-based companies that have the technology and that wish to participate in California's endeavors could come to the state and take part; and (2) that complementary businesses from each state, in which there were potential synergies, could work together on a project, either in California or NRW, that would contribute to the Hydrogen Highway (T. Cackette, pers. comm., 16 November 2005).

Standardization was also an issue for California. The state has a fairly large emphasis on that through the CFCP, which is discussing the standardization of procedures of nozzles, of safety requirements and the like, for fueling cars and buses (T. Cackette, pers. comm., 16 November 2005). The state is also developing standards for first responders; if there is an accident, the question is what do you do with the hydrogen vehicle and how do you train people on how to cut open a car that has hydrogen tanks if people are still inside it? While there are still areas that probably would remain local issues, such as permits for citing facilities, there are other areas, such as that of codes and standards for the hardware, where there is a lot that can be learned. 'These issues take quite a bit of effort, so they are not something that a state would want to embark upon too many times independently' (T. Cackette, pers. comm., 16 November 2005).

IMPLEMENTATION AND GENERAL RESULTS

Not long after the formalization of the partnership a couple of significant events occurred in both states. One month after the MoU signing, Gov. Schwarzenegger appointed Lloyd as Cal/EPA secretary. Although Cackette had already taken over the primary partnership duties, the implication that Lloyd, the original partnership driver in California, would be even less involved in the partnership, can only have been a loss.

On the other side of the Atlantic, six months after the signing of the agreement, the NRW government became conservative for the first time in 39 years. But despite the new government's eagerness to implement major changes, and despite the changing of the name (and direction) of the Ministry to the Ministry for Economics and Energy, Ziolek was confident that there would not be any major changes to the overall policy regarding hydrogen and fuel cells (pers. comm., 12 September 2005). And by one year after the signing, there had been some bilateral contact between companies. But this was considered confidential information (A. Ziolek, pers. comm., 12 September 2005). This fulfilled one goal of the MoU: the establishment of cooperation between different stakeholders; that is, between businesses, research institutes, and environmental and other private organizations. In addition, both CARB and the FCHN had been in contact with each other and had informed one another about activities, meetings and upcoming events (A. Ziolek, pers. comm., 12 September 2005).

But the overall results to that point were minimal. Both sides acknowledged this and had their ideas on where the hold-up lay. Ziolek pointed to NRW's elections, even though he did not expect them to hinder the partnership, and to California's recall elections, although NRW's delegations from 2002 to 2004 were unhindered by this and despite the fact that the actual elections were completed by October 2003, a year before the signing of the official document. There were election repercussions, such as Lloyd's appointment to Cal/EPA. Ziolek also suggested that California may be less interested in international activities than other states and countries (pers. comm., 12 September 2005).

Cackette hinted at his lack of time to dedicate to the implementation of the partnership and, correspondingly, to the lack of a qualified person that he could hand it to, which was why he inherited the project to begin with (T. Cackette, pers. comm., 16 November 2005). The task of implementing the partnership was just a fraction of Cackette's duties; he had 'a big organization to run' and did not have the time to do 'all the detail work' (pers. comm., 16 November 2005). This issue, however, was part of a larger problem, Cackette believed: the lack of an internal organizational set-up for hydrogen in the state government.

Cackette primarily attributed the slow start to this institutional deficiency: 'These things only succeed if you have identified teams or groups of people to follow-up on' (pers. comm., 16 November 2005). When the document was signed in 2004, the state had more of a 'virtual organization' around hydrogen, not really anything 'centralized' (pers. comm., 16 November 2005). By July 2005, CARB had put together a division with 'a hydrogen focus, such as zero-emission focus, that's got a hydrogen element, to implement the hydrogen highway' (T. Cackette, pers. comm., 16 November 2005). 'And so we now have an organizational unit that we can identify as people that have direct responsibility for helping hydrogen infrastructure develop in California. With that I think we will be able to, at the working level, start having a more meaningful and substantive relationship with NRW.'

In addition to the early lack of organizational structure and Cackette's competing priorities, there was uncertainty because of NRW's change of government. But that cleared up, on both sides, when it quickly became apparent that no significant changes would occur (T. Cackette, pers. comm., 16 November 2005). Moreover, one could argue that the change in government was positive for the partnership as the new NRW Minister President, Jürgen Rüttgers, and Gov. Schwarzenegger knew each other, had a good working relationship and both supported the agreement (A. Ziolek, pers. comm., 20 October 2008). Furthermore, Cackette also shared Ziolek's impression that California is simply less active when it comes to international activities. As discussed, NRW had made about four trips to California prior to and for the signing of the MoU starting in 2002. California, conversely, had not yet reciprocated by 2005 despite a couple of opportunities and invitations (T. Cackette, pers. comm., 16 November 2005). Elaborating on this, Cackette said:

> There were a couple opportunities to do it, but it just didn't fit into our schedules. It's difficult too; I think the US side tends to travel internationally less than . . . the Europe side would. It's just a little harder to jump on a plane and go to some event in Europe than it perhaps is coming the other way. (pers. comm., 16 November 2005)

There was, however, one trip that was planned for Lloyd, but he had to cancel it at the last minute. Nonetheless, Californian delegates had still planned to try to travel to Germany in the future (T. Cackette, pers. comm., 16 November 2005).

Despite these hindrances, and after the formation of the new organization within CARB, the two parties renewed their interest and started to explore opportunities for collaboration (T. Cackette, pers. comm., 16 November 2005). Cackette said that it was important that the information exchange develop into something more meaningful. This comment, however, unveils another reason for the hold-up in the implementation – that there was no concrete project or plan established during the delegations, nor during the MoU drafting and signing. Upon elaboration, a couple of other potential reasons for the difficulties became clear. As Cackette explained:

> In all these kinds of things you got to find something where both parties have a need and . . . are benefiting. If it's just pure information exchange, they don't tend to be very meaningful. We're looking for something we could work on together that would benefit us both . . . [where] we both have a need. (pers. comm., 16 November 2005)

Not only does it appear that there was not a concrete plan, but it did not seem that California saw the benefit for itself in the partnership.

Moreover, Cackette said the partnership could not only be between businesses if it is to succeed (pers. comm., 16 November 2005):

> [T]he other option where they tend not to work is if it just happens to be that the MoU (or the partnership) cements an opportunity . . . between a couple of companies that have common interest . . . that doesn't need the hand holding of government to make that happen. It can't be that, 'gee we created an opportunity here' and they go off and do it on their own. (pers. comm., 16 November 2005)

But if the idea is to co-fund projects with business, Cackette said that the state does not have the money or the structural set-up for that:

> What we don't have is any kind of large pot of money that co-funds activities with businesses. And we don't have a deeper infrastructure within government and university links as I kind of sense NRW does, where there's more of a global plan to try to move something forward. In California, this is much more decentralized. (pers. comm., 16 November 2005)

Over the next couple of years, despite a couple of activities between the partners, neither side believed there had been significant progress (A. Bevan, pers. comm., 23 September 2008; T. Cackette, pers. comm., 23 September 2008; A. Ziolek, pers. comm., 20 October 2008). At some point after the hydrogen organization was established within the agency, Cackette handed the partnership to Analisa Bevan, chief of the Sustainable Transportation Technology Branch in CARB (T. Cackette, pers. comm., 23 September 2008). After that, the bulk of the activity was information exchanges via e-mail, such as announcements of upcoming events (A. Bevan, pers. comm., 23 September 2008; T. Cackette, pers. comm., 23 September 2008).

That said, there was another trip that NRW delegates took to California in 2007 (A. Ziolek, pers. comm., 20 October 2008). Furthermore, there was one trip taken by the successor to Lloyd at CARB, Dr Robert Sawyer, CARB's Executive Officer, Catherine Witherspoon, and Cackette, to NRW, in which the three delegates visited car manufacturers and one of the university sites and met with NRW officials (T. Cackette, pers. comm., 23 September 2008; A. Ziolek, pers. comm., 20 October 2008) (it should be noted that by this time Lloyd was no longer in public office). During that visit, there were discussions of what the next steps could be. NRW officials suggested to develop more of a political connection between the two states (agency to ministry; A. Ziolek, pers. comm., 20 October 2008), to have California legislators visit Germany to see what was going on, to see what some of the business opportunities were that were being developed in advanced transportation technology (T. Cackette, pers. comm., 23 September 2008). But the visit was not really followed up on in terms of any serious progress (T. Cackette, pers. comm., 23 September 2008; A. Ziolek, pers. comm., 20 October 2008).

These later developments provide additional insights into where the implementation problems lay. First, one can eliminate a couple of the original thoughts, as they became no longer applicable. A hydrogen-related division was set up in CARB and Cackette was able to pass the partnership on to the head of that section. Moreover, there was no more doubt concerning NRW's 2005 elections. The remaining beliefs – that there was uncertainty as to the ways to work together, that the Californian elections played a role and that California is less likely to travel internationally – remained over time and were elaborated upon.

Both sides came to see that the partners were a mismatch in organizational aims, approaches and interests (which is why there was uncertainty as to the ways to work together). NRW (the FCHN) is very focused on being a government–industry kind of cooperative that builds business and technology in NRW; its participants have an economic approach – they are looking for economic perspectives to set up a new economy based on hydrogen and fuel cells (T. Cackette, pers. comm., 23 September 2008; A. Ziolek, pers. comm., 20 October 2008). CARB, conversely, develops regulations and forces businesses to come up with hydrogen, or with clean cars, with zero emissions (for which there is a huge, high-priced market for the manufacturers that want to abide by the regulations and sell cars in California) (A. Ziolek, pers. comm., 20 October 2008). It is less focused on the business aspect and more centered on whether this technology can do something for pollution or GHGs; this is not to say that the business component is not considered at CARB, but it is not the agency's top project or objective (T. Cackette, pers. comm., 23 September 2008). As Cackette stated, 'While we share interest in fuel cells and hydrogen technology, our objectives seem to be different, at odds with each other' (pers. comm., 23

September 2008). As Ziolek stated, '[T]he way policy is made in California and NRW is absolutely different; so the mechanism to introduce these kinds of technologies is most different' (pers. comm., 20 October 2008).

Ziolek admits that they did not completely understand this incongruity in approaches when they set up the partnership:

> [W]e are working with industry; we try to set up industry workshops, we try to link industrial development, NRW companies with California companies and this is something CARB is simply not able to do because they are doing regulation from a governmental perspective. They don't have any objective to create a new industry, or they even don't even have the tools to do so, they don't have the budget to support [such] projects. That's a general different approach between the two organizations. (pers. comm., 20 October 2008)

But NRW also simply wanted to learn from California because it was one of the main drivers of the hydrogen and fuel cell technology through its Hydrogen Highway project, which had clear benchmarks for what the state considered to be zero-emission vehicles and the clear technical objectives for fueling stations. NRW believed that there was a lot that it could benefit from in this regard (A. Ziolek, pers. comm., 20 October 2008). But this also changed because of changes in state regulations and thus objectives, which were caused by the difficult political situation in the state: first, the change in administrations after the recall election delayed the time it took to come up with the ambitious targets which, second, ultimately were not agreed to by the state legislature (A. Ziolek, pers. comm., 20 October 2008). This is to say that while it was not the turmoil of the elections themselves, it was certain subtle changes afterwards that had detrimental effects.

Cackette indicated that it was not completely clear at the beginning what the intent of the partnership was, nor was there a complete understanding of where the partnership might go (pers. comm., 23 September 2008). Moreover, the Californians have found that if there is real symmetry, then really no formal agreement is needed anyway. The partners had tried earlier to scope out whether it made sense to do demonstrations of certain cars or fuel cell-like vehicles, for instance fork lifts, in both states; seeing demonstrations done in a different way would be complementary (that would foster the development of technology producers and first-tier suppliers for hydrogen technologies), but these ideas never took off. Cackette explained that these activities are happening at various levels, they do not seem to depend on a US–German partnership to make them happen; and the reason that they are happening is because either somebody thinks there is a market for them or companies want to demonstrate their project and are able to depend on some (closer) local or federal government or other businesses or interests to partner with. In other words, NRW is not needed for objectives in California to be achieved (pers. comm., 23 September 2008).

Besides the fundamental differences in objectives, Cackette believes that there are also some major disparities in how a US state government views the world outside of its federal borders compared to how a European subnational-level government (or smaller country) does. While groups of people frequently come to California to do fact-finding, fact-gathering, investigative type of work, it does not seem to occur very easily in the reverse (T. Cackette, pers. comm., 23 September 2008). Cackette explained that smaller European countries have had to deal more with other countries and understand how they work to succeed. Accordingly, NRW and their affiliated officials seem to have the ability and much more freedom to fund and take on international activities. Conversely, for states like California, there has not been the historic protocol of going abroad – the concentration has mostly been within the state itself. It is not easy to get funding to leave the country. Cackette said, '[T]o go to a foreign country in California you have to go write pages and beg and plead your case to be able to fly out of the country. It's not treated like a normal thing' (pers. comm., 23 September 2008). Accordingly, the budget issue is a reflection of the fact that it is not a high priority, other than at the very top level (T. Cackette, pers. comm., 23 September 2008).

While it may be true that regions like NRW are more internationally oriented – the FCHN has state funding for international collaboration, for traveling, for workshops, for international relations in general – officials in NRW have come to find over time, from all of their international collaborations, that even this is not sufficient funding to run their international collaborations well (A. Ziolek, pers. comm., 20 October 2008). Ziolek believes that for such partnerships there should at least be €500000 available for each per year; there should be a concrete budget for these kinds of endeavors; this would make a difference on the results (pers. comm., 20 October 2008):

> From today's perspective, what would be a recommendation, even if it's difficult to realize, is that before you sign an MoU, you should allocate a budget for the collaboration. And before you are [spending time] to come up with concrete additions or projects or collaboration, you should be sure that you are able to finance this collaboration. This really caused a lot of frustration if people spend work to set up a proposal and working on a project, on a common project, and at the end the government says sorry guys, it's a good idea, but we don't have the money to pay for it. (A. Ziolek, pers. comm., 20 October 2008)

In sum, in order for the partnership to be rekindled, something of 'very common interest', and in which there were mutual benefits, would have to arise (T. Cackette, pers. comm., 23 September 2008). In addition, it would have to be a concrete project (A. Bevan, pers. comm., 23 September 2008); it could not subsist on an information exchange alone. 'Nobody has the energy just to have a meeting every once and awhile and exchange some information. There has got to be something concrete' (T. Cackette, pers. comm., 23 September 2008). And regarding information exchanges, a formal agreement is not necessary for that either; it happens naturally by meeting people with similar interests at conferences; that is, the normal networking of people in the same field (A. Bevan, pers. comm., 23 September 2008).

The California officials admit that they had not brought enough to the table and that it is 'too hard to get us motivated' (T. Cackette, pers. comm., 23 September 2008). And if this is true, Cackette believes the NRW officials may not think, in turn, that they can get something beneficial from California (pers. comm., 23 September 2008). Either that or they themselves have not found an obvious project to propose.

Despite the realizations that the collaboration was not working out, it still lingered on for a while. As stated, NRW planned on attempting more of a ministry-to-agency perspective and so officials in the state planned to travel once again to California to prepare this (A. Ziolek, pers. comm., 20 October 2008). The German state also hoped to initiate some additional activities on the topic of hydrogen and fuel cells. Moreover, in hosting the 18th World Hydrogen Energy Conference in May 2010, NRW planned to invite Schwarzenegger, who had connections to the NRW minister-president, which was expected to provide an opportune forum for possible future activities between the states. NRW wanted to look at different approaches to the California government. Furthermore, NRW set up an international organization called the International Partnership for the Hydrogen Economy, in which both Germany and the United States are members as well as different subnations. Finally, NRW and its Canadian colleagues were planning to set up an international hydrogen highway project that it was believed might be another area in which California may participate (A. Ziolek, pers. comm., 20 October 2008).

There may have been one other hindrance to the partnership's implementation: the loss of Lloyd. Lloyd was the original driver of the partnership and it can therefore be assumed that he saw a benefit in it. Otherwise, this would imply that the dozens of people involved in the formation of the partnership (in the delegations), or at least the handful of officials, including Lloyd, were somehow blind to its futility. And that NRW continued trying to find an angle (later the agency–ministry link or another governmental angle with California) implies they did see or believe there was still some kind of potential for the collaboration.

But over the ensuing years, essentially no progress was made. No officials from California made an effort to join WHEC 2010 in Essen. NRW decided to finally close the book on the partnership and moved away from official collaboration on the state level in California towards bilateral contacts between companies and institutes mostly in Europe and Japan. Ziolek says he does not blame California (pers. comm., 18 December 2011). Furthermore, despite all of the difficulties on the California side, Ziolek says the interest of the new NRW government (May 2010) in international collaboration has also significantly decreased (and the technology focus on transportation). This is to conclude that 'the important drives on both sides are not active anymore'.

ANALYSIS

The entire process of the partnership up to the MoU signing is an example of type II multi-level governance. This means that the globalized international system is a structural condition for the formation of the partnership. For starters, NRW's and California's primary reason for forming the partnership, to further their respective ecological modernization goals, accordingly reflected the decentralization of certain responsibilities to lower governmental levels – particularly, the subnational promotion of their own economies beyond their borders – and the influence of other governmental levels on these goals. These ecological modernization objectives were the outcome of fulfilling policy goals in both states. NRW was trying to restructure its economy, particularly the energy sector (from fossil fuels to renewable energies), and had thereby set up the NRW State Initiative on Future Energies, out of which came the Fuel Cell and Hydrogen Network NRW, which was designed to promote the hydrogen and fuel cell industry to create jobs in the state. California announced its decision to create a Hydrogen Highway, which takes cutting-edge technology and expertise in the field of hydrogen and fuel cells and helps to generate jobs, businesses and industries in the state. In addition to these diffusion goals, there was a general interest in learning from one another, particularly NRW from California.

These state policies, when further broken down, are shown to link to the complexities of economic and environmental globalization as well as to the international measures that were made to address some of the global problems. In referring to the motivations for wanting to draw lessons and/or push transfer, we see some coercive elements from this case study that was triggered by different multi-level approaches and processes stemming from the United Nations Conference on Environment and

Development (UNCED). The policy interests surrounding the partnership reflect (political) regulatory and ideational competition, as stimulated by the Western oil dependence, the UNCED and the United Nations Framework Convention on Climate Change (UNFCCC), as the partners refer to such 'independence of fossil fuels', 'sustainable economic development' and 'reduced greenhouse gases' as part of their reasoning for their frontrunner and pusher efforts and joint promotion of hydrogen and fuel cells. Other multi-level factors for NRW prompting reforms to make the state a leader in future energies (leading to the partnership) included economic globalization, which put the state's prominent heavy energy industry into difficulties, together with federal mandates and incentives (to fulfill the international and climate change agendas) that encouraged renewable energy and discouraged fossil fuel energy. Moreover, the partnership reflects (economic) regulatory competition, as stimulated by the global fuel cell market. NRW had ecological modernization goals for its hydrogen and fuel cell technologies. All of these factors can also be seen as situative in their efforts to create a lead market in hydrogen and fuel cells.

The frontrunner standing of both states was also a factor in NRWs resolve to form a cooperative agreement with California and in California's agreeing to it (in seeing the benefit, initially). NRW was interested in California's ecological modernization policies, particularly its ZEV program. Known for policies that force technology, California's hydrogen and fuel cell efforts, for example its Hydrogen Highway initiative, came out of its far-reaching 1990 LEV (ZEV) program. There was the minor mutual frontrunner interest in achieving consistent codes and standards. And being a frontrunner in the technology itself was also crucial. NRW, for instance, could not further develop or sell its products somewhere that was not at a similar level or where such products could not be used; and vice versa, in the construction of California's cutting-edge Highway, the latest innovative products would be needed.

Other important factors were the drive and willingness of the players as well as the number of trips and delegations that NRW took to California leading up to the MoU signing. These trips provided impetus through face-to-face interactions among the would-be partners, and the networking. They also served as a vital forum from which a case could be found and made to form the partnership. What is more, considering all of the political turmoil in California during the course of the NRW delegations, that the partnership was not based on politics (overall) or political parties may have been another contributing factor that led to the successful union.

The primary key players were Ziolek, Lloyd, Dahlen, Cackette, Horstmann and Steinbrück. The secondary key player, someone not directly involved in the making of the partnership but nonetheless important to its creation in some way, was Nurdin. The primary key institutions were the FCHN, CARB and the NRW Ministry. The secondary institutions were the World Fuel Cell Council, the US Fuel Cell Council as well as the numerous businesses and research institutes that participated in the transatlantic meetings.

Breaking it down as to exactly what types of people and institutions were involved and how the entire process functioned further demonstrates multi-level governance in this partnership. The idea to establish a partnership with the agency of a subnational government in another country to advance specific front-running industries and policies stemmed from a non-public official, Ziolek, who runs the public–private network organization, Fuel Cell and Hydrogen Network NRW, which receives funding from the public (the subnational state and the supranational EU) and private sectors. This non-public official worked together with the state through the FCHN's liaison to the ministry, Dahlen, who worked on the political components, for example getting support and endorsement from the state minister, Horstmann (and Steinbrück). Ziolek then networked to establish a dialog with the CARB chairman, Lloyd. Once NRW had a receptive ear in California, it then took several NRW delegations to California, to examine synergies and make the case for the collaboration. The businesses and cross-sectoral, multi-level research institutes that were involved in these visits, especially from within the FCHN alone, contributed to the reaching of the agreement. After the case was made, Lloyd had delegated the hammering-out of the partnership to Cackette, a top executive officer at CARB. Thus, in addition to the MLG dimensions, these findings also show, as in every case study, that this partnership was the fruit of personal efforts, which corresponds to the bounded rationality of the motivations. It also shows that the partnerships require policy entrepreneurs, who in this case were Ziolek and Lloyd.

The implementation stage and subsequent achievements of the partnership were negligible, but with the minor exceptions of some cooperation between businesses as well as one NRW delegation to California and one trip of three Californian delegates to NRW. There are several potential reasons for this outcome. There was an unequal drive between the parties. California did not have much commitment to it. One deterrent was that there did not seem to have been a concrete plan that was made at the time of the agreement, or a plan to make a plan, which is naturally detrimental. The partners ultimately saw themselves as a mismatch because of different organizational aims and interests. The partnership was too business-centered for CARB (not what the agency focuses on). Another disincentive was the fact that such types of international activities were not historic protocol for CARB and therefore not institutionally easy.

In addition to these points was the possible factor that the loss of Lloyd was a blow to the partnership (assuming Lloyd agreed to it because he had a vision). It also speaks to the notion that the absence of policy entrepreneurs in the implementation stage is a key factor as to how well the partnership is carried out. But that Cackette kept the partnership going and even minimally kept up with it (even traveled once to NRW) also indicates that he was not completely dismissive of it. Moreover, as NRW kept trying to keep the partnership going over the years, and even tried to look for other approaches to the California government, shows that the representatives on that side really believed there was potential between the state governments.

That the partnership has lived on despite the odds against it is testimony to the necessity of non-political agents in running it. But even though the partnership was not politically charged, the elections did indirectly contribute to its slowdown. For starters, that both parties mentioned the elections as one of the reasons why the partnership had been held up, even though in reality these elections did not hinder the partnership, except perhaps for a decrease in efficiency due to position reshuffling and the like, indicated that psychological brakes were applied to a degree due to this uncertainty. Furthermore, there were ultimately a couple of detrimental repercussions from the California elections: (1) the promotion of Lloyd to Cal/EPA one month after the MoU signing, followed by his resignation about a year later; and (2) the changes in certain state regulations and objectives in which NRW was interested.

Potentially one of the most damaging factors during the implementation process was the lack of delegations and face-to-face meetings after the signing of the agreement. It took three years for NRW to take a delegation back to California. This detail jumps out compared to the lead up to the MoU signing, where NRW made three or four trips within a two-year period prior to the formation of the partnership. Whereas such delegations contributed to the making of the case, they also would have contributed to the construction of a plan had a similar amount of effort been applied.

In sum, while the structure of Type II multi-level governance was a condition for forming the partnership, once the partnership was formed, this form of governance significantly dissipated on the California side. This was because it was run by one person in a government agency who saw fundamental flaws in the partnership. Conversely, the partnership was not anchored down (in California) in the more traditional institutional fashion. What if Cackette had inherited a partnership that had been tied to a clear-cut legally established program, with funding, goals and accountability? Thus it was ultimately based too much on individual people, whims and external factors. This suggests that it is difficult to sustain a partnership without formal institutionalization, which requires more than an MoU. On the other hand, if the partnership had to go through this type of justification beforehand, it probably would not have been created if the partners really were a mismatch from the outset.

NOTES

1. After the elections in May 2005, the ministry became the Ministry for Economic Affairs and Energy.
2. Public benefit funds come from charges on customers' electricity bills and/or through mandated payments from the companies themselves and are used for energy efficiency programs or renewable energy projects.
3. Today there are 30 members, including the US Department of Energy (DOE), the US Environmental Protection Agency (EPA) and the US Department of Transportation (DOT) as well as local transit agencies.
4. Efficient Energy Use and Utilization of Inexhaustible Sources of Energy.

9. Analysis and implications

This book aimed to establish some generalizations about the environmental partnerships that began emerging in the 1990s between US and German states based on the following questions: What are the common driving factors leading to US and German states forming environmental partnerships? What are the results of the arrangements? What supports and hinders such partnerships in the implementation process? Finally, what are the roles that these innovative US–German environmental partnerships at the subnational level play in global environmental governance for sustainable development in a multi-level system?

The partnerships came about in part because of structural changes in the international system, in which a multi-level governance system within which subnational-level governments, including US states and German *Länder*, play a larger role in environmental and particularly economic areas has arisen. States and *Länder* have acquired larger roles in reference to their respective national governments and the international sustainable development agenda in these two areas. Within these structural changes, the executive branch of the states gained the primary role when it comes to international activities. There were coercive pressures to act and form the partnerships. They were affected by ideational and regulatory (both political and economic) competition caused by economic and communications globalization, the international agenda on sustainable development and climate change; a perceived lack of adequate federal-level policy in these areas, ideological influences from outside multi-level advocacy groups, recognition by subnational actors that they are indispensable players in multi-level governance (MLG) and their desire to play a prominent (even frontrunner and/or pusher) role in this policy dynamic.

These driving factors correspond on the whole to the studies cited in Chapter 1 in this volume regarding what drives states, cities and public–private transnational arrangements to take the lead on climate change and other environmental matters. It is in the context of a growing array of such sub-state activities that the US and German partnerships emerged. They were not only driven by the aforementioned multi-level structural factors, including the common pursuit of the international sustainable development goals, but also by reasons specific to the partners involved relative to issues in their state/*Land*. The unique features ranged from lesson drawing regarding similar environmental problems or promoting policy that benefited a certain environmental technology that was important to the particular state/*Land*, to jointly working on a standard with the intention of pushing it internationally. In all cases, the partners were pioneer states in terms of the policies they were pursuing. As with pioneering cities, they showed more of a reach into the multi-levels of government and ability to pursue projects. The aims of these partnerships are more unique, however, for their tremendous drive to set and push for standards, in many instances at all levels of government.

The California–Bavaria (1995) partnership revealed the diffusion mechanism of both regulatory and ideational competition. In terms of political competition, California was trying to diffuse its Environmental Technology Certification Program (CalCert) both horizontally and ver-tically, pushing it all the way to the International Organization for Standardization (ISO), which was in the process of developing a series on environmental management system (EMS) standards. This policy was also linked by global trade and thus economic competition. To this end, California and Bavaria had ecological modernization plans for their envi-ronmental technology industries and were employing strategies to create lead markets; the partnership was a stepping stone to these ends. Both states tie their ecological modernization goals to globalization, causing economic challenges in their regions (a situative factor) and their conse-quential aims to pair environmental protection with economic growth and thus promotion of environmental technology industries. Bavaria, home to BMW, was particularly interested in learning more about California's Low Emission Vehicles (LEV) program and its fuel cell developments. With its reputation of sparking the worldwide diffusion of technology in the past, it seemed this might also happen with the LEV program as the policy had already forced fuel cell technology in California. In terms of ideas, California wanted to learn from Germany in reconciling an envi-ronmental economy. In the 1990s, the German *Länder* took the lead in Germany on implementing the Rio principles.

The Wisconsin–Bavaria partnership had a deep multi-level dynamic in its influences, which included ISO's EMS standards and the EU's Eco-Management and Audit Scheme (EMAS) standards as well as the epistemic community Multi-State Working Group on Environmental Performance (MSWG) (also working on an acceptable EMS policy), in the sense that Wisconsin wanted to learn from Bavaria (ideational competition) but it also wanted to be a frontrunner with its innovative Green Tier policy (regulatory and political competition), which employed a policy featuring EMSs plus compliance. Bavaria was an even bigger competitor. Already a frontrunner, Bavaria tried to influence or push both the European Union (EU), at different times, and the ISO, until this day, as well as to internationally diffuse its reform policy, the Environmental Pact, which utilizes the EU's EMAS. Wisconsin was involved in this competition, also a frontrunner, but more so through the MSWG (and only initially regarding influencing the ISO). These aims were also prompted by global trade (economic competition) as both states referred to their drive to pursue some type of EMS approach to allow businesses in the state to be as competitive as they could be in the face of tough global competition and a push towards worldwide sustainable development. Finally, Bavaria's policies were linked to its ecological modernization aims, as the state also planned to diffuse its technologies and environmental policies. Bavaria (and to a smaller degree Wisconsin), was vigorously pursuing the establishment of lead markets. The same mechanisms were in place regarding California–Bavaria (2000). The only difference was that it was more mutual, unlike the 1998 partnership, in which Wisconsin was in more of a learning position. This partnership was born out of the MSWG.

These subnational governments were also acting because of the lack of adequate polices from their federal governments – this criticism seemed to be stronger in the United States. For Bavaria, there was a discrepancy between EU and ISO standards, which has detrimental trade effects for companies if they have to contend with different sets of standards; as well as a mistrust of Bavaria's pact by the EU. It bears mentioning that in Wisconsin, the Environmental Protection Agency (EPA) played an enabling role in other ways, having signed agreements with the state so it could enact its innovative reforms. Wisconsin, Bavaria and the EPA were all involved in the MSWG, a state-dominated epistemic community, to work on these issues.

The Maryland–Schleswig–Holstein partnership was primarily driven by ideational competition, as prompted by a transnational advocacy network that included representatives from the federal EPA, the Böll Foundation, the states of Maryland and Schleswig–Holstein, and the German Green Party. This network supported the agenda of the United Nations Conference on Environment and Development (UNCED) and the Kyoto Protocol. Fulfillment of these international objectives were also cited in their Memorandum of Understanding (MoU) through aims such as conserving energy, reducing greenhouse gases, preserving ecosystems, promoting sustainable economic development, and developing innovative policies and technologies in biomass, 'green' buildings, wind energy and Maryland's innovative Smart Growth and Chesapeake Bay Programs. There was also a drive because of lack of US federal climate change action.

Furthermore, for Maryland, this ideational drive and thus urge to form the partnership stemmed from the globalization of communications. Because of the high volume of international attention Maryland received for its Smart Growth and Chesapeake Bay Program projects, this structural factor contributed to its then budding interest in international partnerships (leading it to Schleswig–Holstein) as it clued it into the value of joint international learning and to the realization of its role as an important environmental protection policy actor in a multi-level system. For its part, Schleswig–Holstein may have been driven by ecological modernization, specifically regarding its wind energy industry, which resulted, in part, from state and federal climate change laws that were aiming to fulfill international obligations under the Kyoto Protocol.

Finally, the California– North Rhine–Westphalia (NRW) partnership reveals that the diffusion mechanism of (political) regulatory and ideational competition was at work, as stimulated by the collective Western demand to become more independent from fossil fuels, the UNCED and the United Nations Framework Convention on Climate Change (UNFCCC), as the partners refer to such situative factors as the 'independence of fossil fuels', 'sustainable economic development' and 'reduced greenhouse gases' as part of their reasoning for their frontrunner and pusher efforts and joint promotion of hydrogen and fuel cells. Additional multi-level factors for NRW that prompted reforms to make the state a leader in future energies (which led to the partnership) included economic globalization, which put the state's very prominent heavy energy industry into difficulties, together with federal mandates and incentives (to fulfill the international and climate change agendas) that encouraged renewable energy and discouraged fossil fuel energy. Moreover, the partnership reflects (economic) regulatory competition, as stimulated by the global fuel cell market. NRW had ecological modernization goals for its hydrogen and fuel cell technologies. California was an international frontrunner in fuel cell policy and technology, already playing a sort of sovereign role on the world stage. As stated above, known for policies that force technology, California's hydrogen and fuel cell efforts, for example its Hydrogen Highway initiative, came out of its far-reaching 1990 LEV program. Both states were employing tactics to create a lead market.

Thus, when looking at the influence and content of the partnerships, there is a clear multi-level dynamic. In the first three partnerships, there were both vertical and horizontal diffusion processes starting at the international level[1] (most of the time a two-way process, sometimes including the national level, but in many cases not), in which the subnational governments were seeking a frontrunner role on a specific policy that corresponded to the ISO's EMS standards and the EU's EMAS, which are offshoots or a part of the UNCED regime. The other partnerships were spreading ideas horizontally.

The partnerships largely fit the characterization of Hooghe and Mark's (2003) characterization of Type II multi-level governance (MLG), which means they were structurally voluntary, 'task specific', and based on a common need to work together; they were also flexible in design and intersecting (not nested). In addition to the many influential jurisdictions that formed a kind of 'marble cake', there was also cross-jurisdictional and/or cross-sectoral actor involvement in partnership formation or implementation. Representing the state, however, was always the executive branch. In the California–Bavaria (1995) partnership, the actors in its creation were the secretary or minister of two subnational governments from two countries and an official from the German federal government. For Wisconsin–Bavaria (1998), there were two bureaucrats and two secretaries or ministers of the two governments, and secondarily, the governor or minister-president and a high-level cabinet member (who later became an energy executive). The actors involved in the implementation of the partnership are uncountable, crossing all sectors and including different governmental agencies in Wisconsin. In the California–Bavaria (2000) partnership, the MSWG, two California Environmental Protection Agency (Cal/EPA) officials, two Bavarian ministerial officials and a consultant from an environment and energy consultancy firm were instrumental. Maryland–Schleswig–Holstein came together out of a transnational advocacy coalition, which consisted of state officials from the United States and Germany, as well as a federal official and non-governmental entities. Finally, NRW–California involved officials from the public–private Fuel Cell and Hydrogen Network NRW (FCHN) and California and, secondarily, businesses and other stakeholders.

Structural elements alone do not explain the circumstances behind why these particular partnerships formed. As the policy transfer literature points out, both structural and agency components determine why a party decides to embark on policy transfer. And, indeed, these partnerships showed themselves to be the work of policy entrepreneurs. Not only were the partnerships themselves quite novel, but the policies these particular people were pursuing, advocating or building coalitions in were innovative. As each respective partner was working on the same or similar innovative policies, they could use the other to gain support at home, as part of a policy network, and help to shape the terms of policy debates. Thus, the formation of the partnerships was the result of policy entrepreneurs who were specifically interested in policy learning or policy diffusion. Decisions to look abroad to gain support are examples of the bounded rationality elaborated in Dolowitz and Marsh's (2000) continuum, which pinpoints the agency and structural reasons for policy transfer ranging from voluntary to coercive. While not quite voluntary, bounded rationality shows that actors were driven by their subjective desires, yet in response to multi-level coercive elements, such as and in these cases for legitimacy of a policy idea in an interdependent world.

The partnerships were very much a personal endeavor of these agents. Taking a more human approach and building relationships and networking is one of the characteristics of policy entrepreneurs. In each partnership, connections were first made on the personal level – the main players either got to know each other personally, or they were introduced by way of personal connections. The partnerships between Wisconsin–Bavaria and California–Bavaria (2000) represent the former, while California–Bavaria (1995), Maryland–Schleswig–Holstein and California–NRW represent the latter. In the case of the Wisconsin–Bavaria partnership, the two drivers of the partnership, Jeff Smoller, a special assistant to the DNR secretary, and Dr Matthias Weigand, a legal advisor to the Ministry for Regional Development and Environmental Affairs, met each other at an event, which was the beginning of a long cooperation and friendship between the two. For the California–Bavaria (2000) partnership, the primary players, Dr Robert Stephens, Assistant Secretary for Environmental Management and Sustainability at Cal/EPA, and Weigand got to know each other through mutual work at the MSWG, which led to discussions and the realization of common objectives between the two states. Regarding the partnerships that came about as the result of personal connections, in the case of the California–Bavaria (1995) partnership, Cal/EPA Secretary, James Strock, developed an ongoing dialog and a personal friendship with the German Consul, Ruprecht Henatsch, who then connected Strock to Minister Dr Thomas Goppel when the opportunity arose. In Maryland–Schleswig–Holstein, MDE Secretary, Jane Nishida, had a working relationship with the EPA's Dale Medearis, the German Green Party's Reinhard Bütikofer and the Heinrich Böll Foundation, who, in turn, had connections with Schleswig–Holstein's Minister Klaus Müller. As for NRW, FCHN Director, Dr Andreas Ziolek, networked through the World Fuel Cell Council to connect with California Air Resources Board (CARB) Chairman, Dr Alan Lloyd. As is understood of policy entrepreneurs, they networked and took advantage of windows of opportunity.

In addition to structure and agency, timing and circumstances were determining factors in the formation of the partnerships. In most partnerships, since they were driven by certain players (and their connections), there was the element of the right people being in the right place at the right time. Policy entrepreneurs are aware of the right moments and try to find the right venues to create this moment. In California–Bavaria (1995), a set of burgeoning economic circumstances and the rise of the information technology (IT) economy in California led the German *Länder*, one delegation of which was led by Goppel, to California, and correspondingly to the Consulate. With the assistance of Henatsch, who was already in discussions with Strock, a window of opportunity presented itself. Regarding the Wisconsin–Bavaria partnership, the two key players were attending the same event in California and were sitting next to each other and struck up a conversation; and since the Wisconsin Department of Natural Resources (DNR) was exploring similar ideas to those presented by Bavaria, the discussion ensued from there. California–Bavaria (2000) had Stephens and Weigand, part of the same epistemic community, the MSWG, which provided a venue for discussions of a partnership. Regarding Maryland–Schleswig–Holstein and California–NRW, it was not circumstantial in terms of venue, but rather in terms of the right connected combination of leaders at the helm at the same time. This factor became even more apparent when the partnerships fell apart after the key players left the positions they were in.

Another necessary condition for the formation of a partnership was the matching or complementary innovative interests (policy and/or technology) between the state and *Land*. Working on an innovative or cutting-edge policy implies that the state is alone or among only a small number of states that are doing the same. Thus, upon discovering that their would-be partner was working on a similar or complementary issue, it was a compelling reason to collaborate. In every single case, both parties had frontrunner mentalities in the areas in which they were pursuing the partnership, and in some cases in a more generalized sense. In the California–Bavaria (1995) partnership, one of the main mutual attractions was that they were both leading states, not only in their respective countries but in the world, in environmental policy and technology. Furthermore leaders from both sides were pushing through reforms to reconcile the environment and the economy and, with the help of their frontrunner reputations, could use each other to support their agendas. In the cases of Wisconsin–Bavaria and California–Bavaria (2000), the parties were testing and developing a kind of hybrid EMS that took into consideration both EMAS and the ISO's standards (or EMSs that incorporate a compliance component with legal standards). Maryland and Schleswig–Holstein had complementary innovative programs and technologies to share in urban development, watershed management, 'green' buildings and wind energy policies and technologies. Finally, the states of California and NRW both had complementary cutting-edge policies and technologies in hydrogen and fuel cells.

Another common thread running through each of these partnerships was that they all had, in one way or another, an economic component. There were simple economic interests in cooperation. In many instances this was a direct goal, but in most cases it was an additional incentive to the stated aims. In the case of California–Bavaria (1995), the partners were clearly promoting their environmental technology businesses. Regarding Wisconsin–Bavaria and California–Bavaria (2000), the EMS policy they were advancing was a way to make business more efficient and competitive. This was also to help transatlantic trade and to mutually promote environmental technologies. In Maryland–Schleswig–Holstein there were hopes regarding the wind energy industry on the German side, and some smaller business hopes on the US side concerning a wind company and a solar company, and job creation related to manufacturing wind turbines. Finally, the California–NRW collaboration was to help foster the development of the hydrogen and fuel cell technologies, including export markets.

While policy and technology (economic) interests were the most prominent reasons that the two subnational transatlantic states formed a partnership, there were other ways in which the states were uniquely matched that helped to seal this bond. In all of the partnerships there was agreement that the two states in some way were a natural match-up. The California–Bavaria (1995 and 2000) partners have a parallel history of being leaders in their respective countries in environmental protection, having served as a model for other states and the federal government. Both states have leading economies on a global scale and were pursuing leadership in the business of environmental technology (California had claimed 8 percent of the global trade by 1993). Both had a propensity for pushing the envelope. Wisconsin and Bavaria emphasized their cultural and historical linkages as a psychological bond. This similar heritage led to earlier partnerships and connections, which in turn enhanced the connection and made it seem like a natural extension of an already ongoing relationship. Participants in the Maryland–Schleswig–Holstein partnership emphasized their similar geography and thus analogous environmental problems, as well as comparable leadership and thus a like-minded will of both states' leaders. In the case of California–NRW, NRW representatives believed that the two states had a similar way of thinking.

Another key to the successful formation of the partnerships was personal meetings and/or delegations. Strock met Goppel at the German Consulate in San Francisco; Smoller met Weigand at a transatlantic meeting in Palo Alto; Stephens met Weigand through their mutual membership and work through the MSWG; Nishida met Müller in Schleswig–Holstein; and Ziolek met Lloyd and Tom Cackette, Chief Deputy Executive Officer at CARB, who was in charge of the partnership, on NRW's trips to California. In the specific cases of Maryland–Schleswig–Holstein and

California–NRW, there was a tremendous amount of work – time, energy, the number of people involved – that went into the formation of these partnerships. In these two cases, one can really say that the lead-up began several years prior to the actual official signing. Maryland commenced its effort with its exchange program with two other US states and three German states. This was followed up by transatlantic networking and a trip by Nishida to meet Müller, and again followed by a Maryland delegation to Schleswig–Holstein. Likewise, NRW took several delegations to California prior to the partnership to make its case.

In essentially all of the cases, there was outside assistance, to greater or lesser degrees, in helping to form the partnerships. California–Bavaria (1995) had the help of the German federal government by way of its Consul General, Henatsch, in San Francisco. In the Bavaria–Wisconsin partnership, Edward Quevedo, who was a major player (consultant) in the field of environmental management, among other areas, working with BMW, and a key player in the MSWG, provided a forum, a transatlantic partnership network meeting, at which Smoller and Weigand came together. For the California–Bavaria (2000) partnership, Quevedo gave assistance and the MSWG provided a forum out of which something could develop. The Maryland–Schleswig–Holstein partnership had without a doubt the most outside help. It had one German foundation (Heinrich Böll), one US-based non-governmental organization (NGO) (the Center for Clean Air Policy, CCAP), the US federal level (Medearis at the EPA) and the German Green Party (Bütikofer). And the partnership between California and NRW had the assistance of an NGO (Marcus Nurdin at the World Fuel Cell Council). (See Table 9.1.)

Considering all of the efforts that went into setting up these partnerships, it is surprising that the only one that can arguably be considered to have been successful to any significant extent was that between Wisconsin and Bavaria. As for the others, very little was accomplished. The partnership with the worst results was California–Bavaria (2000), which essentially never moved beyond a paper agreement. The remaining partnerships did not fare all that much better. All exchanged information, whether in person or by other means, and possibly extended some contacts (California–NRW may have resulted in a small number of business connections), but most (except for Wisconsin–Bavaria) did not yield many or long-lasting results. At most, California–Bavaria (1995) and Maryland (2002) found that the partnership (through exchanges) helped in validating their respective reform efforts and consequently helped push them along. But the dismaying consensus, however, when looking at the overall outcome, was that they did not work out.

While there is a growing literature on subnational environmental

Table 9.1   Factors enabling the formation of the partnerships

Partnership	Multi-level structural influences	Policy entrepreneurs (networking)	Right timing, circumstances	Matching innovative interests	Economic component	Perceived 'natural' match	Personal meetings (delegations)	Outside assistance
CA–BA (1995)	x	x	x	x	x	x	x	x
WI–BA (1998)	x	x	x	x	x	x	x	x
CA–BA (2000)	x	x	x	x	x	x	x	x
MD–S-H (2002)	x	x	x	x	x	x	x	x
CA–NRW (2004)	x	x	x	x	x	x	x	x

activities, and some on subnational regional agreements and transnational networks, there had been little research on whether these initiatives have much impact or are sustainable in the long run. While the research in this study only addresses this question in relation to state-to-*Länder* initiatives, the implications of these findings suggest the need for further research into these questions. This study provides groundwork from the conclusions reached when comparing the less successful partnerships to the more successful Wisconsin–Bavaria partnership, as some key differences become apparent.

The comparisons showed that while the loss of the politically appointed partnership drivers is detrimental to the partnerships, they may still survive if there is a person involved who is not politically appointed (a bureaucrat). For example in the case of California–Bavaria (1995), the loss of Strock in his public position meant the loss of the partnership; there was no one else who had any significant involvement in the partnership or interest in carrying it forward. In the case of California–Bavaria (2000), even though it never really got off the ground, when Sec. Winston Hickox and Asst. Sec. Stephens left their positions any hopes for reviving the partnership were gone.

In Maryland–Schleswig–Holstein, Maryland lost its key politically appointed player, Nishida, before the partnership was even realized. It continued in large part because a bureaucrat, Mitchell, was the one actualizing the partnership behind the scenes; Mitchell was a key player and an enthusiast of the partnership. After Nishida left, he presented the partnership to the acting secretary who agreed to continue with it. This partnership took another blow when the administration changed hands a couple of months after the partnership was formed, effectively leaving no one, politically appointed or otherwise, with any involvement in the partnership left to carry it through. While there was no one left on the Maryland side, the non-political key player on Schleswig–Holstein's side, Alfred Eberhardt, carried the partnership through (later followed by Dirk Scheelje), and even through elections in that state, until contacts were formed again with Maryland. But the Maryland side did not see its value; they did not actively work on it or make it a priority. The partnerships clearly were driven by certain players. The state has yet to get anything substantial under way again. In reality, the partnership was fatally immobilized by the loss of the key political players and one of the key bureaucratic players early on. That said, bureaucrats on the other side, nonetheless, managed to keep it alive at least in name.

The California–NRW partnership was also carried forward by a bureaucrat, Cackette, who was handed the task of creating the partnership and kept it alive, at least in name, long after CARB Chair Lloyd left office.

It is uncertain what would have happened had Lloyd, the driver, remained in his position (he left one month after the signing). What is known is that Cackette did not see a value in it and was not motivated by it (also because it was not institutionalized, as explained below). One can assume that the one who wanted to create it, Lloyd, would have had motivations to keep it going.

In the case of Wisconsin and Bavaria, Smoller, who was not politically appointed, was able to keep the partnership afloat through three changes in secretaries. Finally, after nine years, one secretary did not agree to it, yet Smoller on his own and with other interested parties outside the state managed to keep it smoldering. Ultimately, with another change in administration, he brought the partnership back to the forefront. Fortunately, not only was Smoller a bureaucrat but he was the driving player in Wisconsin. Likewise Weigand, his counterpart in Bavaria, was the same.

Thus while it is necessary to have a key player who is not politically appointed involved in the partnership, there are a couple of caveats. First, approval from the succeeding agency head is necessary. The bureaucrat therefore has to have the ability to make the case for the partnership, which is discussed below. And second, there still has to be a driver involved on both sides. This finding demonstrates that the presence of policy entrepreneurs subsequent to the formation of the partnership, into its implementation stage, is a key factor as to how well the partnership is carried out.

In addition to the necessity of having a key player working on the partnership who is not politically appointed, the cross-analysis of the partnerships reveals that such arrangements need to have concrete goals and an implementation plan that includes regular face-to-face meetings. One major incident stands out in all of the partnerships, except for Wisconsin and Bavaria. For all of the effort that it took to form them, there was strikingly little follow-up on implementation. This shows that although policy entrepreneurs make a difference in the implementation phase of the partnership, especially in lieu of institutionalization, their strength lies more in the agenda-setting phase. In the California–Bavaria (1995) partnership, there was some traveling between the two department and ministry leaders, but that was the extent of their diplomacy. In the California–Bavaria (2000) partnerships, while steps were taken between Stephens and Weigand in concretizing the Memorandum of Understanding (MoU) and implementing it, a work plan was established, there was still little effort to carry it out; that is about all that happened in the course of approximately three years.

Since the Maryland–Schleswig–Holstein (2002) partnership collapsed shortly after it was created, it cannot be categorically criticized for not having set concrete goals, since it hardly had a chance. That said, it did assemble a delegation for the occasion of signing the agreement, which would have been a good time to establish some specific aims. Then, in later years, as Schleswig–Holstein tried to build it back up, they made very minimal efforts. Scheelje came to understand exactly this – that concrete projects (and the procurement of funding) are essential.

The California–NRW partnership is possibly the most perplexing case regarding minimal implementation efforts, considering how much exertion went into forming the partnership on NRW's side (four delegations). Not only was no implementation plan created, but there were no further delegations for three years and then there still were no plans or specific goals established, which was very much lamented on the Californian side (although that side did not put forth the effort needed to counter this complaint). Interestingly, in this case and that of Maryland–Schleswig–Holstein, the key players on the German side caught on to this fact and tried to adjust by thinking about presenting some concrete plans to the other side.

The Wisconsin–Bavaria partners not only immediately created an implementation plan, identifying the areas of focus, but they also assessed the plan between 2001 and 2004, after which they created a second implementation plan for the next phase. Furthermore, they had constant face-to-face meetings and delegations, at least one a year, often more. Comments made by those who are more engaged in such international endeavors, including Maryland's John Mitchell, Maryland Department of the Environment's (MDE) international activities coordinator, who now works in international projects at the EPA, concluded that regular face-to-face meetings are essential, at least once a year, and that without such meetings, without traveling, it is outright impossible to work internationally. Face-to-face meetings not only help to solidify the partnership, as explained by officials in these partnerships, but they also help to cultivate interest in it and to maintain its vibrancy. Moreover, such contact reinforces concrete projects and vice versa. It would be futile to constantly meet without reason, and it would be detrimental to have projects without meeting much. If an agenda between the two parties is laid out and another meeting is scheduled, the work will get completed because of the pressures of having to meet again.

Finally, the partnerships need to be institutionalized (beyond the formal MoU) into the legal structures of the states. This supports Dolowitz and Marsh's (1996) findings that the constraints of institutions and structures on agents' transferring policies is decisive. The lack of institutionalization was a problem in every single partnership on the US side and to a (lesser) degree on the German side. But it takes both sides for an effective partnership. In the United States, this is because they were not formally institutionalized into the state apparatus. True institutionalization in the states – namely, the establishment of an actual program which several people would be focusing on and spending most or much of their time on – would have to be in the budget. This means that it would have to be approved by the legislature or come out of the agency's discretionary funds, which are either limited, meaning that maybe a minimum of one person could work actively on the partnership or travel, or are not easily accessible for such activities. And as revealed, there are significant barriers to states getting approval to work internationally. There is still an entrenched mentality that such work is a junket, which is why the case has to be made, as discussed below. While there is always the possibility of getting funding from outside sources, that is a difficult, uncertain avenue that poses ethical barriers. Furthermore, funders are not interested in putting up money to states that are not willing to put up any of their own. This tells the funder that the state partners are not taking their own project seriously enough. On the German side, while the partnerships were at least institutionalized to a greater degree (except for in Schleswig–Holstein), they still did not have enough resources for them. The idea of finding a concrete project was understood as a way to secure funding. The following sums up each partnership regarding this struggle.

In the California–Bavaria (1995) partnership, there was some traveling between the two department and ministry leaders, using a small amount of funds, but that was the extent of their activities. Henatsch, Consul General for Germany, who helped facilitate the partnership, unequivocally stated that its failures were due to the lack of institutionalization and funding on both sides; in other words there was not enough available money to carry out a serious exchange of delegations, regular meetings and the like. Regarding the Wisconsin–Bavaria partnership, only Smoller received some funding, but he also paid out of his own pocket, which is a characteristic of a policy entrepreneur. All of the other delegates either paid for themselves, or were helped by businesses or foundations. This was due to institutional resistance in Wisconsin regarding such international activities, which are still scrutinized among the status quo. Bavaria, for its part, had some institutionalized funding, albeit not limitless. It was not as blatantly a problem since Bavaria did not do major delegations.

In the California–Bavaria (2000) partnership, the same explanation was given by the key player in California, Stephens, who explained how the state's budget problem was the reason the partnership ran into trouble. Stephens emphasized that while he was able to spend time on the partnership traveling and giving his support to it, a state-to-state partnership cannot exist with the sole efforts of one person and there has to be money to support it. Such partnerships, Stephens found, constantly face institutional resistance, in terms of both legislative funding and of the innovative idea itself, which is seen as a threat to the system. In this case, the problem seemed to be on California's side; or at least, the partnership did not last long enough to see if Bavaria would hold up the end of its bargain.

The Maryland–Schleswig–Holstein partnership further revealed the difficulties of institutionalization. The establishment of the partnership was in great part the product of the energy and resources of many outside sources. As with other partnerships, state officials said that it is hard to be approved for funding for international travel, that there is still a stigma associated with it from within the establishment, and that it is not seen as something that could be beneficial. The partnership took a hit when all of the key players in Maryland left their government positions after the state elections that were held shortly after the MoU signing. Their leaving in effect closed the policy window. Although it originally appeared that this lack of institutionalization of the partnership had only to do with Maryland because of the dramatic change in administrations, the same holds true for Schleswig–Holstein. Even though the environmental ministry has a department for international affairs and climate change, there really was no concrete institutionalization – no responsible person or specific funds for it. And what funding existed was very limited. Thus, while Schleswig–Holstein had been successful in keeping the partnership alive in name, it had few resources to aggressively follow up and re-establish the partnership. And in Maryland, the partnership did not become institutionalized in the state and thus there were insufficient resources including personnel to put into it.

Finally, the California–NRW partnership hit its first obstacle as there was no institutional structure for it in California. The person assigned to the partnership had very little time for it. Later, the problem seemed to be that the Californians perceived little value in it. This was coupled with the problem that there were no concrete projects or goals. Again, had the partnership been institutionalized, there would have been accountability pressures to resolve these issues (it would have been established with goals), or the partnership would not have come into existence if there really was no value in it in the first place. Moreover, as with almost all of the other partnerships, the Californian official in charge of the partnership said that it is not easy to get funding to leave the country – that there are institutional roadblocks because it is not seen as 'a normal thing'. There was also not enough money in NRW; the driver estimated that between €0.5 million and €1 million would be necessary for such a partnership per year.

Interestingly, the reasons why these partnerships were not institutionalized in the US states were that the state officials involved in them understood that going through the formal channels of the state apparatus would not be worthwhile, because they said that those invested with the powers of authorizing (funding) such activities either distrusted the real reasons for particular activities (such as delegations abroad) or did not see the value in international activities in general (they did not believe that there was much to be gained beyond state borders). Such partnerships, it was disclosed, as well as innovative programs in general, constantly run up against resistance: financial resistance through the legislature, or conceptual resistance in the sense of trying to change the existing system. And since states are cashed-strapped, most of the actors did not bother trying this route.

Stephens, one of the key players of the California–Bavaria (2000) partnership, reflected on how it is possible to overcome the problem of getting the partnership institutionalized, which he saw as an essential condition for its success. The key agents of the partnerships have to make the case for it. In reflecting upon the 2000 partnership, Stephens said that he would have spent more time making the case to the governor, the legislature, the NGOs and the business community, as to why the direction of the current environmental policy, legal structure and regulatory system needed changing, and as to how a necessary part of figuring out what needs to be done to get where to the state needs to be in the long term is to look at what others are doing for ideas – and that the partnership is one small means to this end. This is what Wisconsin did, which secured an informal institutionalization, as is discussed below.

THE EXAMPLE OF WISCONSIN

While this tactic of making the case did not win Wisconsin formal institutionalization for its partnership, it is ultimately what made the difference for the success of the partnership as it helped the state to acquire, instead, an informal institutionalization. First, the partnership's agents in Wisconsin quickly coupled the partnership to their regulatory reform efforts (they moved fast and worked hard on both simultaneously so that they corresponded to one another). Second, the actors achieved a successful cross-sectoral outreach (including other state agencies and representatives from the legislative branch, as well as other sectors of society such as business, media, academia and NGOs), which not only resulted in widespread, aggregate support for the partnership and the reform (creating shared values), but also served as a funding source. Third, the agents were able to play the partnership and the reform policy off of each other, gaining more authority for both. Fourth, the partnership acquired legitimacy from the fact that the Green Tier reform policy was moving through formal institutionalization (in other words, legislative) channels. Fifth, the partnership secured institutional footing through its staying power (gaining stability over time is akin to an informal institutionalization) and successes. This durability was due in large part to the reasons as discussed above: (1) that there was a key driver (both in the formation and the implementation phases), Smoller, who was in a non-politically appointed position; (2) that Smoller was able to carry the partnership through three (ultimately four) changes of secretaries (linking its importance to policy, as stated above); (3) that each new secretary agreed to it and supported it (except for Matt Frank); (4) that the case, indeed, was compelling (the reform, and thus the partnership, was seen as important, and the timing was right); and (5) that the partners quickly drafted an implementation plan and had regular face-to-face meetings and delegations (a predictable pattern). And (6), what became an informal institutionalization of the partnership, in turn, contributed to its momentum and thus success. Still, some believe it could have been even more successful had it been formally institutionalized.

While certain state actors can form a state-to-state international partnership based on their personal preference and with the support and influence of outside actors, the results demonstrate that they need to be institutionalized into the state structure. Such partnerships cannot sustain themselves on agents, circumstances and external factors. And the one that did, Wisconsin and Bavaria, was really a Herculean task. Interestingly, this finding also corresponds to the literature on multi-level governance. It supports the idea that a multi-jurisdictional and layered ('marble cake') Type II MLG may be embedded in the structures of Type I, which is more in the traditional legal fashion with the different branches of government within a multi-tiered ('Russian doll') federal-type system. Type II actually needs to function within the parameters of Type I if it is to function effectively. Otherwise, the partnerships show that the executive branch of government at the state level – which gained a larger role in the international arena and is connected to others in the spectrum that Type II MLG covers – and the legislative branch, which is still anchored in the traditional federalism form of policymaking and therefore more representative of Type I, are at odds with each other. Yet the two branches are dependent on each other to create policy.

These findings also speak to the prominence of institutions over agency, as is theorized in the 'new institutionalism' literature. The state allowed the officials to create a partnership, by way of an MoU, but constrained them from implementing it without going through further institutional channels. This supports the notion that a policy entrepreneur can initiate a partnership to draw lessons and transfer policy but will have difficulty in sustaining it without formal institutionalization. These findings show that the entrepreneur may be able to impact the institution, as was shown in the case of Wisconsin and as some interviewees believe to be possible, by making the case, as outlined above. These findings suggest that the literatures on policy transfer and diffusion do not focus enough attention on the importance of institutionalization. And as such international cooperation at the subnational level has its own set of enabling and hindering factors, they also suggest that there needs to be more differentiation between theorizing on diffusion and theorizing on partnerships or cooperation. (See Table 9.2.)

Based on these findings, this study concludes that both multi-level structural and agency components (of the executive) drive certain states and *Länder* to form a partnership to learn and/or transfer innovative policies and technology. Structurally, they are driven by ideational and regulatory competition stemming from factors including certain international agendas, certain components of globalization such as economic and communication, outside multi-level advocacy groups and their increased roles in the MLG structure. They are also driven by policy entrepreneurs and/or the personal motivations of specific individuals. They also formed because the timing and circumstances were right, the states had matching innovative interests and there were economic interests. Moreover, the two states saw themselves as a 'natural match', the agents had become personally familiar (through personal meetings or exchanges) and they were assisted by some outside source or sources.

But while their dynamic and their formation was in the spirit of MLG, they do not tend to work out, conversely, because they are of this nature – they are not institutionalized into the state system. This makes them dependent on the availability of the people who established them. While an informal type of institutionalization could suffice to make a functional partnership, as was shown in Wisconsin–Bavaria, the effort required to do this is tremendous and therefore unlikely to be made. Moreover, not only does funding from outside sources have ethical problems, but it would not be enough anyway to maintain a partnership. Conversely, outside sources are not interested in funding partnerships that are unwilling to fund themselves. This is to say that, overall, these findings suggest that we are being too positive about international subnational cooperation. These partnerships reveal that this budding style of governance looks better on paper than in reality. That said, there is still a small glimmer of hope that this outlook may improve. Many of the problems stem from naivety or ignorance on implementation, as such partnerships are relatively novel (there were no precedents). But knowledge about such partnerships is

Table 9.2   Factors enabling the implementation of the partnerships

Partnership	Involvement of a bureaucrat	Agreement of future secretaries	Always a driver on both sides	Concrete goals	Implement- ation plan	Regular face-to- face meetings	Funding	Institutional -ization (formal) making the case	Institutional- ization (informal) making the case
CA–BA (1995)		N.A.				x			
WI–BA (1998)	x	(until 2007)		x	x	x	x		x
CA–BA (2000)		N.A.							
MD–S–H (2002)	x		x				x		
CA–NRW (2004)	x		x				x		

194

being acquired and as some of the actors themselves have shown, lessons are being learned.

GENERAL IMPLICATIONS

The findings of this book have relevancy beyond these specific cases because they help to shed insight into similar problems found in other non-national public–private transnational arrangements. The arguments made here correlate with critiques of the governing capacities of such partnerships and networks for being too dependent on national or European funding, and for lacking the authority necessary to bring about substantive changes, leaving standard-setting to governments alone – in other words to Type I structures. This study provides lessons learned on what can be done to make such arrangements better.

These lessons can also provide some guidelines on future collaborations between the EU and California where some hopes for a global environmental protection based on MoU collaboration are pinned. The EU has taken up the role of being a global leader in environmental regulations, and California is a regulatory policy leader in the United States and influences other states, and the federal and international levels. Because California has been instrumental in spreading European policies in the United States, many leading figures in the field have come to the consensus that absent intergovernmental agreement this is the best avenue to achieving transatlantic and, ultimately, global regulatory cooperation. Given that neither the EU nor California is a sovereign state, MoUs are considered the best and only way to collaborate even though it is understood that the degree to which an MoU can be an effective policy instrument remains uncertain (Vogel and Swinnen, 2011).

This study suggests that one should not put too much hope on paper partnerships alone and should focus attention on either institutionalizing those partnerships or finding other effective means to move them forward, such as proposing and working on concrete projects that can garner funding. The same needs for institutionalization apply to Europe, as an MoU also does not guarantee that a directive or a regulation will follow. Nonetheless, if MoUs are chosen as the best way to secure cooperation between the two governing bodies, policymakers can take the lessons learned from this study and amend the sample MoU provided to decrease the emphasis on the soft governance of information exchange and similar activities, and to follow more concrete steps towards institutionalization. Partners should establish specific projects, draft implementation plans and have regular face-to-face meetings. The advocates of the partnership have to make the case for its utility to the powers that be. All of these components can help the partnership take on substance and lead to meaningful actions.

NOTE

1. The foundation for the ISO EMS standards was modeled on policies of a handful of countries, not including the United States or Germany.

References

Abbruzzese, J., J. Barmach, S. Jones, K. Klick, J. Maldonado, M. Steinhilber, et al. (2002), *Keeping Pace: An Evaluation of Maryland's Most Important Environmental Problems and What We Can Do to Solve Them*, University of Maryland Environmental Law Clinic, Baltimore, MD, available at http://www.law.umaryland.edu/specialty/environ ment/documents/frosh-report.pdf.

Aldecoa, F. and M. Keating (eds) (1999), *Paradiplomacy in Action: The Foreign Relations of Subnational Governments*, London, UK and Portland, OR, USA: Frank Cass.

Andonova, L.B., M.M. Betsill and H. Bulkeley (2009), 'Transnational Climate Governance', *Global Environmental Politics*, 9 (2), 52–73.

Andrews, R., N. Darnall, D. Gallagher, J. Villani, S. Keiner, E. Feldman, et al. (1999), *National Database on Environmental Management Systems: The Effects of ISO 14001 Environmental Management Systems on the Environmental and Economic Performance of Organizations* (Project Summary 1), University of North Carolina, Chapel Hill, NC and Environmental Law Institute, Washington, DC.

Bäckstrand, K. (2008), 'Accountability of Networked Climate Governance: The Rise of Transnational Climate Partnerships', *Global Environmental Politics*, 8 (3), 74–102.

Barringer, F. (2007). 'Ruling Undermines Lawsuits Opposing Emissions Controls', *New York Times*, 3 April, available at http://www.nytimes.com/2007/04/03/us/03impact.html?_r=1&oref=slogin.

Barringer, F. (2009), 'EPA Grants California the Right to Enforce Emissions', *New York Times*, 20 June, available at http://www.nytimes.com/2009/07/01/business/energyenvironment/01webwaiver.html?_r=1& ref=us.

Bavarian Ministry of Economic Affairs, Infrastructure, Transport and Technology (MEAITT) (2005), *Bavaria High-Tech Center Environmental Technology*, Munich: Bayern International.

Bavarian Ministry of Economic Affairs, Infrastructure, Transport and Technology (MEAITT) (2009), *Invest in Bavaria*, MEAITT, Munich, available at http://www.invest-in-bavaria.in/whybavaria.htm (accessed 2 July 2009).

Bavarian State Government (n.d.), *Political life: Environmental Protection*, Bavarian State Government, Munich.

Bavaria State Ministry for Regional Development and Environmental Affairs (MRDEA) and California Environmental Protection Agency (Cal/EPA) (1995), *Memorandum of Understanding to Create the Bavaria–California Clean Technologies Working Group.*

Bavaria State Ministry for State Development and Environmental Affairs (MSDEA) and California Environmental Protection Agency (Cal/EPA) (2000), *Memorandum of Understanding to Create the Bavaria–California Regulatory Innovations Partnership.*

Bavarian State Ministry of the Environmental and Public Health (MEPH) (2004), 'Schnappauf: Bayerns Umweltpakt wird zum transatlantischen Exportschlager', MEPH, Munich, 12 October.

Bennett, C. (1991a), 'How States Utilize Foreign Evidence', *Journal of Public Policy*, 11 (1), 31–54.

Bennett, C. (1991b), 'Review Article: What is Policy Convergence and What Causes It?', *British Journal of Political Science*, 21 (2), 215–233.

Bennett, C. (1992), *Regulating Privacy: Data Protection and Public Policy in Europe and the United States*, Ithaca, NY: Cornell University Press.

Berry, F.S. and W.D. Berry (1990), 'State Lottery Adoptions as Policy Innovations: An Event History Analysis', *American Political Science Review*, 84 (2), 395–415.

Berthold, M. (2004), 'Foreword', in M. Berthold (ed.), *Approaches Challenges Potentials: Renewable Energy and Climate Change Policies in US States and German Lander – Opportunities for Transatlantic Cooperation and Beyond*, Washington, DC: Heinrich Boll Foundation North America.

Betsill, M.M. and H. Bulkeley (2004), 'Transnational Networks and Global Environmental Governance: The Cities for Climate Protection Program', *International Studies Quarterly*, 48 (2), 471–493.

Biermann, F. and K. Dingwerth (2004), 'Global Environmental Change and the Nation State', *Global Environmental Politics*, 4 (1), 1–22.

Blankenship, K. (2003), 'Mathias Boat Trip in 1973 Launched Chesapeake Cleanup Effort', *Bay Journal*, 1 July, available at http://www.bayjournal.com/article.cfm?article=1170.

Blatter, J.K. (2001), 'Debordering the World of States: Towards a Multi-Level System in Europe and a Multi-Polity System in North America? Insights from Border Regions', *European Journal of International Relations*, 7 (2), 175–209.

Bomberg, E. (2009), 'Governance for Sustainable Development: The United States and the European Union Compared', in M.A. Schreurs, H. Selin and S.D. VanDeveer (eds), *Transatlantic Environment and*

Energy Politics: Comparative and International Perspectives, Farnham, UK and Burlington, VT, USA: Ashgate, pp. 21–40.

Bonfante, J. and D. Seidman (1990), 'California Greenin'', *Time*, 26 February, available at http://www.time.com/time/magazine/article/0,9171,969466,00.html.

Borger, J. (2001), 'Bush Kills Global Warming Treaty', *Guardian Unlimited*, 29 March, available at http://www.guardian.co.uk/environment/2001/mar/29/globalwarming.usnews.

Brouwer, S., D. Huitema and F. Biermann (2009), 'Towards Adaptive Management: The Strategies of Policy Entrepreneurs to Direct Policy Change', paper presented at the conference on Human Dimensions of Global Environmental Change in Amsterdam, December.

Brown, R.S. (1999), 'The States Protect the Environment', *ECOStates*, Summer.

Bulkeley, H. and M.M. Betsill (2003), *Cities and Climate Change: Urban Sustainability and Global Environmental Governance*, London, UK and New York, USA: Routledge.

Bundesverband der Deutschen Industrie / Federation of German Industries (BDI) (2007), 'Werner Schnappauf als Neuer BDI-Hauptgeschäftsführer Nominiert', BDI, Hamburg, 5 September, available at http://www.presseportal.de/pm/6570/1043932/werner-schnappauf-als-neuer-bdi-hauptgeschaeftsfuehrer-nominiert.

Bunkley, N. (2006), 'California Sues 6 Automakers over Global Warming', *New York Times*, 21 September, available at http://www.nytimes.com/2006/09/21/business/21auto.html?ex=1316491200&en=e1823cd05f9e6f57&ei=5088&partner=rssnyt&emc=rss.

Busch, P.-O., H. Jörgens and K. Tews (2006), 'The Global Diffusion of Regulatory Instruments: The Making of a New International Environmental Regime', in M. Jänicke and K. Jacob (eds), *Environmental Governance in Global Perspective: New Approaches to Ecological and Political Modernization*, Berlin: Freie Universität Berlin, pp. 123–144.

California Air Resources Board (CARB) (1990), 'California Air Resources Board to Consider Nation's First Emission Standards for "Ultra-Clean" Cars and Fuels', CARB, Sacramento, CA, 26 September, available at http://www.arb.ca.gov/newsrel/nr092690.htm.

California Air Resources Board (CARB) (1997), *Meeting before the California Air Resources Board*, Board Hearing Room, CARB, Sacramento, CA, 24 April, available at http://www.arb.ca.gov/board/mt/mt042497.txt.

California Air Resources Board (CARB) (2000), 'ARB Cuts Emissions from Transit Buses', CARB, Sacramento, CA, 24 February, available at http://www.arb.ca.gov/newsrel/nr022400.htm.

California Air Resources Board (CARB) (2004), 'ARB Approves Greenhouse Gas Rule', CARB, Sacramento, CA, 24 September, available at http://www.arb.ca.gov/newsrel/nr092404.htm.

California Air Resources Board (CARB) (2008a), *Key Events in the History of Air Quality in California*, CARB, Sacramento, CA, available at http://www.arb.ca.gov/html/brochure/history.htm (accessed 13 April 2009).

California Air Resources Board (CARB) (2008b), *Zero Emission Vehicle Incentive Programs*, CARB, Sacramento, CA, available at http://www.arb.ca.gov/msprog/zevprog/zip/zip.htm (accessed 23 September 2009).

California Air Resources Board (CARB) and North Rhine–Westphalia Ministry of Energy and Spatial Planning, November (MESP) (2004), *Memorandum of Understanding on Hydrogen and Fuel Cell Cooperation.*

California Climate Action Registry (n.d.), available at http://www.clima teregistry.org/ABOUTUS/Legislation/ (accessed 2 March 2007).

California Energy Commission (CEC) (1998), *Executive Summary; 1997 Global Climate Change: Greenhouse Gas Emissions Reduction Strategies for California Volume 1*, P500-98-00IV1, California Energy Commission, Sacramento, CA, available at http://infohouse.p2ric.org/ref/07/06221/global_climate_change/97GLOBALVOL1.PDF.

California Energy Commission (CEC) (2009a), *California's Renewable Energy Programs*, CEC, Sacramento, CA, available at http://www.energy.ca.gov/renewables/ (accessed 22 September 2009).

California Energy Commission (CEC) (2009b), *History of California's RenewableEnergy Programs*, CEC, Sacramento, CA, available at http://www.enrgy.ca.gov/renewables/history.html (accessed 22 September 2009).

California Environmental Protection Agency (Cal/EPA) (1996a), 'ISO 14000 Examines California Certification Standards for Environmental Performance', Cal/EPA, Sacramento, CA, 14 August, available at http://www.calepa.ca.gov/PressRoom/Releases/1996/C2896.htm.

California Environmental Protection Agency (Cal/EPA) (1996b), 'California's Environmental Technology Certification Program Named Finalist in 1996 Innovations Awards Program', Cal/EPA, Sacramento, CA, 11 September, available at http://www.calepa.ca.gov/PressRoom/Releases/1996/C3096.htm.

California Environmental Protection Agency (Cal/EPA) (1996c), 'Cal/EPA and Environment Canada Join the Advancement of the Environmental Technology Certification', Cal/EPA, Sacramento, CA, 9 October, available at http://www.calepa.ca.gov/PressRoom/Releases/1996/C3696.htm.

California Environmental Protection Agency (Cal/EPA) (1996d),

'California's Environmental Technology Certification Program Wins 1996 Innovations in American Government Award', Cal/EPA, Sacramento, CA, 3 December, available at http://www.calepa.ca.gov/PressRoom/Releases/1996/innov.htm.

California Environmental Protection Agency (Cal/EPA) (1997), 'Cal/EPA's Partnership with Environment Canada Reaches Milestone with Launching of Canadian Environmental Technology Verification', Cal/EPA, Sacramento, CA, 10 June, available at http://www.calepa.ca.gov/PressRoom/Releases/1997/OS2197.HTM.

California Environmental Protection Agency (Cal/EPA) (1998), 'BP Solar Receives Cal/EPA Seal of Approval for Thin-Film Solar Energy Product', Cal/EPA, Sacramento, CA, 18 September, available at http://www.calepa.ca.gov/PressRoom/Releases/1998/bpsolar.htm.

California Environmental Protection Agency (Cal/EPA) (2000), 'Cal/EPA Launches Pilot Environmental Management Projects', Cal/EPA, Sacramento, CA, 6 June, available at http://www.calepa.ca.gov/PressRoom/Releases/2000/c500.htm.

California Environmental Protection Agency (Cal/EPA) (2005a), 'Cal/EPA Environmental Management Systems Innovation Initiative: Purpose of the Multi-State Workgroup', Cal/EPA, Sacramento, CA, 19 April, available at http://www.calepa.ca.gov/EMS/Archives/Workgroups/MultiState/ default.htm.

California Environmental Protection Agency (Cal/EPA) (2005b), 'Cal/EPA Secretary Alan C. Lloyd Honored at London Fuel Cell Conference', Cal/EPA, Sacramento, CA, 4 October, available at http://calepa.ca.gov/pressroom/Releases/2005/PR16-100405.pdf.

California Environmental Protection Agency (Cal/EPA) (2006a), *Environmental Technology Home Page*, Cal/EPA, Sacramento, CA, available at http://www.calepa.ca.gov/EnviroTech/.

California Environmental Protection Agency (Cal/EPA) (2006b), *The History of the California Environmental Protection Agency*, Cal/EPA, Sacramento, CA, available at http://www.calepa.ca.gov/About/History01/calepa.htm.

California Fuel Cell Partnership (CFCP) (n.d.), *History*, CFCP, West Sacramento, CA, available at http://cafcp.org/node/82 (accessed 22 September 2009).

'California Fuel Cell Partnership' – Demonstration Project with 50 Fuel Cell Vehicles (1999), *HyWeb Gazette*, 4 May, available at http://www.netinform.net/H2/Aktuelles_Detail.aspx?ID=2420.

California Office of the Attorney General (CAG) (2004), 'Attorney General Lockyer Files Lawsuit to Reduce Global Warming Emissions from Five Largest Polluters: *California Joins Seven Other States, New*

York City in Groundbreaking Action', CAG, Sacramento, CA, 21 July, available at http://oag.ca.gov/news/press-releases/attorney-general-lockyer-files-lawsuit-reduce-global-warming-emissions-five-0.

California Office of the Governor (2000), 'Governor Davis Signs Legislation to Protect Ratepayers', Office of the Governor, Sacramento, CA, 30 September 30.

California Office of the Governor (2004a), 'Governor Schwarzenegger Announces the California Hydrogen Highways Network', Office of the Governor, Sacramento, CA, 20 April.

California Office of the Governor (2004b), 'Governor Schwarzenegger Appoints Alan Lloyd Secretary of the Environmental Protection Agency', Office of the Governor, Sacramento, CA, 16 December.

California Office of the Governor (2006), 'Gov. Schwarzenegger, British Prime Minister Tony Blair Sign Historic Agreement to Collaborate on Climate Change, Clean Energy', Office of the Governor, Sacramento, CA, 31 July.

Canaleta, C.G., P.P. Arzoz and M.R. Gárate (2004), 'Regional Economic Disparities and Decentralisation', *Urban Studies*, 41 (1), 71–94.

Center for Clean Air Policy (CCAP) (2002), *State and Local Climate Change Policy Actions*, CCAP, Washington, DC.

Center for Clean Air Policy (CCAP) (2003), *State and Local Leadership on Transportation and Climate Change*, CCAP, Washington, DC.

Center for Climate and Energy Solutions (C2ES) (2003), *Automakers Drop California Zero Emissions Lawsuit*, C2ES, Arlington, VA, available at http://www.c2es.org/us-states-/news/2003/automakers-drop-california-zero-emissions-lawsuit.

Center for Climate and Energy Solutions (C2ES) (2004), *States Litigate for Utility Emissions Reductions*, C2ES, Arlington, VA, available at http://www.c2es.org/us-states-regions/news/2004/states-litigate-utility-emissions-reductions.

Cerny, P.G. (1996), 'Globalization and Other Stories: The Search for a New Paradigm for International Relations', *International Journal*, 51 (4), 617–637.

Cerny, P.G. (1997), 'Paradoxes of the Competition State: The Dynamics of Political Globalization', *Government and Opposition*, 32 (2), 251–274.

Chernotsky, H.I. and H.H. Hobbs (2001), 'Responding to Globalization: State and Local Initiatives in the Southeastern United States', *Passages: Interdisciplinary Journal of Global Studies*, 3 (1), 57–82.

Clapp, J. (2005), 'The Privatization of Global Environmental Governance: ISO 14000 and the Developing World', in D.L. Levy and P.J. Newell (eds), *The Business of Global Environmental Governance*, Cambridge, MA: MIT Press, pp. 223–248.

Clarke, N. (2010), 'Town Twinning in Cold-War Britain: (Dis)continuities in Twentieth Century Municipal Internationalism', *Contemporary British History*, 24 (2), 173–191.

Clean Energy States Alliance (CESA) (2004), 'US Clean Energy State Funds Participate in Germany's International Conference for Renewable Energy', CESA, Montpelier, VT.

Cohen, J.R. (2002), 'Maryland's "Smart Growth": Using Incentives to Combat Sprawl', in G. Squires (ed.), *Urban Sprawl: Causes, Consequences and Policy Responses*, Washington, DC: Urban Institute Press, pp. 293–324.

Database of State Incentives for Renewables and Efficiency (DSIRE) (n.d.), 'California Incentives for Renewable Energy', DSIRE, Raleigh, NC, available at http://www.dsireusa.org (accessed 2 March 2007).

Daykin, T. (2002), 'How's Economy? Depends on Sector: Tourism Healthy in State since Attacks, but Other Industries Ailing', *JS Online*, 11 September.

de Boer, S. (2002), *Canadian Provinces, US States and North American Integration: Bench Warmers or Key Players?*, Institute for Research on Public Policy, Montreal, available at http://www.irpp.org/choices/archive/vol8no4.pdf.

Deeg, R. (1996), 'Economic Globalization and the Shifting Boundaries of German Federalism', *Publius*, 26 (1), 27–52.

Deutch, J., J.R. Schlesinger and D.G. Victor (2006), *National Security Consequences of US Oil Dependency*, Independent Task Force Report No. 58, Council on Foreign Relations, New York, available at http://www.cfr.org/content/publications/attachments/EnergyTFR.pdf.

Dolowitz, D. (1997), 'British Employment Policy in the 1980s: Learning from the American Experience', *Governance*, 10 (1), 23–42.

Dolowitz, D. (1998), *Learning from America: Policy Transfer and the Development of the British Workfare State*, Brighton, UK and Portland, OR: Sussex Academic Press.

Dolowitz, D. and D. Marsh (1996), 'Who Learns What from Whom: A Review of the Policy Transfer Literature', *Political Studies*, 44 (2), 343–357.

Dolowitz, D. and D. Marsh (2000), 'Learning from Abroad: The Role of Policy Transfer in Contemporary Policy-Making', *Governance*, 13 (1), 5–24.

Donfried, K.E. (1996), 'Government and Politics', in E. Solsten (ed.), *A Country Study: Germany*, Washington, DC: Library of Congress, Chap. 7, available at http://lcweb2.loc.gov/frd/cs/detoc.html#de0120.

Drezner, D.W. (2001), 'Globalization and Policy Convergence', *International Studies Review*, 3 (1), 53–78.

EnergieAgentur.NRW (n.d.-a), *Innovation*, EnergieAgentur.NRW, NRW State Initiative on Future Energies, Düsseldorf, available at http://www. energieland.nrw.de/about_us/innovation_e.htm (23 May 2006).

EnergieAgentur.NRW (n.d.-b), *Objectives of the Fuel Cell and Hydrogen Network North Rhine–Westphalia*, EnergieAgentur.NRW, Fuel Cell and Hydrogen Network NRW, Düsseldorf, available at http://www. fuelcell-nrw.de/index.php?id=25&L=4 (accessed 23 September 2009).

EnergieAgentur.NRW (2004), 'Klimaschutzvereinbarung zwischen Kalifornien und NRW', EnergieAgentur.NRW, Düsseldorf, 19 November, available at http://www.ea-nrw.de/_infopool/info_details. asp?InfoID=2701.

EnergieAgentur.NRW (2007), *North Rhine–Westphalia. Economic Structure and Climate Protection. At a First Glance*, EnergieAgentur. NRW, Düsseldorf, available at http://www.energieagentur.nrw.de/_ database/_data/datainfopool/EAN-BeginnersGuideRZ.pdf.

Energy Strategy for Transportation Started in Germany (1998), *HyWeb Gazette*, 13 May, available at http://www.netinform.net/H2/Aktuelles_ Detail.aspx?ID=2527.

Environmental and Energy Study Institute (EESI) (2000), *Fuel Cell Fact Sheet*, EESI, Washington, DC.

Environmental Council of the States (ECOS) (n.d.-a), *ECOS Founders Award*, ECOS, Washington, DC, available at http://www.ecos.org/ section/_alumnicorner/_foundersaward.

Environmental Council of the States (ECOS) (n.d.-b), *Renewable Energy Program*, ECOS, Washington, DC, available at http://www.ecos.org/content/innovations/detail/1986?text=& sustainable=&goal=&solution=&media=&state=5&results=detailed&l imit=25&orderby=score (accessed 22 September 2009).

European Commission (EC) (2009a), *EMAS – The European Eco-Management and Audit Scheme*, EC, Brussels, Belgium, available at http://ec.europa.eu/environment/emas/about/summary_en.htm (accessed 13 May 2009).

European Commission (EC) (2009b), *The History of EMAS*, EC, available at http://ec.europa.eu/environment/emas/about/history_en.htm (accessed 6 July 2009).

European Environment Agency (EEA) (n.d.), *Best Practices Network for Sustainable Development*, EEA, Copenhagen, available at http://bpn. ew.eea.europa.eu (accessed 14 September 2007).

European Hydrogen Association (EHA) (2000), *EHA Founding*, EHA, Brussels.

European Union (EU) (2002a), 'Commission to Launch High Level Group on Hydrogen and Fuel Cell Technologies', EU, 10 September.

European Union (EU) (2002b), 'Commission Launches High Level Group on Hydrogen and Fuel Cells', EU, 10 October, available at http://europa.eu/rapid/pressReleasesAction.do?reference=IP/02/1450&format=HTML&aged=0&language=EN&guiLanguage=en.

Evans, M. and J. Davies (1999), 'Understanding Policy Transfer: A Multi-Level, Multi-Disciplinary Perspective', *Public Administration*, 77 (2), 361–385.

Facts and Figures from NRW: Brimming over with Energy (2005), available at http://www.regional-renewables.org/cms/upload/pdf/NRW_505%20 FaktenLZE-en.pdf (accessed 10 May 2006).

Frey, B.S. and R. Eichenberger (1999), *The New Democratic Federalism for Europe: Functional Overlapping and Competing Jurisdictions*, Cheltenham, UK and Northampton, MA, USA: Edward Elgar.

Fry, E.H. (1998), *The Expanding Role of State and Local Governments in US Foreign Affairs*, New York: Council on Foreign Relations Press.

Fry, E.H. (2004), 'The Role of Subnational Governments in the Governance of North America', IRPP Working Paper No. 2004-09d, Institute for Research on Public Policy, available at http://www.irpp.org/wp/archive/NA_integ/wp2004-09d.pdf.

Fuel Cell Standardization Body Being Created (1998), *HyWeb Gazette*, 18 December.

Furmankiewicz, M. (2007), 'International Cooperation of Polish Municipalities: Directions and Effects', *Journal of Economic and Social Geography*, 98 (3), 349–359.

'Future of Hydrogen Technologies' – Dealt with in a Question in the German Parliament (1998), *HyWeb Gazette*, 13 July, available at http://www.netinform.net/H2/Aktuelles_Detail.aspx?ID=2512.

Geiger, S. (2003), 'Fuel Cells in Germany – A Survey of Current Developments', *Fuel Cell Today*, 18 June.

German Hydrogen Association (DWV) (1998), *HyWeb Gazette*, 27 January.

German Ministry: Hydrogen to Come in 30 to 50 Years at the Earliest (1997), *HyWeb Gazette*, 1 April, available at http://www.netinform.net/H2/Aktuelles_Detail.aspx?ID=2627.

German Parliament Enacts Law on Combined Heat and Power Systems Including Fuel Cells (2002), *HyWeb Gazette*, 2 February, available at http://www.netinform.net/h2/Aktuelles_Detail.aspx?ID=2008.

Germany: Introduction of Alternative Fuels (1998), *HyWeb Gazette*, 2 March.

Giddens, A. (1981), *A Contemporary Critique of Historical Materialism in Power, Property and the State*, vol. 1, Berkeley: University of California Press.

Glendening, P. (2001), *Sustaining Maryland's Future with Clean Power, Green Buildings and Energy Efficiency*, Executive Order 01.01.2001.02, State of Maryland, available at http://www.mde.state.md.us/assets/document/EO-0101200102.pdf.

Goetz, K.H. (1995), 'National Governance and European Integration: Intergovernmental Relations in Germany', *Journal of Common Market Studies*, 33 (1), 91–116.

Gray, V. (1973), 'Innovation in the States: A Diffusion Study', *American Political Science Review*, 67 (4), 1174–1185.

Greenhouse, L. (2006), 'Justices' First Brush with Global Warming', *New York Times*, 29 November, available at http://www.nytimes.com/2006/11/30/washington/30scotus.html?ei=5090&en=e0449316c48396b8&ex=1322542800&partner=rssuserland&emc=rss&pagewanted=all.

Gress, F. and R. Lehne (1999), 'Länder Governance in a Global Era: The Case of Hesse', *Publius*, 29 (4), 79–97.

Gunnarsson, J. (2003), 'Local Business Alliances and Regional Empowerment in EU Policy Networks', *Perspectives on European Politics and Society*, 4 (3), 501–528.

Haas, P.M. (1989), 'Do Regimes Matter? Epistemic Communities and Mediterranean Pollution Control', *International Organization*, 43 (3), 377–403.

Hassett, S. (2004), Remarks in Munich, Wisconsin Department of Natural Resources, Madison, WI.

Hassett, S., N. Kedzie and M. Miller (2004), 'Wisconsin's Green Tier Law', *Innovation, Management Systems and Trading Committee Newsletter*, 4, 10–18.

Hatch, M.T. (2007), 'The Europeanization of German Climate Change Policy', paper preseented at the EUSA Tenth Biennial International Conference, Montreal, May, available at http://aei.pitt.edu/7897/1/hatch-m-06b.pdf.

Helsinki University of Technology (TKK) (n.d.), *History of Fuel Cells and Current Trends*, TKK, Helsinki, available at http://www.tkk.fi/Units/AES/projects/renew/fuelcell/fc_1.html (accessed 22 April 2013).

Herbert, W. and K. Blechschmidt (2001), 'Instruments and Actions of the German Federal States towards Climate Protection', paper presented at the ECEEE (European Council for an Energy Efficient Economy), Summer, available at http://www.eceee.org/conference_proceedings/eceee/2001/Panel_1/p1_9/paper.

Hey, C. (2005), 'EU Environmental Policies: A Short History of the Policy Strategies', in S. Scheuer (ed.), *EU Environmental Policy Handbook: A Critical Analysis of EU Environmental Legislation*, Brussels: European Environmental Bureau, pp. 18–30.

Hira, A. and R. Hira (2000), 'The New Institutionalism: Contradictory Notions of Change', *American Journal of Economics and Sociology*, 59 (2), 267–282.

Höhn, B. and E.-C. Stolper (2004), 'State Approaches and Initiatives for Renewable Energy – The Case of North Rhine–Westphalia', in M. Berthold (ed.), *Approaches Challenges Potentials: Renewable Energy and Climate Change Policies in US States and German Lander – Opportunities for Transatlantic Cooperation and Beyond*, Washington, DC: Heinrich Boll Foundation North America, pp. 43–47.

Hooghe, L. and G. Marks (2003), 'Unraveling the Central State, But How? Types of Multi-Level Governance', *American Political Science Review*, 97 (2), 233–243.

Ikenberry, G.J. (1990), 'The International Spread of Privatization Policies: Inducements, Learning and "Policy Band Wagoning"', in E. Suleiman and J. Waterbury (eds), *The Political Economy of Public Sector Reform and Privatization*, Boulder, CO: Westview Press, pp. 88–110.

Immisch, T. (ed.) (2002), 'Europe's Powerhouse', *Welcome Special*, 5–9.

International Council on Clean Transportation (ICCT) (2006), 'Alan Lloyd, Former Secretary of California EPA, Joins the International Council on Clean Transportation as President', ICCT, 1 March.

IPHE Established by 15 Member States in Washington (2003), *HyWeb Gazette*, 17 December, available at http://www.netinform.net/H2/Aktuelles_Detail.aspx?ID=1760.

Jacob, K. and A. Volkery (2006), 'Modelling Capacities for Environmental Policy-Making in Global Environmental Politics', in M. Jänicke and K. Jacob (eds), *Environmental Governance in Global Perspective: New Approaches to Ecological and Political Modernization*, Berlin: Freie Universität Berlin, pp. 67–94.

Jänicke, M. (1983), 'Beschäftigungspolitik', *Natur*, 4, 58–59.

Jänicke, M. (1985), *Preventive Environmental Policy as Ecological Modernization and Structural Policy*, IIUG Discussion Paper, International Institute for Environment and Society.

Jänicke, M. (2006a), 'Ecological Modernisation: New Perspectives', in M. Jänicke and K. Jacob (eds), *Environmental Governance in Global Perspective: New Approaches to Ecological and Political Modernization*, Berlin: Freie Universität Berlin, pp. 9–29.

Jänicke, M. (2006b), 'Trend Setters in Environmental Policy: The Character and Role of Pioneer Countries', in M. Jänicke and K. Jacob (eds), *Environmental Governance in Global Perspective: New Approaches to Ecological and Political Modernization*, Berlin: Freie Universität Berlin, pp. 51–66.

Jänicke, M. and K. Jacob (2004), 'Lead Markets for Environmental Innovations: A New Role for the Nation State', *Global Environmental Politics*, 4 (1), 29–46.

Jänicke, M. and K. Jacob (2006), 'Lead Markets for Environmental Innovations: A New Role for the Nation State', in M. Jänicke and K. Jacob (eds), *Environmental Governance in Global Perspective: New Approaches to Ecological and Political Modernization*, Berlin: Freie Universität Berlin, pp. 30–50.

Jeffery, C. (1996), 'Towards a "Third Level" in Europe? The German Länder in the Union', *Political Studies*, 44 (2), 253–266.

Joint EPA/State Agreement to Pursue Regulatory Innovation (1998), *Federal Register*, 63 (86), pp. 24784–24796, available at http://www.epa.gov/fedrgstr/EPA-GENERAL/1998/May/Day-05/g11799.htm.

Jörgensen, K. (2002), 'Policymaking for Ecological Sustainability in Federal States: The Examples of the German Bundesländer and the US States', AICGS/DAAD Working Paper, American Institute for Contemporary German Studies, available at http://www.aicgs.org/site/wp-content/uploads/2011/10/jorgensen.pdf.

Jörgensen, K. (2006), 'Sub-National Trans-Atlantic Lesson-Drawing Related to Governance for Sustainable Development', in M. Jänicke and K. Jacob (eds), *Environmental Governance in Global Perspective: New Approaches to Ecological and Political Modernization*, Berlin: Freie Universität Berlin, pp. 145–164.

Junker, K.W. (2004), 'Conventional Wisdom, De-emption and Uncooperative Federalism in International Environmental Agreements', *Loyola University Chicago International Law Review*, 2 (1), 93–116.

Justices Reject Lawsuit against Power Companies (2011), *Daily Hampshire Gazette*, 21 June.

Kaiser, R. (1999), 'The Internationalization of Subnational Politics: How Regional Integration Affects Federal Systems – The Case of Germany and the US', paper presented at the conference on International Institutions: Global Processes – Domestic Consequences, Durham, NC, April.

Kaiser, R. (2002), 'Subnational Governments in International Arenas – Paradiplomacy and Multi-Level Governance in Europe and North America', presentation given at the Fifth Symposium of the International Political Science Association on Globalization, Nations and Multi-Level Governance: Strategies and Challenges, Montréal, October.

Kaiser, R. (2005), 'Sub-State Governments in International Arenas: Paradiplomacy and Multi-Level Governance in Europe and North America', in G. Lachapelle and S. Paquin (eds), *Mastering Globalization:*

New Sub-States' Governance and Strategies, London, UK and New York, USA: Routledge, pp. 90–103.

Kassulke, N. (2002), 'The Complex Business of Keeping the Lights On: Smart Energy Policy Takes More Than Flipping a Switch. Germany Provides Lessons',*Wisconsin Natural Resources Magazine*, December, available at http://dnr.wi.gov/wnrmag/html/stories/2002/dec02/energy. htm.

Kassulke, N. (2003), 'A Fresh Look at Energy: Renewable Energy and Conservation are Bigger Parts of the Energy Mix in Germany. Can We Do It Here?', *Wisconsin Natural Resources Magazine*, February, available at http://dnr.wi.gov/wnrmag/html/stories/2003/feb03/energy.htm.

Kedzie Named to Green Tier Mission to Bavaria (2004), WisPolitics.com, 24 September, available at http://wispolitics. com/1006/9_24greentiermission.pdf.

Kern, K. (2008), 'Sub-National Sustainable Development Initiatives in Federal States in Germany', in S. Baker and K. Eckerberg (eds), *In Pursuit of Sustainable Development: New Governance Practices at the Sub-National Level in Europe*, London, UK and New York, USA: Routledge, pp. 122–144.

Kern, K. and H. Bulkeley (2009), 'Cities, Europeanization and Multi-Level Governance: Governing Climate Change through Transnational Municipal Networks', *JCMS*, 47 (2), 309–332.

Kern, K., H. Jörgens and M. Jänicke (2001), 'The Diffusion of Environmental Policy: A Contribution to the Globalisation of Environmental Policy', Discussion Paper FS II 01 – 302, Social Science Research Center Berlin, available at http://skylla.wz-berlin.de/pdf/2001/ ii01-302.pdf.

Kern, K., C. Koll and M. Schophaus (2007), 'The Diffusion of Local Agenda 21 in Germany: Comparing the German Federal States', *Environmental Politics*, 16 (4), 604–624.

Kern, K. and J. Monstadt (2008), 'The Re-Scaling of Subnational Energy and Climate Change Policy in Europe', paper presented at the International Studies Association Annual Convention on Bridging Multiple Divides in San Francisco, CA, March.

Kingdon, J.W. (1984), *Agendas, Alternatives, and Public Policies*, New York: Longman.

Knigge, M. (2005), *Transatlantic Environmental Cooperation on the Subnational Level*, Ecologic: Berlin, available at http://www.ecologic.de/ download/verschiedenes/2005/transatlantic_cooperation_subnational. pdf.

Knodt, M. (2004), 'International Embeddedness of European Multi-Level Governance', *Journal of European Public Policy*, 11 (4), 701–719.

Kraemer, R.A. (2003), 'Preface', in D. Medearis and B. Swett (eds), *International Best Practice and Innovation: Strategically Harvesting Environmental Lessons from Abroad*, Ecologic: Berlin, p. 3, available at http://www.ecologic.de/download/verschiedenes/2003/medearis_swett. PDF.

Kraemer, R.A. (2007), 'Federalism and Environmental Regulation in Germany and the EU', in R.A. Kraemer and M.A. Schreurs (eds), *Federalism and Environmentalism in the United States and Germany*, AICGS Policy Report 31, Washington, DC: American Institute for Contemporary German Studies, pp. 6–32.

Kraft, M.E. and D. Scheberle (1998), 'Environmental Federalism at Decade's End: New Approaches and Strategies', *Publius*, 28 (1), 131–146.

Ladi, S. (2001), 'Globalization and Policy Transfer: The Secrets of Success and the Realities of Failure', paper presented at the Hellenic Social Policy Association Conference on Social Policy in Greece and the European Union: New Challenges, Trends and Reform Prospects at the University of Thrace, Greece, May.

Lafferty, W.M. and K. Eckerberg (eds) (2009), *From the Earth Summit to Local Agenda 21: Working towards Sustainable Development*, London: Earthscan.

Lafferty, W.M. and J. Meadowcroft (2000), 'Patterns of Governmental Engagement', in W.M. Lafferty and J. Meadowcroft (eds), *Implementing Sustainable Development: Strategies and Initiatives in High Consumption Societies*, Oxford, UK and New York, USA: Oxford University Press, pp. 337–422.

Leading Fuel Cell Organizations Reach Co-operation Agreement (2003), *HyWeb Gazette*, 6 November.

Lecours, A. (2002), 'When Regions Go Abroad: Globalization, Nationalism and Federalism', paper presented at the conference on Globalization, Multilevel Governance and Democracy: Continental, Comparative and Global Perspectives in Kingston, Ontario, May.

Liefferink, D. and M.S. Andersen (1998), 'Strategies of the "Green" Member States in EU Environmental Policy-Making', *Journal of European Public Policy*, 5 (2), 254–270.

Liptak, A. (2007), 'Suit Blaming Automakers over Gases Is Dismissed', *New York Times*, 18 September, available at http://www.nytimes.com/2007/09/18/us/18pollute.html?_r=1&hp&oref=slogin.

Lotze-Campen, H. (2001), 'A Sustainability Geoscope: Observing, Understanding and Managing the Sustainability Transition', Berlin, available at http://www.pik-potsdam.de/members/hlotze/geoscope_report_international_berlin_oct01.pdf.

Lyall, C. and J. Tait (2004), 'Foresight in a Multi-Level Governance Structure: Policy Integration and Communication', *Science and Public Policy*, 31 (1), 27–37.

March, J.G. and J.P. Olsen (1984), 'The New Institutionalism: Organizational Factors in Political Life', *American Political Science Review*, 78 (3), 734–749.

Marks, G. (1992), 'Structural Policy in the European Community', in A.M. Sbragia (ed.), *Euro-Politics: Institutions and Policymaking in the 'New' European Community*, Washington, DC: Brookings Institutions, pp. 191–224.

Maryland Department of the Environment (MDE) (n.d.), *Partnership with MUNF of Schleswig–Holstein*, MDE, Baltimore, MD, available at http://www.mde.state.md.us/programs/CrossMedia/MDE InternationalActivities/Pages/Programs/MultimediaPrograms/interna tional/schleswig-holstein.aspx.

Maryland Department of the Environment (MDE) and Schleswig–Holstein Ministry for Environment, Nature, and Forestry (MUNF) (2002), *Memorandum of Understanding, Maryland Department of the Environment–Schleswig–Holstein Ministry for Environment, Nature, and Forestry*, available at http://www.schleswig-holstein.de/UmweltLandwirtschaft/ DE/NachhaltigeEntwicklungEineWelt/02_InternationalesEuropa/03_ Partnerschaften/01_Maryland/PDF/Memorandum__blob=publication File.pdf.

McCown, T.L. (2005), 'Policy Entrepreneurs and Policy Change: Strategies beyond Agenda Setting', paper presented at the annual meeting of the American Political Science Association in Washington, DC, September.

Medearis, D. and B. Swett (2003), *International Best Practice and Innovation: Strategically Harvesting Environmental Lessons from Abroad*, Ecologic: Berlin, available at http://www.ecologic.de/down load/verschiedenes/2003/medearis_swett.PDF.

Meyer, G.E. (1999a), Speech given at the US–German State Leadership Conference Environmental Policy Challenges for the 21st Century in Washington, DC, March, available at http://www.dnr.state.wi.us/org/ caer/cea/bavaria/phase1/gmremarks.htm (accessed 19 September 2011).

Meyer, G.E. (1999b), 'A Green Tier for Greater Environmental Protection', Wisconsin Department of Natural Resources, Madison, WI.

Michigan Department of Environmental Quality, and Multi-State Working Group on Environmental Performance (MDEQ & MSWG) (2005), *Eco-Innovation 21: The Local/Global Imperative – The 2005 Multi-State Working Group Conference*.

Milford, L., A. Schumacher, C. Brooks and M. Berthold (2004), *Preliminary Report on the Clean Technology Implementation Network*

(CTIN) State Funds Delegation to "Renewables 2004", Clean Energy States Alliance, Montpelier, VT.

Ministerium für Umwelt, Natur und Forsten des Landes Schleswig–Holstein (MUNF) (2002), 'Minister Müller Eröffnet Kabinettssitzung im US-Staat Maryland', MUNF, Kiel, Schleswig–Holstein, 9 August, available at http://www.schleswig-holstein.de/ArchivSH/PI/MUNF/2002/Maryland_0802.html.

Mintrom, M. (1997), 'Policy Entrepreneurs and the Diffusion of Innovation', *American Journal of Political Science*, 41 (3), 738–770.

Mintrom, M. and S. Vergari (1998), 'Policy Networks and Innovation Diffusion: The Case of State Education Reforms', *Journal of Politics*, 60 (1), 126–148.

Müller, E. (2005), 'Changes in Environmental Legislation – Regulatory Innovation', speech given at the conference on Environmental Law in a Connected World at the University of Wisconsin-Madison, January, available at http://www.dnr.state.wi.us/org/caer/cea/bavaria/phase2/01312005mueller.pdf (accessed 19 September 2011).

Müller, K. (2002a), 'Perspectives for the Environmental Partnership between Maryland and Schleswig–Holstein', speech presented to the US delegation in Tönning, Germany, July.

Müller, K. (2002b), 'Schleswig–Holstein – Towards Sustainability', speech presented in Maryland, August.

Müller, K. (2004), 'Schleswig–Holstein and its Role in Environmental Policy and Renewable Energies', speech presented to the US delegation in Kiel, Germany, March.

Müller, K. (2005), 'Sub-National Strategies for Development and Deployment of Innovative Technologies. Wind, Solar and Biomass/Biofuels', speech presented at the Montreal Strategic Climate Change Workshop on Sub-National Strategies for Clean Energy Investment, Technology Deployment and Innovation in Montreal, October.

Multi-State Working Group on Environmental Performance (MSWG) (2007), 'Climate, China, Europe: Shaping Environmental Policy and Practices', MSWG, Portland, OR, 15 May.

National Hydrogen Association (NHA) (n.d.), *About the NHA*, NHA, Washington, DC, available at http://www.hydrogenassociation.org/about/index.asp (assessed 2 May 2007).

Natural Resources Conservation Authority (NRCA) (n.d.), *Towards a National EMS Policy and Strategy – Major Country Report*, NRCA, Government of Jamaica, available at http://www.nrca.org/policies/ems/reports/EMS%20Major%20Country%20Report.doc.

New England Governors and Eastern Canadian Premiers (NEP/ECP)

(2001), *Climate Change Action Plan 2001*, available at http://www.gov.pe.ca/photos/original/eef_climate2001.pdf.

New Jersey Department of Environmental Protection (NJDEP) (1998a), 'Commissioner Shinn Outlines Global Warming Initiative Focused on Sea Level Rise', NJDEP, Trenton, NJ, 23 April, available at http://www.state.nj.us/dep/newsrel/releases/98_0046.htm.

New Jersey Department of Environmental Protection (NJDEP) (1998b), 'Environmental Officials from the Netherlands and New Jersey Agree to International Partnership', NJDEP, Trenton, NJ, 5 June, available at http://www.nj.gov/dep/newsrel/releases/98_0072.htm.

New York State Energy Research and Development Authority (NYSERDA) (n.d.), *Hydrogen Fact Sheet: History of Hydrogen*, NYSERDA, Albany, NY, available at http://www.getenergysmart.org/Files/HydrogenEducation/3HistoryofHydrogen.pdf (accessed 19 September 2011).

New York State Energy Research and Development Authority (NYSERDA) (2002), '2002 State Energy Plan Released', NYSERDA, Albany, NY, 19 June.

New York State Office of the Attorney General (NYAG) (2003), 'States, Cities, Environmental Groups Sue Bush Administration on Global Warming, Challenge EPA's Refusal to Reduce Greenhouse Gas Pollution', NYAG, Albany, NY, 23 October, available at http://www.ag.ny.gov/press-release/states-cities-environmental-groups-sue-bush-administration-global-warming-challenge.

Newmark, A.J. (2002), 'An Integrated Approach to Policy Transfer and Diffusion', *Review of Policy Research*, 19 (2), 151–178.

NRW-Energieministerium (n.d.), *NRW State Initiative on Future Energies*, NRW-Energieministerium, NRW State Initiative on Future Energies, Düsseldorf, available at http://www.innovations-report.com/html/profiles/profile-1246.html (accessed 19 September 2011).

O'Connor, J. (1991), 'On the Two Contradictions of Capitalism', *Capitalism Nature Socialism*, 2 (3), 107–109.

Office of the Premier, Gauteng Provincial Government (2001), *Gauteng and Bavaria to Increase Cooperation*, Office of the Premier, Johannesburg.

Ohmae, K. (1993), 'The Rise of the Region State', *Foreign Affairs*, 72 (2), 78–87.

Owens, S. and R. Cowell (2011), *Land and Limits: Interpreting Sustainability in the Planning Process*, London: Routledge.

Pembina Institute (2002), 'Canada Lags behind US States in Climate Change Action – Canadian Complaints of US Inaction Unfounded', Pembina, Canada, 17 May, available at http://www.pembina.org/media-release/1038.

Pennsylvania Department of Environmental Protection (PDEP) (1999), 'MSWG Discusses Glatfelter's Certification', PDEP, Harrisburg, PA, 4 June.

Perkmann, M. (2005), *Cross-Border Cooperation as Policy Entrepreneurship: Explaining the Variable Success of European Cross-Border Regions*, CSGR Working Paper No. 166/05, Centre for the Study of Globalisation and Regionalisation, available at http://wrap. warwick.ac.uk/1953/1/WRAP_Perkmann_wp16605.pdf.

Peters, B.G. (2005), *Institutional Theory in Political Science: The 'New Institutionalism'*, London, UK and New York, USA: Continuum International.

Pew Center on Global Climate Change (n.d.-a), *Clean Energy Incentive Act*, Pew Center, Arlington, VA, available at http://www.pewclimate. org/node/4130.

Pew Center on Global Climate Change (n.d.-b), *Greenhouse Gas Standards for Vehicles*, Pew Center, Arlington, VA, available at http://www.pew climate.org/node/4151.

Pew Center on Global Climate Change (n.d.-c), *States with Renewable Portfolio Standards*, Pew Center, available at http://pewclimate.org/ what_s_being_done/in_the_states/rps.cfm (accessed 31 August 2007).

Pew Center on Global Climate Change (2004), *Climate Change Activities in the United States: 2004 Update*, Pew Center, Arlington, VA, available at http://www.pewclimate.org/docUploads/74241_US%20Activities%20 Report_040604_075445.pdf.

Pew Center on Global Climate Change (2006), *Learning from State Action on Climate Change: June 2006 Update*, Pew Center, Arlington, VA, available at http://www.pewclimate.org/docUploads/States%20 Brief%20June%202006.pdf.

Piattoni, S. (2008), 'Multi-Level Governance: A Conceptual Analysis', paper presented at the Societa' Italiana di Scienza Politica (SISP) annual meeting in Pavia, Italy, September.

Porter, M.E. and C. van der Linde (1995), 'Green and Competitive: Ending the Stalemate', *Harvard Business Review*, 73 (5), 120–134.

Purdum, T.S. (1999), 'Pete Wilson Reflects on One More, Elusive Rung', *New York Times*, 16 January.

Rabe, B.G. (2000), 'Power to the States: The Promise and Pitfalls of Decentralization', in N.J. Vig and M.E. Kraft (eds), *Environmental Policy*, Washington, DC: CQ Press, pp. 32–54.

Rabe, B.G. (2002), *Greenhouse and Statehouse: The Evolving State Government Role in Climate Change*, Pew Center on Global Climate Change, Arlington, VA, available at http://www.pewclimate.org/doc-Uploads/states_greenhouse.pdf.

Rabe, B.G. (2006), *Race to the Top: The Expanding Role of US State Renewable Portfolio Standards*, Pew Center on Global Climate Change, Arlington, VA, available at http://pewclimate.org/docUploads/ RPSReportFinal.pdf.

Rabe, B. (2007), 'Beyond Kyoto: Climate Change Policy in Multilevel Governance Systems', *Governance: An International Journal of Policy, Administration, and Institutions*, 20 (3), 423–444.

Rabe, B. (2008), 'States on Steroids: The Intergovernmental Odyssey of American Climate Policy', *Review of Policy Research*, 25 (2), 105–128.

Rabe, B. (2009), 'Second-Generation Climate Policies in the States: Proliferation, Diffusion, and Regionalization', in H. Selin and S.D. VanDeveer (eds), *Changing Climates in North America: Institutions, Policymaking, and Multilevel Governance*, Cambridge, MA: MIT Press, pp. 67–86.

Regional Greenhouse Gas Initiative: An Initiative of the Northeast and Mid-Atlantic States of the US (RGGI) (n.d.), available at http://www. rggi.org (accessed 30 August 2007).

Reinhold, R. (1991), 'California Stalemate Ends in a Budget', *New York Times*, 18 July.

REN21 Renewable Energy Policy Network for the 21st Century (REN21) (2005), *Renewables 2005 Global Status Report*, REN21, Paris.

REN21 Renewable Energy Policy Network for the 21st Century (REN21) (2011), *Renewables 2011 Global Status Report*, REN21, Paris, available at http://www.ren21.net/Portals/0/documents.

Resources/110929_GSR2011_FINAL.pdf.

Richards, C. (2004), 'Devolution in France: The Corsican Problem', *European Public Law*, 10 (3), 481–501.

Robertson, D.B. (1991), 'Political Conflict and Lesson-Drawing', *Journal of Public Policy*, 11 (1), 55–78.

Rogers, E.M. (1995), *Diffusion of Innovations*, New York: Free Press.

Rose, R. (1991), 'What is lesson drawing?', *Journal of Public Policy*, 11 (1), 3–30.

Rose, R. (1993), *Lesson-Drawing in Public Policy: A Guide to Learning across Time and Space*, Chatham, NJ: Chatham House.

Rosenau, J. (2000), 'Change, Complexity and Governance in a Globalizing Space', in J. Pierre (ed.), *Debating Governance: Authority, Steering, and Democracy: Authority, Steering, and Democracy*, Oxford, UK and New York, USA: Oxford University Press, pp. 167–200.

Rowlands, I.H. (2009), 'Promotion of Renewable Electricity in the United States and the European Union: Policy Progress and Prospects', in M.A. Schreurs, H. Selin and S.D. VanDeveer (eds), *Transatlantic*

Environment and Energy Politics: Comparative and International Perspectives, Farnham, UK and Burlington, VT: Ashgate, pp. 145–164.

Salon, D., D. Sperling and D. Friedman (1999), *California's Partial ZEV Credits and LEV Program*, UCTC No. 470, University of California Transportation Center, Berkeley, CA, available at http://www.uctc.net/papers/470.pdf.

Savage, R.L. (1985), 'Diffusion Research Traditions and the Spread of Policy Innovations in a Federal System', *Publius*, 15 (4), 1–28.

Scherf, J., J. Hass and S. Gander (2000), 'Editorial', *Für eine Lebenswerte Stadt: Ein Transatlantischer Austausch*, Heinrich-Böll Stiftung, Berlin, pp. 5–6.

Schnappauf, W. (1998) *Statement by State Minister Dr Werner Schnappauf*, Wisconsin Department of Natural Resources, Madison, WI, December, available at http://www.dnr.state.wi.us/org/caer/cea/bavaria/phase1/statement.htm. (accessed 19 September 2011).

Schnappauf, W. (1999), 'The Implementation of Agenda 21 in the German Laender and the American Federal States', speech given at the German–American conference of *Länder*/Federal States, Washington, DC, March.

Schnappauf, W. (2003), 'A State Government Perspective on the Bavarian Environmental Pact', speech given at a conference of businesses and industries participating in the Environmental Pact in Munich, April.

Schnappauf, W. (2004), Speech given at the Bavarian Business Association's New Year's reception in Augsburg, Germany, January.

Schneider, M. and P. Teske (1992), 'Toward a Theory of the Political Entrepreneur: Evidence from Local Government', *American Political Science Review*, 86 (3), 737–747.

Schreurs, M.A. (2008), 'From the Bottom Up: Local and Subnational Climate Change Politics', *Journal of Environment and Development*, 17 (4), 343–355.

Schreurs, M.A. (2010), 'Federalism and the Climate: Canada and the European Union', *International Journal*, 66 (1), 91–108.

Schreurs, M.A., H. Selin and S.D. VanDeever (2009), 'Conflict and Cooperation in Transatlantic Climate Politics: Different Stories at Different Levels', in M.A. Schreurs, H. Selin and S.D. Vandeveer (eds), *Transatlantic Environment and Energy Politics: Comparative and International Perspectives*, Farnham, UK and Burlington, VT, USA: Ashgate, pp. 165–185.

Selin, H., and S.D. VanDeever (2005), 'Canadian–US Environmental Cooperation: Climate Change Networks and Regional Action', *American Review of Canadian Studies*, 35 (2), 353–378.

Selznick, P. (1996), 'Institutionalism "Old" and "New"', *Administrative Science Quarterly*, 41 (2), 270–277.

Sereno, J. (2002), 'German Lessons: In Search of a Way to Meet Energy Demands without Damaging the Environment, a Wisconsin Delegation Travels to Germany to See How It's Done', *Wisconsin State Journal*, 3 February.

Shoup, A. (2009), 'Emissions Trading Ins and Outs', *Online NewsHour*, 17 March, available at http://www.pbs.org/newshour/indepth_coverage/ science/globalwarming/emissions_update.html.

Smoller, J. (n.d.), 'Energy as a Partnership: Germany's Shared Responsibility Model', *Energy Watch*, WI, available at http://www.ener- gywatchwi.com/Mag2_Content/Smoller.pdf (accessed 22 November 2004).

Smoller, J. (2006), 'Environmental Results through Innovative Policy and Law', speech given at the Bavarian Business Association in Munich, January.

Some States Flirt with Europe on Carbon Controls (2004), *USA Today*, 16 December.

Southern Maryland Electric Cooperative (SMECO) (n.d.), *Customer Choice: Fact Sheet on Electric Industry Restructuring*, available at http://www.smeco.com/choice/factsheet.html (accessed 28 August 2008).

State of Bavaria (n.d.), *Partnership Bavaria-Shandong*, State of Bavaria Shandong Office.

State of California (1993), *Environmental Technologies, California Statute ch. 1306*, available at http://www.leginfo.ca.gov/cgi-bin/statquery (accessed 18 September 2011).

Still, T.W. (2002), 'Converting Talk into Energy: Applying Germany's Energy Success to Wisconsin', *Wisconsin State Journal*, 21 April.

Stinchcombe, A.L. (1997), 'On the Virtues of the Old Institutionalism', *Annual Review of Sociology*, 23, 1–18.

STMUGV – Bayerisches Staatsministerium für Umwelt, Gesundheit und Verbraucherschutz (n.d.-a), *Einführung*, STMUGV, Munich.

STMUGV – Bayerisches Staatsministerium für Umwelt, Gesundheit und Verbraucherschutz (n.d.-b), *Sustainable development: Global action*, STMUGV, Munich.

STMUGV – Bayerisches Staatsministerium für Umwelt, Gesundheit und Verbraucherschutz (2000), *Environmental Pact of Bavaria – Sustainable Economy in the 21st Century: Agreement Between the Bavarian State Government and the Bavarian Business Community Concluded on October 23, 2000*, STMUGV, Munich.

Stoiber, E. (1994a), 'Mut zu Neuem: Chancen ergreifen, Zukunft sichern

Identität wahren', address given at the Bavarian State Parliament in Munich, December.

Stoiber, E. (1994b), 'Offensive Zukunft Bayern', address given at the Bavarian State Parliament in Munich, July.

Stoiber, E. (1995), 'Umweltinitiative Bayern – Kooperativer Umweltschutz Nachhaltige Entwicklung Ökologischer Wohlstand', address given at the Bavarian State Parliament in Munich, July.

Stoiber, E. (2003), Speech presented at the Environmental Pact midpoint commemoration in Munich, April.

Stone, D. (2000a), 'Learning Lessons, Policy Transfer and the International Diffusion of Policy Ideas', CSGR Working Paper, Centre for the Study of Globalisation and Regionalisation, available at http://poli.haifa.ac.il/~levi/res/stone-2000.pdf.

Stone, D. (2000b), 'Non-Governmental Policy Transfer: The Strategies of Independent Policy Institutes', *Governance*, 13 (1), 45–70.

Tews, K. (2006), 'The Diffusion of Environmental Policy Innovations: Cornerstones of an Analytical Framework', in M. Jänicke and K. Jacob (eds), *Environmental Governance in Global Perspective: New Approaches to Ecological and Political Modernization*, Freie Universität Berlin, pp. 97–122.

Thompson, T.G. (1991), 'A Governor's Perspective on Trade', *Business America*, 112, 13–15.

Thompson, T.G. (1998a), Remarks at the signing of the Wisconsin–Bavaria Regulatory Reform Working Partnership in Munich, December.

Thompson, T.G. (1998b), 'Benevolent Judgment and Actions: Transatlantic Cooperation and Commerce', address given at Herbert Quandt Foundation Transatlantic Dinner in Munich, December.

Torinus, J. (2004), 'Bavaria Won't Go Back to Micro-Regulation', *JS Online*, 16 October, available at http://www3.jsonline.com/bym/news/oct04/267239.asp.

Treber, M., C. Bals and G. Kier (n.d.), 'Climate Policy in Germany: A Brief Overview', presentation, Germanwatch, Bonn, available at http://www.germanwatch.org/folien/cliger-e.ppt.

Umweltminister Thomas Goppel Antwortet Rosolar (1995), *Sonnenpost*, March, p. 8, available at http://rosolar.de/assets/files/sonnenpost_pdfs/sonnenpost-1995-3.pdf.

Union of Concerned Scientists (UCS) (n.d.), *Renewable Energy Tax Credit Saved Once Again, But Boom–Bust Cycle in Wind Industry Continues*, UCS, Cambridge, MA.

Union of Concerned Scientists (UCS) (2008), *Clean Vehicles; Backgrounder; California's Zero Emission Vehicle Program: Problems and Potential*, UCS, Cambridge, MA.

United Nations (UN) (n.d.), *Implementation in Germany of the Decisions of the 1992 World Summit on Environment and Development in Rio de Janeiro*, UN, available at http://www.un.org/jsummit/html/prep_process/national_reports/ger_natl_assess_0107.pdf.

United Nations (UN) (1997), *UN Conference on Environment and Development (1992)*, UN, available at http://www.un.org/geninfo/bp/enviro.html.

United Nations Economic Commission for Europe (UNECE) (2001), *Hydrogen-Fuelled Vehicles*, 42 GRPE, Informal Document no. 11, available at http://www.unece.org/trans/doc/2001/wp29grpe/TRANS-WP29-GRPE-42-infl1.doc.

United Nations Environment Programme (UNEP) (n.d.-a), *National/Sub-National Relationships in Federal Systems: State/Environmental Protection Agency Enforcement Agreements in the United States*, UNEP, Division of Environmental Law and Conventions.

United Nations Environment Programme (UNEP) (n.d.-b), *Vertical Designation of Enforcement Responsibilities for Enforcing Pollution-Control Laws in the United States*, UNEP, Division of Environmental Law and Conventions.

United Nations Framework Convention on Climate Change (UNFCCC) (2004), *United Nations Framework Convention on Climate Change: The First Ten Years*, UNFCCC, Bonn, available at http://unfccc.int/resource/docs/publications/first_ten_years_en.pdf.

University of California, Davis (UC Davis) (2000), *Secondary Benefits of the Zero-Emission Vehicle Program*, Institute for Transportation Studies, UC Davis, Davis, CA, available at http://www.arb.ca.gov/msprog/zevprog/2000review/zevbenrd.doc.

University of Madison-Wisconsin (UW) (n.d.), 'Wisconsin's Green Tier Draws on Bavaria's Experience', *Wisconsin Style: New Approaches to Regulatory Innovation*, La Follette School of Public Affairs, UW, Madison, WI, available at http://www.lafollette.wisc.edu/research/envi ronmentalpolicy/bavaria.html.

US Census Bureau (2002), *Wisconsin: 2000*, C2KPROF/00-WI, Census Bureau, Washington, DC, available at http://www.census.gov/prod/2002pubs/c2kprof00-wi.pdf.

US Department of Commerce (DOC) (2000), *Gross State Product 1992–98: High-tech Manufacturing and Business Services Boost Growth in Western States*, DOC, Bureau of Economic Analysis, Washington, DC, available at http://www.bea.gov/newsreleases/regional/gdp_state/2000/pdf/gsp_0900.pdf (19 September 2011).

US Department of Energy (DOE) (n.d.), *President's Hydrogen Fuel Initiative: A Clean and Secure Energy Future*, DOE Hydrogen Program, available at http://www.hydrogen.energy.gov/presidents_initiative.html (accessed 20 May 2007).

US Department of Energy (DOE) (1996), *1996 Annual Report: IEA Agreement on the Production and Utilization of Hydrogen*, US Office of Scientific and Technical Information, Oak Ridge, TN, available at http://www.osti.gov/bridge/servlets/purl/775568OznsMo/webview able/775568.pdf.

US Department of Energy (DOE) (1999), *Realizing a Hydrogen Future: Hydrogen Technical Advisory Panel Recommendations*, DOE/GO-10099-906, DOE, National Renewable Energy Laboratory, Washington, DC, available at http://www.hydrogen.energy.gov/pdfs/brochure.pdf.

US Department of Energy (DOE) and United States Council for Automotive Research (USCAR) (2002), 'FreedomCAR: Energy Security for America's Transportation', agreement between Department of Energy and United States Council for Automotive Research, available at http://www.hydrogen.energy.gov/pdfs/freedomcar_agreement_2002. pdf.

US Energy Information Administration (EIA) (2011), *International Energy Outlook 2011*, DOE/EIA-0484(2011), EIA, Washington, DC, available at http://www.eia.gov/forecasts/ieo/pdf/0484(2011).pdf.

US Environmental Protection Agency (EPA) (1997), *EPA Strategic Plan*, EPA/190-R-97-002, EPA, Washington, DC.

US Environmental Protection Agency (EPA) (1999), 'Wisconsin Regulatory Flexibility Agreement Reached', EPA, Washington, DC, 5 February, available at: http://yosemite.epa.gov/opa/admpress.nsf/b1ab 9f485b098972852562e7004dc686/76b9fce4a6e943bc8525670f0069179e? OpenDocument.

US Environmental Protection Agency (EPA) (2000), *Innovative Treatment Technology Developer's Guide to Support Services*, Office of Solid Waste and Emergency Response, EPA 542-B-99-008, EPA, Washington, DC, available at http://www.epa.gov/swertio1/download/supply/devgde4ed. pdf.

US Environmental Protection Agency (EPA) (2002), *Partnerships and Progress: EPA State and Local Climate Change Program, 2001 Progress Report*, Office of Air and Radiation, EPA/430/R-02/002, EPA, Washington, DC.

US Environmental Protection Agency (EPA) (2006), *Greenhouse Gas Emission from the US Transportation Sector, 1990–2003*, Office of Transportation and Air Quality, EPA 420 R 06 003, EPA, Washington, DC, available at http://www.epa.gov/otaq/climate/420r06003.pdf.

US Environmental Protection Agency (EPA) (2007), *Climate Change – State and Local Governments, State Action Plans*, EPA, Washington,

DC, available at http://www.epa.gov/climatechange/wycd/stateandlo-calgov/state_action.html#CO (29 August 2007).

US Environmental Protection Agency (EPA) (2008), *Environmental Management Systems (EMS)*, USEPA, Washington, DC, available at http://www.epa.gov/ems (accessed 13 April 2009).

US Environmental Protection Agency (EPA), North Carolina Department of Environment and Natural Resources, New Hampshire Department of Environmental Services, Oregon Department of Environmental Quality, Pennsylvania Department of Environmental Protection, Illinois Environmental Protection Agency, Arizona Department of Environmental Quality, California Environmental Protection Agency (Cal/EPA), Wisconsin Department of Natural Resources (1998), *EPA and State Regulatory Framework for EMS Pilot Projects*, available at http://infohouse.p2ric.org/ref/01/00323.pdf.

US Fuel Cell Council Formed (1998), *HyWeb Gazette*, 10 November, available at http://www.netinform.net/H2/Aktuelles_Detail.aspx?ID=2483.

US General Accounting Office (GAO) (1997), *Global Warming: Information on the Results of Four of EPA's Voluntary Climate Change Programs*, GAO/RCED-97-163, GAO, Washington, DC, available at http://www.gao.gov/archive/1997/rc97163.pdf.

US Signs Global Warming Treaty (1998), *CNN.com*, 12 November.

USA: Hydrogen Future Decided Upon (1997), *HyWeb Gazette*, 1 April, available at http://www.netinform.net/h2/Aktuelles_Detail.aspx?ID=2642.

VanDeveer, S.D. (2010), 'Multilevel Governance Perspectives from North America Climate Politics', paper presented at the Multilevel Approaches to Environmental Regulation in the Age of Nanotechnology in Boston, Massachusetts, May, available at http://pubpages.unh.edu/~sdv/Nano_MLG_and_NAm%20v5.pdf.

Vogel, D. and J.F.M. Swinnen (eds) (2011), *Transatlantic Regulatory Cooperation: The Shifting Roles of the EU, the US and California*, Cheltenham, UK and Northampton, MA, USA: Edward Elgar.

Vogel, D., M. Toffel and D. Post (2005), 'Environmental Federalism in the European Union and the United States', in F. Wijen, K. Zoeteman and J. Peters (eds), *A Handbook of Globalization in Environmental Policy: National Governments Interventions in a Global* Arena, Cheltenham, UK and Northampton, MA, USA: Edward Elgar, pp. 247–276.

Wälti, S. (2009), 'Intergovernmental Management of the Environmental Policy in the United States and the EU', in M.A. Schreurs, H. Selin, and S.D. VanDeveer (eds), *Transatlantic Environment and Energy Politics: Comparative and International Perspectives*, Farnham, UK and Burlington, VT: Ashgate, pp. 41–54.

Washington State Department of Natural Resources (WSDNR) (2004), 'Lands Commissioner Doug Sutherland Praises New Law to Reduce Greenhouse Gases: Sutherland Says Legislation Will Help the Environment and Create a New Source of Funding for Washington's Schools', WSDNR, Olympia, WA, 31 March.

Weidner, H. and L. Mez (2008), 'German Climate Change Policy: A Success Story with Some Flaws', *Journal of Environment and Development*, 17 (4), 356–378.

Weissbach, A. (2000), *Environmental Pact Bavaria*, Wisconsin Department of Natural Resources, Madison, WI.

Western Cape Government (2004), *International Cooperation Agreements of the Western Cape*, Western Cape Government, Cape Town, available at http://www.capegateway.gov.za/eng/pubs/public_info/I/57572 (21 January 2008).

Williamson, M. (2004), 'Mark Williamson: A Business Perspective on the Delegation to Germany', *WisBusiness.com*, 8 October, available at http://wisbusiness.com/index.iml?Article=24986.

Wisconsin Department of Natural Resources (DNR) (n.d.-a), *Bavarian Environmental Pact: Achievements to date: 1995*, DNR, Madison, WI, available at http://www.dnr.state.wi.us/org/caer/cea/bavaria/phase1/communities/achievements1995.pdf (accessed 11 March 2009).

Wisconsin Department of Natural Resources (DNR) (n.d.-b), *Emerging World Environmental Leaders' Network: Collaboration and Innovation for 21st Century Results*, DNR, Madison, WI.

Wisconsin Department of Natural Resources (DNR) (n.d.-c), *Report: Phase One Implementation Plan: Bavaria-Wisconsin Regulatory Reform Working Partnership*, DNR, Madison, WI.

Wisconsin Department of Natural Resources (DNR) (n.d.-d), 'Wisc. Governor Signs Historic EMS Agreement with Bavaria', *International Environmental Systems Update*, DNR, Madison, WI.

Wisconsin Department of Natural Resources (DNR) (n.d.-e), *Wisconsin–Bavaria Regulatory Reform Working Partnership*, DNR, Madison, WI.

Wisconsin Department of Natural Resources (DNR) (1998), *Progress Report on the Cooperative Environmental Agreement Legislation*, DNR, Madison, WI, available at http://dnr.wi.gov/org/caer/cea/ecpp/reports/1998annualreport.pdf (accessed 19 September 2011).

Wisconsin Department of Natural Resources (DNR) (1999), 'Wisconsin, Bavaria Sign First International Innovations Pact', *The Reinvention Report*, DNR, Madison, WI, 1 January, available at http://www.dnr.state.wi.us/org/caer/cea/bavaria/phase1/article2.pdf (accessed 19 September 2011).

Wisconsin Department of Natural Resources (DNR) (2004), *Phase Two: Implementation Plan*, DNR, Madison, WI.

Wisconsin Department of Natural Resources (DNR) (2005a), *Green Tier: Frequently Asked Questions (FAQs)*, DNR, Madison, WI.

Wisconsin Department of Natural Resources (DNR) (2005b), *Green Tier Background and History*, DNR, Madison, WI.

Wisconsin Department of Natural Resources (DNR) (2008a), *Phase One – Implementation Plan*, DNR, Madison, WI.

Wisconsin Department of Natural Resources (DNR) (2008b), *Frequently Asked Questions (FAQs)*, DNR, Madison, WI.

Wisconsin Department of Natural Resources (DNR) and Bavaria State Ministry for Regional Development and Environmental Affairs (MRDEA) (1998), *Memorandum of Understanding to Create the Wisconsin–Bavaria Regulatory Reform Working Partnership*.

Wisconsin Department of Natural Resources (DNR) and US Environmental Protection Agency (EPA) (1999), *Memorandum of Agreement between the Wisconsin Department of Natural Resources and the United States Environmental Protection Agency Concerning Implementation of the Joint State/EPA Agreement to Pursue Regulatory Innovation and the Wisconsin Environmental Cooperation Pilot Program*.

Wisconsin Energy Corporation (WEC) (n.d.), *WEC Management Team: James R. Klauser*, WEC, Milwaukee, WI.

Wisconsin Office of the Governor (2004), 'Governor Doyle Signs Green Tier Legislation, Four Other Bills: Measure Marks the Last Major Bill the Governor Called for in His "Grow Wisconsin" Economic Development Plan', Office of the Governor, Madison, WI, 16 April.

World Fuel Cell Council (WFCC) (n.d.), available at http://www.fuelcell world.org/article_flat.fcm?articleid=72&subsite=1172 (accessed 2 May 2007).

WWF (2003), 'Rising Tide: Growing Momentum on Global Warming in the US', paper presented at the Ninth Conference of the Parties to the Climate Convention Meeting in Milan, Italy, December, available at http://assets.panda.org/downloads/uswwfreportrisingtide.doc.

Index